Brian Donlevy,
the Good Bad Guy

Brian Donlevy, the Good Bad Guy

A *Bio-Filmography*

DEREK SCULTHORPE

McFarland & Company, Inc., Publishers

Jefferson, North Carolina

ALSO BY DEREK SCULTHORPE
Van Heflin: A Life in Film (McFarland 2016)

Frontispiece: Brian Donlevy at home with his pet dachshund Snoops. Publicity shot from *Photoplay,* 1943.

LIBRARY OF CONGRESS CATALOGUING-IN-PUBLICATION DATA

Names: Sculthorpe, Derek, 1966– author.
Title: Brian Donlevy, the good bad guy : a bio-filmography / Derek
    Sculthorpe.
Description: Jefferson, N.C. : McFarland & Company, Inc., Publishers,
    2017. | Includes bibliographical references and index. | Includes
    filmography, along with theater, television and radio credits.
Identifiers: LCCN 2016054330 | ISBN 9781476666570 (softcover : acid
    free paper) ♾
Subjects: LCSH: Donlevy, Brian. | Actors—United States—Biography.
Classification: LCC PN2287.D5225 S38 2017 | DDC 791.4302/8092
    [B] —dc23
LC record available at https://lccn.loc.gov/2016054330

ISBN (print) 978-1-4766-6657-0
ISBN (ebook) 978-1-4766-2658-1

BRITISH LIBRARY CATALOGUING DATA ARE AVAILABLE

Front cover: Donlevy publicity still for *Kiss of Death* (1947)

Printed in the United States of America

McFarland & Company, Inc., Publishers
  Box 611, Jefferson, North Carolina 28640
  www.mcfarlandpub.com

Acknowledgments

With many thanks to Bela G. Lugosi, Jr., for his kindness. Thank you especially to Carey Federer of Sheboygan Falls for taking so much time out on my behalf. With grateful thanks to Tammie Kahnhauser, Education Technician, Nimitz Library, Annapolis, Maryland, for her valuable assistance. Thank you to Jon Whitehead and Joe Smith for the chance to see so many obscure movies. Thanks as always to my family for their constant support.

Table of Contents

Acknowledgments   v

Preface   1

1. "Mention my name in Sheboygan"   3

2. Broadway: "Mr. Donlevy is between engagements"   12

3. Hollywood at Last: The Fox Years   28

4. *Beau Geste* and Beyond   46

5. The Great Donlevy   55

6. The War Years: Riding High at Paramount   74

7. "Gentlemen, this is my wife..."   90

8. The Postwar Years   97

9. *Impact* and the Early 1950s   117

10. Radio and Television   131

11. Quatermass to the Rescue   137

12. Fade Out   150

13. Happiness with Lillian   160

Epilogue   163

Appendices   165
   Filmography 165 • Theater 169 • Radio 170 •
   Television 174 • Recordings 178

Chapter Notes   179

Bibliography   195

Index   201

Preface

"...the man they see on the screen isn't me at all."[1]

Brian Donlevy was one of the most dependable character actors during Hollywood's golden era. Whether as a crime boss or a D.A. he had an immediate presence that was hard to miss and was more often than not a tough guy. But he had something else besides, some elusive quality that made him strangely likable. Working at a time when good and bad were clearly delineated, he was more often than not in the latter camp and therefore bound to end up dead and not getting the girl. On the rare occasions when he was still standing at the end (and *rarer* occasions when he was standing with the girl), it was almost too much of a surprise. Even when he got to play the good guy and had a chance to get the girl, he usually lost her. In *Canyon Passage* he lost Susan Hayward to Dana Andrews; in *The Trouble with Women* he loved Teresa Wright but she fell for Ray Milland, and in *Fighting Coast Guard* he was a gallant officer and gentleman who courted Ella Raines but lost her to Forrest Tucker, a roughneck who took women for granted.

At one stage of his career, Donlevy played the baddie so often that when he was cast in Fritz Lang's *Hangmen Also Die!*, it was immediately presumed that he would be the hangman! Perhaps audiences preferred to see the narrow-eyed Donlevy murdering Jane Darwell, rifling through Gary Cooper's pockets when he was dead, about to shoot Joel McCrea in the back or stamping on Don Ameche's face. Maybe then the balance of the universe was restored. They might have been surprised to know how gentle he was in real life according to those who knew him: a doting father, generous to a fault, a poet at heart, and a vegetarian who never hunted because he could not bring himself to hurt any living thing.

Sadly, his vulnerability was seldom revealed on screen and he was too often used—and allowed himself to be used—as shorthand for a tough

1

villain who gets his comeuppance. When he was given the chance to play against type or let his guard down, he was a different and far more interesting actor.

His vulnerability informed much of his finest work on screen: the all-too-human Joe McClure with his very apparent physical and emotional deficiencies that rendered his demise so chillingly memorable and sad in *The Big Combo*; the weak gambling addict George Camrose in *Canyon Passage* whose friend believes in him despite everything; his world-weary Walter Williams, seeing at last the sunlit uplands and wanting to start life new in *Impact* but sensing that fate is against him.

He could be light too, and in *The Remarkable Andrew* and *The Great McGinty* he displayed a fine comedic touch which he had honed during his Broadway years when he almost exclusively worked in comedy. But then he could be the black-hearted Markoff in *Beau Geste,* the gallant war hero of *Wake Island*, the brusque space scientist Prof. Quatermass and the unassuming immigrant who makes good in King Vidor's *An American Romance*. A natural for satire, he did not mind sending up his own tough guy image as he did so splendidly as the chain-smoking captain in *Song of Scheherazade*. He had a gift for satire which was not recognized often enough. Few others could say they had appeared to effect with such notable comedic talents as Bert Lahr, Eddie Cantor, Gracie Fields, Red Skelton and Jerry Lewis. Donlevy worked for many of the finest directors of the time, including Fritz Lang, Henry Hathaway, Preston Sturges and Cecil B. DeMille.

Donlevy had a quality that made him believable no matter what he was called on to do. He had authority, and even as a youth he was never cast as less than a corporal.

There have been profiles of Donlevy over the years in books where he was featured amidst ten or a dozen other actors. This is the first book solely dedicated to him. Most writers have tended to overlook his time on Broadway. In this book, I hope to resurrect one of the almost forgotten actors of his era and renew interest in his time and the media in which he worked. I was able to watch almost all of his films, heard many of his radio performances and saw much of his television work. I consulted a wide range of books and every article and interview possible. I contacted all those I could find who knew him. This is my tribute to an undervalued actor who stands for all those who are unlikely ever to be recalled from the mists of time. I hope to give him his due and provide a comprehensive and human assessment of his life and career. If I can pique the curiosity of those who might never have heard of him, my work will have been worthwhile.

1

"Mention my name in Sheboygan"

"Oh sure, he was a swell kid ... full of pep ... always had to have something doing."
— "Here's the Real Brian Donlevy Without All the Press Agent Malarkie," *The Milwaukee Journal*, March 5, 1940, 1

A number of cities like to claim Brian Donlevy as their native son, but the evidence suggests that Waldo Bruce Donlevy was born in Cleveland, Ohio, on February 9, 1901.[1] His fabled birth on the Emerald Isle, the son of a whiskey distiller, was a little embroidery on the rather more prosaic truth. His father Thomas Henry Donlevy, employed in the woolen industry all his working life, knew nothing of the secrets of making whiskey. He was a sober-minded individual who might have balked at the suggestion. At the time of Waldo's birth, his father was a traveling salesman in the same business that was his life's work.

Thomas had married on February 16, 1899, in Winchendon, Massachusetts.[2] He was 48 at the time and this was his second marriage. His wife, 26-year-old Rebecca Parks, had been born in Portadown, Armagh, in Ireland, and arrived in America two years earlier.[3] A local Irish newspaper recently reported that Donlevy was born in Castle Street, Portadown.[4] This address may have had some connection to his mother's family, but all official records contradict the assertion including government, naval and army records. In August 1944, *The Milwaukee Journal* printed a letter received from the adjutant general of the National Guard in Madison, Wisconsin:

> Dear Sir: Our records show that Waldo Donlevy was born in Cleveland, Ohio. When I was adjutant of the 127th Infantry I always considered Donlevy as our outstanding bugler.
> Yours Very Truly,
> Col. Byron Beveridge[5]

The son of Christopher and Ellen Donlevy, Thomas Henry was born on August 18, 1851, in Connecticut. Christopher was a farm laborer born in Cork, Ireland, in 1826; he arrived in the U.S. around the time of the Irish potato famine.[6] His parents were Peter and Bridy Dunleavy, the spelling of the surname often altered over the years. The Dunleavys are descended from four families known as the Princes of Ulidia. They were mostly centered in the counties of Cork, Mayo and Sligo. The name means "fortress on the hill," or "chief of the mountain."[7]

Christopher settled in Southbridge, Worcester, Massachusetts, around 1848 and married a local girl, Ellen Gilliman. She was the daughter of Englishman Brian Gilliman and his wife Ann *née* Riley.[8] Christopher and Ellen had five sons and two daughters. Peter and Frank worked on the railroad; James, Martha and Christopher worked in a woolen mill. Christopher Sr. died of consumption at the age of 66 in 1892, his wife Ellen died in 1909, at age 80.

Thomas attended public school and then spent four years at a textile school in Boston.[9] He married Elizabeth Murray on February 16, 1885, at St. Peter's Church, Plymouth, Massachusetts. Their son Frank Henry was born two years later. Elizabeth died on September 9, 1890, at age 28 in Coventry, Connecticut, and was buried at Oak Grove Cemetery.[10]

Waldo's earliest years were spent in Ohio and Massachusetts. Although he was born in Cloncore, Cleveland, Ohio, the family was living in Boston by 1903, and later moved to Medway, Massachusetts. Thomas Donlevy was out of work for much of 1909 but was employed the following year.[11] Around 1911 he was offered a job in Beaver Dam, Wisconsin, as superintendent of the Brickner Woolen Mills. Some time after 1912, the family moved to nearby Sheboygan Falls, where a childhood friend remembered that Waldo joined the school in sixth or seventh grade at about age 11 or 12, which would be around 1913 or 1914.[12]

Thomas' life was devoted to the woolen industry, and according to Brian he was one of the founders of the American Woolen Company.[13] Begun in 1899, the company "owned and operated 58 textile mills throughout New England and employed over 40,000 people" during the earlier part of the twentieth century.[14]

According to reports, "the men who worked under Thomas Donlevy found him a genial, kindly man, and his neighbors found him quiet, retiring and a man who minded his own business. He was always friendly, but he didn't encourage questions about himself and his family,"[15] A neighbor remembered that Waldo often visited his father at the mill.[16]

His mother was described as "a fine looking woman noted for her generosity to her neighbors and to the sick."[17] Although it was later implied that she canvassed "house to house selling trinkets," Lester C. Weisse, who administered her estate in 1939, refuted such claims, stating that she "made regular visits to give generously of the delicious food she used to bake."[18] It was said that Waldo resembled his mother and also had her generosity.

Twice Rebecca Donlevy returned to Ireland to visit her sisters in Armagh; the first time was in 1903 when Waldo was two, then again nine years later.[19] These visits appeared to form the basis of later tall tales of whiskey distillers and a romantic Irish background so beloved by Hollywood press agents. Although the Irish part was very true, surely his grandfather, fleeing the terrible famine, saw nothing romantic in it. But whether Waldo was born in Ireland or not is a moot point; he identified strongly with his Irish antecedents with very good reason, and could be justly proud of his heritage. His love of storytelling and his somewhat lonesome, melancholic tendency might be attributable to his Celtic roots. His mother was also very superstitious and passed this trait on. The first superstition he ever mentioned implied that he was supposed to have been born a girl.[20] He said that in his childhood, he became used to fighting once the other boys discovered that he liked to write verse and paint.

Beaver Dam was the hometown of Fred MacMurray, and a possibly apocryphal anecdote relates that as a boy, Waldo cleaned bottles in the bottling factory owned by MacMurray Sr. The story goes that he was fired for being such a vigorous worker that he smashed too many bottles in his eagerness to increase his salary.[21]

Early on, Waldo sought the safety and prestige of a uniform. As a young boy in Beaver Dam, he wanted to join the Scout troop but was told that he was not old enough and to come back in a few years' time. Downcast, he persisted. When he arrived in Sheboygan Falls, he was surprised to discover that there was no scout troop. In time, he and four other boys convinced the men of the town to back the idea, and soon there *was* a Sheboygan Falls scout troop. Already it would seem that there was something convincing about him. Other boys seemed to look up to him because his restless activity always had a sense of direction. "[H]e was a swell kid … full of pep … always had to have something doing," they remarked.[22]

Even before he was a scout, Waldo was fascinated by uniforms and soldiers in general. He often watched the comings and goings at the National Guard headquarters in Beaver Dam. The image that comes across of young Waldo is of a solitary, discontented boy left very much to his own devices, and wishing to escape from the family home as soon as he could. While roaming around Sheboygan Falls after school and on week-ends, he gravitated to the gates of the camp. He haunted the environs of that establishment so often that in time he was adopted as a mascot by the company. He loved the attention and adulation and longed to join the ranks of the Guard as soon as he could.

An early family photograph shows a young Waldo standing stiffly beside his father, a stern-looking but distinguished man with gray hair and a mustache. Thomas, who was 50 when Waldo was born, believed in resolute hard work, and was proud to have never missed a day at the mill.

Other pictures show 15-year-old Waldo in his National Guard uniform, an alert-looking, rather skinny kid with his hat distinctively tilted on the back of his head. This became a familiar trademark of many a Donlevy character on the big screen. In a picture taken a year later, he looks more intent as a private ready for service in France with the 32nd Company.

He graduated from grade school in June 1915 and entered high school that September, but his schooling was soon interrupted. When Company C 32nd Division, 127th Infantry of the National Guard of Wisconsin was ordered to the Mexican border in June 1916, he tried to enlist, but was turned down by Capt. Schmidt on account of his age (he was 15). He asked if he could try again with his parents' consent and if he passed the entrance examination; the captain agreed. "That evening he returned with the written consent of his parents and although he was given a rigid physical," he passed and was accepted.[23] The company's previous bugler did not pass his test and was discharged, so Waldo was appointed. His troop was sent first to Camp Douglas where after two weeks his mother visited him. She became indispensable during the week she spent there mending the soldiers' clothes and darning their socks. The troop went on to the Mexican border but saw little action and was sent back to Sheboygan in the fall of 1916. While stationed there, Waldo had leisure time to write verses. Full of enthusiasm that what he had written was good, and desperate for an audience, he read some to his fellow soldiers. But a company of young recruits is hardly the best judge of literary merit and to his heavy disappointment, "the readings were either drowned in jeers or started fights."[24]

Waldo's elder brother Frank, nicknamed "Spink," also served in the conflict in Company D of the Plymouth, Massachusetts, militia. Posted to Fort Hancock, Texas, he was guarding a bridge out of Rattlesnake Hill one night when a party was fired upon. He managed to apprehend the sniper and captured a deputy sheriff and his assistant; for this act of bravery, he was promoted to corporal.[25] Speaking with natural pride, Thomas Donlevy said he was proud to have both sons in the militia. In civilian life, Frank had a well-paid position as a railroad inspector working in the telegraph office. He was born and lived most of his life in Plymouth and married a local girl, Elsie Carlisle (or Carlish), in 1910. They had two children, Harriet and Thomas. Considering the 14-year age gap between them and the fact that Waldo was only nine when Frank married, it is unlikely the two were close.

Once he was back in Sheboygan, Waldo was restless with the inactivity and bored by constant drilling. He wanted to be where the action was. At that time, the war in Europe had been raging for over two years. In February 1917 he and fellow bugler Edgar Klaick, considered asking for a discharge in order to join the Navy. But by April, war was declared and the troop was mobilized again on July 17. After more drilling and training, they were sent to Camp Douglas the first week in August, and later to Camp MacArthur in Waco, Texas. In October, he wrote home to an old classmate, and captured some of the atmosphere of the camp awaiting news of their posting overseas:

> It's 9:30 and at the opposite end of the mess hall, Chris the cook from the Grand Ice Cream Parlor of Sheboygan is making chili con carne amid a terrible rattle of pots, pans and burning water. Outside the moon is smiling its radiant cheerful light over the broad expanse of prairie dotted with khaki tents.[26]

In December 1917, Waldo and his friend Alan Wade came down with measles and were both laid up in the hospital.[27] In February 1918, the company was sent to France.

Waldo finally went into action in April 1918, but it is uncertain exactly what action he saw. The 32nd Division served at the front line from May until the Armistice on November 11, 1918.[28] The infantry division, known as the Red Arrow, was the first to bridge the Hindenburg Line, and fought in four major offensives including the Battles of Marne and Oise and the Meuse-Argonne Offensive. In this period, the "division was under constant fire with only ten days' rest."[29] They suffered over 13,000 casualties with 11,000 wounded and 2,250 killed in action. They were the only American division to earn a *nom de guerre* from the French—Les Terribles— and the colors of all four infantry regiments were awarded the Croix de Guerre with Palm. This high honor was something that no other National Guard units achieved.[30]

Donlevy was never listed as a sergeant-pilot with the Lafayette Escadrilles as he later claimed, nor was he ever shot down and heroically wounded twice. The Lafayette Escadrilles was an elite group of volunteer pilots formed in March 1916. It comprised only "38 Americans and four French officers."[31] There were also 269 members of the Lafayette Flying

Corps; Donlevy was not listed as one of them. In the postwar period, many thousands claimed to have been members of the elite group.[32] Actually, many more Americans served in the British Royal Flying Corps. The details of his service are sketchy and he appears not to be mentioned in the official regimental histories. He certainly won medals and may well have flown after hostilities had ceased. His main duties were those of bugler with the Quartermaster corps. The bugler was actually very important to an army run on discipline and ruled by strict schedules.

After his time on the front line, Waldo contracted diphtheria in September 1918 and was forced to leave his company.[33] Such infectious diseases were rife in the trenches, which is unsurprising considering the poor sanitation and the way everyone lived in close proximity. A pernicious and potentially deadly illness, diphtheria principally affects the throat and causes a hoarse cough. Waldo spent a long time recovering at Base Hospital 46 in Neufchateau.[34]

When the Armistice was signed in November 1918, the 32nd Company became part of the army of occupation in Germany, in which capacity it served until April 1919. In May, the regiments were sent home piecemeal to Wisconsin. A private in the American Expeditionary Force, Waldo was honorably discharged on May 18.

There is the tantalizing possibility that around this time, Donlevy made his film debut: He appeared in the Crest film production *A Romance of the Air* (1919), directed by Harry Revier, according to the reference books *Celluloid War* and *From the Wright Brothers to Top Gun*. The latter calls *A Romance of the Air* "a slight tale of war fighting in France ... starring Bert Hall and a youthful Brian Donlevy."[35] But most other sources list British actor Brian Darley in the cast, which may account for the confusion. Bert Hall was an experienced pilot who had flown for the Bulgarians as a mercenary in the 1912–13 Balkans Wars and later served in the Lafayette Escadrilles.

After the war, Waldo returned to Sheboygan Falls and the normalcy of high school. Although he had missed out on several years' education and his classmates were often a lot younger than he was, he appeared to enjoy his time at school. By all accounts, the younger children were awed to have a genuine hero in their midst and looked up to him. He threw himself into school life; he played basketball and football, joined the drum and bugle corps, organized dramatics and wrote for the school newspaper. Longing to become a writer, he composed class songs and football verses; from his earliest years he wrote poems and stories prolifically, and was greatly encouraged by his doting mother.[36]

Accounts vary as to his character and demeanor; some say he was "modest and unassuming for all his drive; others [that] he swaggered and domineered."[37] Most likely there was some truth in both observations. Sometimes his later self-aggrandizement did not seem to be entirely the product of over-excited Hollywood press agents. It was said that he had an ambition for West Point and he also claimed to have spent a year at St. John's Military Academy in Delafield, Wisconsin. However, Col. Roy F. Farrand, then president of the academy, disabused anyone of this notion early on, stating clearly that Donlevy had never been a cadet there at any time under any name.[38]

Still dreaming of being a writer, he "turned professional" and as "Don Levy" he contributed a weekly column to the *Sheboygan News*. It was even "whispered that he had sold some stories to pulp magazines," although it was never stated who did the whispering.[39] He often sent his work to magazine editors but if he had been successful, it seems unlikely he could have kept quiet about it. He enrolled in a journalism course at Columbia University but quit after a month when "the professors tore his things to shreds."[40] It became apparent that his future was not in the mundane workaday world of a provincial newspaper office grinding out stories about other people's exploits. His love of writing was overtaken by his love of being someone else. He wrote a play, *Buddies,* which incorporated some of his wartime experiences. Naturally he cast himself as a heroic British RAF pilot officer. With a cast of eighteen and before a capacity audience he was cheered to the rafters.

After Donlevy graduated from high school in June 1921, he tried to join the advertising department of a plant near Sheboygan Falls, but was turned down. He once implied that he attempted to enter West Point but whether he did or not, he definitely applied to the Annapolis, Maryland, naval academy and was accepted. To become a midshipman, it was necessary to pass a stringent medical and to pay fees of $325 for a uniform and text books. He also needed to be officially nominated by a Congressman, and successfully petitioned Edward Voigt.[41] Voigt, a former Sheboygan County district attorney and one-time city attorney of Sheboygan, stood for Congress from 1917 to 1927.

Donlevy passed the medical examination on July 26, 1921, entering the academy in September. From the first, naval discipline did not suit him and he incurred a series of minor infractions during October, November and December.[42] Nor did he endear himself to the upperclassmen when he wore his military medals to academic functions.[43] All first year or sophomore naval students were known as fourth class men or "plebes" and were very much at the bottom of the ladder in the hierarchy. The academy was a very structured, insular community at one remove from the life of the city beyond the gates, and plebes were dealt with harshly if they should contravene school discipline.

At the academy, Donlevy blossomed on the amateur theatrical front. He wrote a musical, took part in several skits, sang and often danced. One of his tutors in seamanship was Don Smith, whom he met many years later while working on *Stand By for Action*; by this time, Smith was a lieutenant commander.[44]

On New Year's Eve 1921, Donlevy went to a dance party at a house in Annapolis, which was strictly against regulations. Some weeks later, during a routine medical exam, it was discovered that he had secondary syphilitic lesions. This meant he could not stay at the academy. Given the choice of dismissal or resignation, he chose the latter. His resignation took effect on March 8, 1922. His commanding officer wrote to his father notifying him that he had resigned but without giving reasons.[45]

Donlevy must have been devastated, not to mention scared, because there was then no treatment or cure for syphilis. The scourge of Europe for centuries, this disease was widespread. There were three types, primary, secondary and tertiary. In the secondary stage, which he had, it becomes latent but can sometimes cause problems with the vital organs and alopecia. However, after two years, it cannot be passed on to others.

At any event, it had already become clear to him that his future did not lie in a naval career. He was not alone; out of the 1300 cadets in his class year, almost a third resigned before they saw their service through. Donlevy later said that he sought to be a flyer and was told he would have to serve four years as a midshipman to qualify. Four years must have seemed like an eternity to someone who had barely served six months. In addition, he seemed to be susceptible to various ailments, despite his apparent robustness, and spent some time in the hospital.

After so much fanfare prior to entering the academy, not to mention the money required, Waldo sought to ameliorate the heavy disappointment of his father, who may have wanted his money back. He returned to Sheboygan and worked as a garage mechanic and as a farmhand.[46] At this point he dropped both Waldo and especially Bruce which he never liked, and adopted the name Brian.

His parents were very disappointed to hear he had left the academy, and his father was not placated to learn that he wished to be an actor. Such a precarious profession was hardly what he had envisaged for his son. But Brian had his own ideas and the approval of his mother.

It had all seemed so much simpler when he was a high school senior; he was looked up to by the younger ones as an adventurer who had been out into the world. The real world might be harder to please, but at this point he decided to head for New York—next stop Broadway.[47] It would not be easy but 20-year-old Donlevy was undaunted. These were heady times and he wanted to be a part of the sophisticated metropolitan world far from the small town life he had known.

2

Broadway:
"Mr. Donlevy is
between engagements"

"Hardship is only amusing in retrospect. If a man still wants to
act when all the theater and screen has done is push him in the
face, he has a real chance of making good."
            —Donlevy interview by Charles K. Moore,
               Lodi News-Sentinel, January 30, 1942, 4.

The Zeitgeist of the 1920s was captured and bottled for all time by F.
Scott Fitzgerald in his classic novel *The Great Gatsby,* published in the
middle of the decade. This distillation of the decadence of the Jazz Age,
the days of flappers, speakeasies and gangsters big and small, was char-
acterized by greed, vanity, hedonism and ennui. Everything seemed like
a reaction to the "war to end all wars," to the failure of Versailles, to Pro-
hibition, to the poverty of ideas in the ruling political class. This effect
was mirrored in Europe, where a generation had already seen too much
on the field of battle and was determined to live each day as though it
might be their last.

Economically, the years of Harding and Coolidge were epitomized
by almost continual boom, so much so that the inevitable bust was all the
harder to bear. But at heart there was a moral vacuum, and all the old cer-
tainties were irrelevant. When huge fortunes could be made overnight,
nothing seemed to have any real meaning, and the Wall Street Crash of
1929 was too much reality for many. The Depression that followed took
a great deal of time and political will to escape and the effects of these
momentous years were felt for a long time.

Like everywhere else, Broadway reflected the vicissitudes of social,
economic and political life albeit in fractured form. Some stage shows

harked back to the end of the previous century for their inspiration, but others sought to show the rapid changes in society. Always the chief motivator was the need to entertain, but the social drama came into its own at this time. Comedy often had the veneer of sophistication but despite itself sometimes showed its vaudeville roots. Stage shows were increasingly in competition with movies during the 1920s; once talkies came in, the tide moved inexorably in favor of the cinema, and many theaters became movie theaters. But for most of these years, Broadway was fueling the rush to the West Coast as every successful show and star was whisked away, thus inadvertently contributing to its own demise.

Twenty-year-old Brian Donlevy arrived in New York in 1922 full of hope that he might sell some of his writing. Armed with a play, *Tantamount,* two novels, some short stories and many poems, he was met by a distinct lack of interest.[1] He took a journalism course at Columbia University and became thoroughly disillusioned about his chances of becoming a writer. To make ends meet, he had a succession of jobs: waiter, bartender, bank clerk, debt collector, canning factory worker. According to his publicity material, he was a deep sea fisherman.[2]

When he first came to New York, he had hopes that he might become a professional boxer. He had enjoyed some success in amateur bouts around Wisconsin and thought he was good enough for the big time. So he called up an old friend who ran a gym. As Donlevy described the scenario:

> They called a broken-down old boy from the other end of the gym and we put on gloves the size of pillows and climbed into one of the rings. Within a minute I knew it wasn't the right business for Mrs. Donlevy's boy. He hit me with everything but the ring posts, and I'm not sure about them. Then he dropped one on my jaw and I woke up in the dressing room.[3]

By far the steadiest occupation he had during the dozen or so years from 1922 was that of insurance salesman. On all official documents he was always listed as this and never as an actor, underlining the precariousness of the acting profession. But his other main source of income was as a model.

Modeling for J. C. Leyendecker

While he had been in France in 1918, Donlevy had noticed a poster by the illustrator J.C. Leyendecker and wrote to compliment him on his work. So began a correspondence between the two men. Leyendecker was noted for his classic style, and his work for Arrow collars was especially esteemed. Mostly he depicted men's fashion; his elegant designs encapsulated the Jazz Age in illustrated form. At that point, photography was not used for advertising the way it would be later. The advantage of artwork in the world of advertising was that it instantly established a mood and sold a lifestyle more effectively than a static photograph ever could, precisely because of the element of imagination.

Once Donlevy arrived in New York, he arranged to meet Leyendecker, who was so impressed by him that he hired him on the spot. There was something in Donlevy's muscular, upright bearing that made him an ideal model. He became one of a succession of Arrow men in the days of detachable collars and high style. He allegedly even modeled once as Cleopatra for a *Saturday Evening Post* cover, albeit heavily disguised, and as Santa Claus for a Christmas "number." He stayed with Leyendecker and his manager Charles Beach at their beautiful New Rochelle, New York, home and he even did the gardening there for bed and board. Beach was Leyendecker's most frequent model. As the artist's biographer observed, "Donlevy had the image Leyendecker sought as a counterpart to Beach and his affected mannerisms: a rigid, military-like demeanor combined with raw toughness."[4]

Before his Broadway career began, Donlevy modeled for illustrator J. C. Leyendecker and even stayed at his palatial house where he did the gardening. He was one of the Arrow collar men of the 1920s. In 2001, a set of U.S. Postal Service stamps were issued to commemorate Leyendecker; on one of them, Brian dances with silent screen actress Phyllis Martingnoni (above).

Leyendecker often used models who later became successful actors, including Neil Hamilton and Fredric March. For some it was a passport to fame, and their faces became so familiar that they had a following in their own right. Donlevy regularly worked for Leyendecker from the early 1920s until the early 1930s, often during the times he was "resting." In February 2001, a set of 34-cent stamps depicted some of Leyendecker's iconic work. One stamp showed a stylish couple dancing and they look as though they had just stepped from the pages of *The Great Gatsby.* The woman was silent screen actress Phyllis Martingnomi, and the man was Donlevy.[5]

Failed Screen Test; His Early Films

After modeling for Leyendecker, Donlevy was in demand by many other illustrators. One of the foremost commercial artists, James Montgomery Flagg, said Donlevy had the "perfect Grecian warrior face."[6] Donlevy appeared in advertisements for cigarettes, socks, soap, Listerine, etc. Buoyed up by such attention, he thought he would try his luck with a screen test. He was tested by film director Christy Cabanne and Pathe News cameraman James Pergola. To his great disappointment, they "turned him down flat" and told him in no uncertain terms that "he couldn't make the grade."[7]

Donlevy took his Arrow collar ad with him to the Pathe studios. At that time they were releasing productions by the Chronicles of American Picture Corporation.[8] Donlevy made his debut in a short historical drama, *Jamestown.* This was the second in an ambitious series of 33 planned films based on the definitive 50-volume *Chronicles of America,* the most authoritative history of the United States up to the Civil War, published by Yale University Press. They were short films, 40 minutes in length, and the original intention was to show them in schools and colleges. But it appears that financial difficulties curtailed the enterprise and only 15 were completed.[9] All were shot at studios in New York. Donlevy had a minor part in *Jamestown,* which was set in 1612 and told the familiar tale of John Smith and Pocahontas. In the fifteenth and final short, *The Eve of Revolution,* he was elevated to the role of Paul Revere during the momentous years between 1765 and 1775. This was adapted for the screen by George Pierce Baker, one of the foremost professors of drama at Yale. The films were shown in 1941 during some early tests for television on channel WNBT in New York.[10]

Donlevy appeared in other films around that time, including two for Pilgrim Pictures. He played a small role in the rather contrived drama

Damaged Hearts (1924), set in the Florida Everglades, about a man who takes it out on the world when he finds that his sister has died at the hands of her affluent benefactors. "The regeneration of a twisted soul, warped by hate, through a woman's love," was how one reviewer summarized it at the time.[11] Among the cast was Tyrone Power, Sr.; his son and Donlevy later appeared in two films. *Damaged Hearts* may be a lost film.

At Paramount's New York studios, Donlevy popped up in the prestigious *Monsieur Beaucaire* (1924) starring Rudolph Valentino, the undisputed idol of the screen. This was based on the novel by Booth Tarkington about a renegade nobleman at the court of Louis XV. The film is set in eighteenth century France and England. Donlevy had a small role as a guest at a ball in the English city of Bath. He is clearly visible in the background dressed as a foppish gentleman; he is wearing a powdered wig, velvet coat and ruffles. He isn't called on to take part in the action and could easily be missed.

Donlevy was given a more prominent role in the Victor Halperin production *School for Wives* (1925). This was based on Leonard Merrick's novel *The House of Lynch,* an old-fashioned melodrama about an unscrupulous wealthy man and his detrimental effect on the lives of the poor. Although the entire chorus of Earl Carroll's Vanities put in an appearance at one stage, the feature was not well-received. "At no time does it ring true or arouse more than mild interest," observed a contemporary critic.[12] Donlevy had so little concern for any of these early silent films that he did not even list them among his credits.[13]

Stage Debut: *What Price Glory?* (1924–26)

Leyendecker continually helped Donlevy, by employing him as a model and by widening his social circle. He introduced Donlevy at the Green Room Club, which had been founded in 1902 for members of the acting fraternity as a way for all those involved in theater—writers, producers, performers and musicians—to meet socially. Donlevy made a number of influential contacts here. One of the most notable was actor Louis Wolheim, fresh from his success in Eugene O'Neill's *The Hairy Ape.* One night over drinks, Wolheim promised Donlevy he would get him a part in his upcoming play *What Price Glory?* Donlevy hung around the following day and again met Wolheim, who had forgotten his drunken promise, but nevertheless honored it, putting in a word for him with producer Arthur Hopkins.[14]

Donlevy duly approached Hopkins for a job and was asked what stage experience he had; "Practically none," he replied.[15] Hopkins liked his military bearing and gave him a small part. Written by Maxwell Anderson and Laurence Stallings, *What Price Glory?* concerned the rivalries between two U.S. Marine regiments in France during the First World War. Stallings was so impressed with Donlevy during rehearsals that he elevated him to the more prominent role of Corporal Gowdy.

The play presented a totally unromantic view of war. Although the characters reflected the familiar camaraderie of such situations, it was presented in a direct, no-nonsense way which gave it a sense of reality that many Broadway productions of the time lacked. Its earthy language was innovative although quite shocking at the time:

> The play's abundant use of profanity caused much controversy. One story tells of a prim, straitlaced woman who, during intermission, bent over to retrieve something from the floor and announced, "I seem to have dropped my goddam program."[16]

"Controversy usually sells tickets, as does excellence, and *What Price Glory?* had both."[17] The show was sold out for most of its year-long run, and by the time it closed in September 1925 it had run a remarkable 435 performances. There followed an almost year-long tour of the country. Donlevy's mother made the trip from Wisconsin to see her son in New York and was there to witness his stage debut. She also spent time with him in Chicago when he first played at the Studebaker Theater in October 1925.[18] His father never showed the remotest interest. When Donlevy returned to New York after the tour, everyone asked him where he had been. It took him many months to get another job.[19]

Excellent Pictures 1926–27

After the nationwide *What Price Glory?* tour ended in early 1926, Donlevy went back to the day job selling insurance. He also did more modeling for Leyendecker and tried once more to make a go of films.

He made several films for Excellent Pictures and featured in a set of six movies built around star George Walsh, younger brother of the director Raoul Walsh. The first in the series was a football story, *The Kick-Off* (1926). There followed in rapid succession *The Broadway Drifter,* about a gentleman-prizefighter, and *The Winning Oar,* set during a spring regatta. Donlevy may have appeared in these, but only partial cast lists are available and some are possible lost films. In *A Man of Quality* (1926), he had his most prominent part to date as the head of a silk smuggling gang and target of a Secret Service operation. "Lurid, improbable, dime novelish," commented one critic, "but good entertainment, well-acted, directed and photographed."[20] The same critic noted that Donlevy made an excellent villain. He played uncredited supporting roles in *Striving for Fortune* (1927), the tale of a financial wizard working for a shipping line, and in *His Rise to Fame* (1927), a stirring story of success in adversity.[21] All were filmed at the studios in New York and relied on a rotating stock company of actors.[22]

Broadway (1927–29)

After Excellent Pictures, Donlevy went back to selling insurance, played in stock and kept trying to find Broadway roles. In April 1927, he landed a part as a naval officer in Vincent Youman's comedy musical *Hit the Deck* and stayed with the show for ten months; it closed in February 1928. This raucous spectacle, set around the docks, introduced a number of songs including "Join the Navy and See the World," "What's a Kiss Among Friends?" and "Sometimes I'm Happy" with lyrics by Irving Berlin. The show was a sell-out for almost a year. (Even before it hit Broadway in April, it had done surprisingly well in a two-week tryout at the Chestnut Street Opera House in Philadelphia.[23])

In May 1928, Donlevy met newspaperman Louis Sobol, an aspiring playwright, and appeared in his farce *The High Hatters* with a young Robert Montgomery.[24] The critics were scathing: "Perhaps a feebler script … has reached Broadway in the past few years but it is not very likely," wrote one of the kinder reviewers.[25] The show very soon closed. Sobol's editor must have had a sense of humor because he promptly made him his newspaper's drama critic. Sobol later wrote an anecdotal memoir of his years on Broadway, and his impressions provide some vivid atmosphere of the era and its characters.

Donlevy next played a prizefighter in *Ringside*. Rehearsals began at the Garrick Theater in Detroit in June 1928.[26] The play was well-received from the opening night in July. It was especially praised for its realism and its "racy, vivid third act" set in Madison Square Garden. "What a kick the New York mob will get out of this baby," declared one critic, and true to form it was a success when it ran at New York's Broadhurst Theater from August to October 1928.[27]

Playing the role of Grace in *Ringside* was Yvonne Grey, a lovely 21-year-old Brooklyn showgirl. She and Donlevy had something of a whirlwind romance and married in Manhattan soon after the show closed on October 5, 1928.[28] Yvonne was in demand; at the same time, she was appearing as Maritza in Ziegfeld's musical comedy *Rosalie* at the New Amsterdam. She had previously been in both *Ziegfeld's Follies* and *George White's Scandals* of 1925 and in the revue *No Foolin'* at the Globe Theater.[29] She had started her career in ballet at the Metropolitan Opera Company, but abandoned operatic ballet because she had ambitions as an actress and eventually planned to play heavy drama roles on screen. Like most chorus girls, she hoped that she would be spotted in a Ziegfeld revue by a big director.[30] The distinction between a Ziegfeld girl and a chorus girl was that the first was described as little more than a clothes horse requiring hardly any dancing ability, "just beauty and costumes," whereas a chorus girl had to be able to dance.[31] Grey once wrote a newspaper article extolling the virtues of the humble lemon as a versatile beautifier and a pick-me-up; "You can hand me a lemon anytime you want to," she declared.[32] Thereafter she often posed for a syndicated beauty column in several newspapers including *The Evening Independent* in Florida. She had also once featured in the famous and eminently collectable magazine *Hessler's Garden of Girls*.

A month after their marriage, Donlevy started in *Rainbow,* a musical set during the California gold rush of 1849, about a man who takes on a new identity after killing a man in a brawl. Although the music was by Oscar Hammerstein II with choreography by Busby Berkeley, *Rainbow* was described as "innovative but unsuccessful."[33] According to a leading music scholar, the show was

> very accomplished with an ambitious libretto by Hammerstein and Laurence Stallings and a blues-jazz score by Vincent Youmans now considered ahead of its time…. Despite some potent scenes and noteworthy songs, *Rainbow* collected only a few compliments from the press and quickly closed.[34]

Donlevy told the story that he got offers for two shows, but his agent talked him out of one and persuaded him to do *Rainbow.* At that time he was making about $225 a week, and on the strength of his agent's assurances he took a year-long lease on a Prospect Place apartment for $250 a month. But it was someone's bright idea to use a donkey on stage. Unsurprisingly, the animal would not cooperate and held up the play for 18 minutes. Donlevy later commented:

> The burro killed it. Most of the audience walked out on the show. I went flat broke, had to live on bran and water. One night, with my rent bill in my pocket, I walked towards the Hudson River. On my way I met the agent. I could have killed him. I told him I was going to jump into the river. He loaned me $200.[35]

The Donlevys were both busy during 1929, Yvonne in the smash hit *Smilin' Through* for practically the whole year. Donlevy, playing in the quiet little comedy *Queen Bee,* "ran away with the show," according to *Variety,* "his stew in the third act wringing laughter in such measure that his performance almost makes the show worthwhile."[36] He was, said another reviewer, "indubitably the best in the cast" and one of those rare actors who could "make a drunk both believable and likeable."[37]

His First Talkies

Between his Broadway engagements, Donlevy made some talkies at the end of the 1920s. He had a small, uncredited role as a reporter in *Gentlemen of the Press* (1929), which marked the feature debut of Walter Huston. Shot in four weeks in January 1929 at the Paramount studios on Long

Donlevy made several movies during his time in New York and had a bit part as a newspaperman in *Gentlemen of the Press* (1929), which was filmed in both sound and silent versions. *Left to right:* Kay Francis, Walter Huston (in his feature debut), Norman Foster, Donlevy.

Island, the movie was released in both sound and silent versions.[38] Donlevy then appeared as the bad boy brother of the title character in the cloyingly sentimental Pathe musical *Mother's Boy* (1929), centering on an Irish-American family and built around the now largely forgotten singer Morton Downey. The story was essentially a reworking of *The Jazz Singer*. Donlevy was again the villain of the piece, a cynical counterpart of the lead. He did not feature too prominently because it was mostly a singing showcase for Downey. This production was praised for its technical competence in sound recording which was then in its early days of development.

Donlevy made only two more film appearances in the next five years. In *Ireno* (1932), a short, Ethel Merman sang a couple of songs in a nightclub set in divorce capitol Reno, Nevada. Donlevy appeared at the beginning in a delightful spot as a drunk. The second was the charming short *The Cinderella Racket,* later retitled *A Modern Cinderella* (1933), filmed by Warner Brothers in their New York studios. Ruth Etting starred as Anita Ragusa, a poor dress shop owner's daughter. She delivers a costume to haughty Carolyn Belmont (Barbara Child) for a fancy dress party at a Park Avenue address. Belmont is not impressed by the costume so Anita models it for her. Anita is mistaken for a guest at the party by a drunk (Donlevy) who takes a shine to her. In the end it turns out that Belmont was really only the maid who thought her mistress had gone out for the evening, but she returns unexpectedly. Mr. Ragusa comes to pick up his daughter and the cab driver is none other than Donlevy. In this slight but jolly tale, Etting got to sing two songs, but it was Donlevy who caught the attention as the drunk. By this time he had perfected his stage act; seldom has such a likable drunk appeared on screen. This 17-minute film and two other Etting shorts can be seen on the Warner Home Video DVD release of *Love Me or Leave Me* (1955).

Man of Broadway (1930–35)

On stage, Donlevy next appeared in the clever comedy *Up Pops the Devil* (September 1930 to January 1931), which received excellent reviews. Critics praised the keen-witted dialogue, one hailing it as "a deftly constructed, splendidly acted play satirizing Greenwich Village Bohemians."[39] Donlevy was among those singled out for praise: "a trunk-packing bit by two stews, Hackett and Donlevy, is one of the funniest scenes in the show." The same critic remarked that the show "makes no claim to greatness but is good fun."[40] *Up Pops the Devil* lasted four months and Donlevy garnered good personal notices; he was even interviewed by the New York press. Around the same time, he received the news from home that his father, nearly 80, had died on January 28, 1931. He had been working at Brickner's woolen mill as usual until a few days earlier. Brian returned to Sheboygan Falls to attend the funeral, which was described in the local press as impressive.[41] He was not among the pallbearers, who were all men with whom Thomas Donlevy had worked.

Stage business was slack for much of 1931 as the economic situation became more serious. Around this time, the Donlevys lived in an apartment at Tudor City and he was often seen walking his two dogs by Ed Sullivan, then a *New York Evening Graphic* sports reporter.[42] The two often met at the New York Athletic Club, where Donlevy would lament his lack of success and confide that he was more than discouraged. Sullivan described him as "always a nice person, quiet, thoughtful."[43] Once a play folded, Donlevy was back at the Athletic Club, where he would swim and work out enthusiastically. Sullivan recalled the young actor's greatest supporter at that time was Paddy, one of the club's rubdown men, an Irishman with a thick brogue. As soon as Paddy learned about the actor's Irish connections, he was a friend for life:

> Paddy divided his allegiance between Jim Barton and Donlevy. He held them up as prime examples of what the Irish could accomplish on stage if they put their minds to it. When they'd tease Paddy about Donlevy's frequent periods of idleness he'd retort with great dignity, "Mr. Donlevy is between engagements."[44]

Donlevy later recalled his years of struggle on Broadway: "There were once four whole days when the only thing that separated my backbone from my stomach was a cup of coffee. It's nice to remember a day when you can take it, but I wouldn't want to do it over again."[45]

After a nine-month lull, Donlevy's next major play was Myron Fagan's light comedy *Peter Flies High,* which started life in a try-out in Detroit in September 1931 and was due to open at the Criterion in New York in October. However, the producers were not satisfied with it and after much revision and a revamp by Frank Craven it opened at the Gaiety Theater on November 9, 1931. The reviews were initially promising, and it was even suggested that it might form the basis for a movie. The verdict was that it had "not much to offer but will probably satisfy as a mild programmer."[46] Then interest waned and the show barely lasted into the following week. In between such failures, Donlevy fell back on his earlier occupation of insurance salesman, at which career he was never especially successful.

Meanwhile, Yvonne played Veronique in the short-lived operetta *Princess Charming* before appearing in *Ziegfeld Follies of 1931.* Her spot in the "Broadway Reverie" was considered one of the show's highlights. These were the last Follies produced during Flo Ziegfeld's lifetime. Ever popular, the revue ran from July to November 1931. It also marked Yvonne's last Broadway appearance.

Donlevy's next big show was *Society Girl* at the Booth Theater, which opened on New Years' Eve 1931. This was a typical tale of its time about a debutante who leads a boxer astray and then leaves him high and dry. It was described by a recent author as the story of a "sophisticated woman in a cheap sex comedy."[47] At the time it was billed as "an amusing evening for Brooklyn and Manhattan and a riotous one for the hinterland."[48] Donlevy was singled out for his "forceful and incisive performance as the manager."[49] He was especially praised for the excellent and subtle way he played the final scene. When Twentieth Century–Fox bought up the film rights for *Society Girl,* Brian was fully expecting to play his original part. But his hopes were dashed once more when his role was given to Spencer Tracy.[50]

In February 1932, Donlevy tried out for a part in Preston Sturges' romantic comedy *Child of Manhattan,* but "after a week of rehearsals Sturges told him he wasn't a good actor and had to let him go."[51] It was somewhat ironic that several years later Sturges sought him as the lead for *The Great McGinty* and said he was a great actor and "a second Spencer Tracy."[52]

Also in February 1932, Donlevy landed a part in *The Inside Story* at the National Theater. This strong political drama concerned racketeers in a Midwest city run by unctuous big shot Louis Corotto (Louis Calhern). Donlevy was said to be a standout as Calhern's assistant, Nick Lipman, in a "carefully prepared and splendidly cast" production.[53] This "dramatically effective" three-act play involved 14 scenes and eight different sets, including three rolling platforms set on steel tracks.[54] Although the early reviews were favorable, business tailed off and the show closed in mid–March 1932 after less than a four-week run.

Donlevy's next play, *The Boy Friend,* began at the Morosco in June 1932. Set in a boarding house run by blowsy Aunt Belle, a one-time chorus girl, this involved some colorful characters and a plot that sounds too complicated for words. One of Belle's indigent chorus girl tenants is Donnie, who is pregnant by "a slippery booking agent [called] Raincoat."[55] Donnie's brother, a wanted gunman from Detroit known as the Eel (Donlevy), loves his sis and comes looking for Raincoat to force him into a shotgun wedding. "Twice Raincoat makes a getaway, once up the fire escape to the roof, which provides a swell curtain line uttered by the Detroiter to the effect that the dope is as near to heaven as he ever will be."[56]

There were two other eccentric characters: a sugar daddy who pretends to drop dead and turns out to be a federal agent in disguise, and a newspaperman so incompetent that he delivers his exclusive story over the phone to a rival paper. This lively melodrama tried to pack in everything. One reviewer noted that Donlevy "plays the tough Eel very well."[57] Another said he was "the hit of the evening … and plays [in a] very legitimate and effective" way, in contrast to the frenetic style of the other players.[58] A "strange mixture teaming with plot," *The Boy Friend* only ran for 15 nights.[59]

Donlevy next replaced Thomas Mitchell in *Honeymoon,* which ended in February 1933.[60] He came in at very short notice and had little time to get into the role. The following month he began in *Three-Cornered Moon,* for which he drew plaudits as the "well-balanced doctor," and seemed "the one sane person" in the misfire comedy.[61] Also in the cast was a young Elisha Cook, Jr., who became a friend. Ruth Gordon received the best notices.[62]

Donlevy had the lead in *Another Man's Son* for the Mariarden Players at the Peterborough Dramatic Festival, held in Providence, Rhode Island in the summer of 1933. It was a hackneyed story about a man who longs for a son and heir and is hoodwinked into bringing up someone else's child. "The acting and dialogue lifted the piece above the average on the first night, but how it will size up on Broadway is a matter of deep conjecture."[63] The show never made it to Broadway. At the Cape Playhouse, Massachusetts, in early September, he started in Rachel Crothers' *Talent,* which featured a young Rosalind Russell. Crothers was one of the most noted female dramatists of her day; her well-constructed plays often explored feminist themes. *Talent* was due to open at the Royale in New York on January 2, 1934, but then the leading lady developed acute laryngitis so the production was abandoned.[64]

Donlevy did particularly well in an adaptation of Denys Amiel's French comedy *Three and One* at the Longacre Theater from October to the end of December 1933. Playing yet another boxer, he was required to perform some knockabout stunts; at one point he had to fall out of bed with his arms full of books. One reviewer called his "superb playing … the saving grace of the piece."[65]

> The acting is first-rate. Brian Donlevy, who has done many pleasing things, is at his liveliest and best as the talkative young athlete constantly being called stupid by his brothers but apparently the brightest of the three.[66]

He was next scheduled to start in the comedy *Sing and Whistle* at the Fulton, but at short notice switched to *Broken Doll* with Spring Byington.[67]

This was retitled *No Questions Asked* and began at the Theater Masque February 5, 1934. The plot followed the travails of a woman who tries to commit suicide while on board a ship, but is saved by a Park Avenue lush who takes her home. When he finds out that she has been left pregnant and abandoned by her lover, he gets drunk, but later returns and asks her to marry him with no questions asked. Although considered a slight piece, it had good dialogue, and Donlevy received decent notices. *Variety* commented that he "has had better jobs, but as Pat's [Byington] suitor he scored."[68] The premiere seemed promising, but bad weather that winter resulted in a short run.

Donlevy was a good friend of fellow cast member Ross Alexander. They were members of a group of six struggling

An early publicity photo of Donlevy, who was once dubbed "the answer to a flapper's dream." During his Broadway years (1924 to 1935), Donlevy mostly played comedy roles. Some of his highlights included *What Price Glory?* (1924–26), *Hit the Deck* (1927–28), *Ringside* (1928), *Up Pops the Devil* (1930–31) and *The Milky Way* (1934).

young Broadway actors who used to meet once a week for lunch. The idea was that the one who had made the best "break" of the week treated everyone. The other members were Owen Davis, Jr., Henry Fonda, James Stewart and Elisha Cook, Jr.[69] There were many weeks when all six bought their own lunches. Davis, son of a Pulitzer Prize–winning dramatist, appeared in a few films including *All Quiet on the Western Front* (1930). After war service, he moved into TV production but was drowned while sailing off Long Island, at age 41.[70] Alexander made several movies including *Captain Blood* (1935) and seemed to have everything going for him. But his life took a downward spiral after his wife Aleta committed suicide and he got into debt. Although he married again, he became depressed and shot himself almost a year later in the same location and with the same gun his wife had used, according to Henry Fonda.[71]

Donlevy took the lead in another light and sophisticated comedy, *The Perfumed Lady*, which first played at the Plymouth Theater in Boston at the end of February 1934. The show was doing fairly well, but suddenly folded after only a week, when it was partially recast. When the play moved to Broadway, critics had few kind words, but noted that Donlevy "did good work."[72] He was used to knockabout antics on stage and became inured to being smashed over the head with a Chinese vase every night and matinee.[73] Despite the naysayers, *The Perfumed Lady* did surprisingly good business and lasted for a month.

Donlevy was second lead to his good friend Hugh O'Connell in *The Milky Way*, "an instant hit and good all summer."[74] The premiere was attended by Lillian Hellman. It featured the "likable Donlevy" as yet another "husky little champion" fighter.[75] Although he was the real fighter, he had to watch crafty milkman O'Connell as he became middleweight champion. Also in the cast was the wonderful Gladys George. Donlevy's character was smacked several times, hit by a cane until it broke and finally floored by a stage punch that was rather too convincing.[76] The reviews were uniformly good: "The script crackles, the action roars by and there's never a let-down throughout."[77] He was praised for his portrayal of "the most horizontal champ ever on the stage." *Variety* commented: "He has been in plenty of shows this season, but this time he has the best chance to stick around the same theater for a while."[78] Even so, it was O'Connell's turn to reap the benefit, and he was whisked off to Hollywood on the strength of his performance.

Even before *The Milky Way* finished its run in August 1934, Donlevy was already rehearsing for the revue *Life Begins at 8:40,* which had a Boston try-out in July. The show looked like a surefire hit from the first night at the Winter Garden in New York: "A large, glittering and enthusiastic audience found this lively, tuneful and jolly entertainment greatly to its liking."[79]

The show featured music by Harold Arlen and lyrics by Ira Gershwin and Yip Harburg. Audiences stayed entertained for the next seven months: The combination of music, dancing and sketches proved an ideal mix, and revues were very popular in both America and Europe at this time. Donlevy featured in five segments. In the sketch "Quartet Erotica," he played the French novelist de Maupassant with the great Bert Lahr as Balzac and Ray Bolger as Italian poet Boccaccio. All of them joined in a song lamenting their decline in potency in the modern age. Lahr and Donlevy combined well in a sketch about the money markets, "A Day at the Brokers," of which one commentator noted that the "market crash is just old enough that audiences who got socked can take the skit and laugh."[80] Donlevy received good reviews for his knockabout comedy routines with the two comics. In a few years, Lahr and Bolger would achieve immortality as the Cowardly Lion and Scarecrow in *The Wizard of Oz* (1939).

Somehow the relationship between Brian and Yvonne petered out. It must have been more than just the attention he was getting from the chorus girls in *Life Begins at 8:40.*[81] Each spent such long hours working on shows, and neither had advanced greatly. Yvonne's career in particular had stalled; she had not appeared in a major show for four years. In early 1934 she traveled to England, returning home in May on the *Champlain.*[82] By the time Brian made the trip to Hollywood a year later, the spring of 1935, his wife did not go with him. In September she travelled again to Europe on the *Britannic,* and arrived back in New York on October 13 where she stayed at the Hotel Tudor registered as Yvonne Grey-Donlevy.[83] After living apart for several months they were divorced in Reno, Nevada, on February 1, 1936, at her instigation, citing cruelty. She was awarded $5000. In October 1936, Yvonne went to London as a dancer in the revue *Transatlantic Rhythm* at the Adelphi Theater on the Strand.[84] There she was spotted by Gastao Raul Nothman, a real estate agent. After a year-long courtship they married at Caxton Hall Register Office, Westminster, on December 10, 1937, in the presence of the ambassador and the Marquis of Queensbury.[85] Yvonne, who was 30, wore a heavy fur coat and a spray of orchids.[86] The couple had a daughter, Susan Belinda Nothman. The erudite Gastao, known as "Bobby," hailed from an old Paulista family. Originally from Brazil, he had been educated in England, and became secretary to the Brazilian ambassador in 1940. He was also editor of and contributor to a number of books published in his native Brazil. Recently it was revealed that during the war, Yvonne was an Intelligence agent for the Special Operations Executive.[87] Bobby, 19 years older than his wife, died in London on March 26, 1958, at age 69.[88] In time, Yvonne retired to the quiet coastal resort of Torbay, Devon, where she died in November 1999 at age 92.[89]

At the end of spring 1935, Donlevy said farewell to Broadway, to his wife, and to the last dozen years of his life. His friends, including James Cagney, had told him that breaking into Hollywood was a lead pipe cinch. But they added the proviso "Don't go until you are asked."[90] Time was passing for the impatient Donlevy, who was not about to wait to be asked. He took a plane out west to the city of dreams where he had longed to be all along.

3

Hollywood at Last:
The Fox Years

"Season after season on Broadway I saw fellows in the same shows with me signed up and whisked away to Hollywood, success and salaries. But it somehow passed me up. Closing one night in Detroit, I hopped a plane to the coast just to see what was wrong."
—"He Wasn't Wanted," *The Brooklyn Daily Eagle*,
January 10, 1937, 66

Tired of waiting for Hollywood to call him, Donlevy flew to Los Angeles and stayed for a spell with his close friend, the actor Hugh O'Connell. He had heard that Paramount had acquired the rights for *The Milky Way* in which they had both appeared, and went straight to the studio hoping to land the same role. To his great disappointment, he learned that it had already been given to William Gargan. Time passed and his money was fast running out. When he only had enough for his fare back to New York, O'Connell lent him $100. After that, Donlevy decided to make things happen. He called Sam Goldwyn's casting director Bob McIntyre, who he knew was a soft touch,[1] and McIntyre gave him the part of a heavy in Howard Hawks' *Barbary Coast* (1935). The role pretty much set the tone for his early career. And Goldwyn offered him a long-term contract, although the exact term was not specified.[2]

Barbary Coast was an atmospheric yarn set in fog-bound San Francisco at the height of the Gold Rush. The town is run by Luis Chamalis (Edward G. Robinson) and his henchmen, especially Knuckles Jacoby (Donlevy), from their headquarters in the Bella Donna saloon. Into this den of iniquity comes New Yorker Mary Rutledge (Miriam Hopkins), who finds that her fiancé is dead and his gold claim gone. After meeting Chamalis, she soon finds herself running the Bella Donna's crooked gambling tables. On the orders of Chamalis, Knuckles kills a man who lost at the roulette wheel. A Chinese witness identifies Knuckles as the killer, but Chamalis has his own resident, rarely sober judge dismiss the case.

Mary becomes dissatisfied with her life and goes horse-riding one day in the rain. She stops out of town near the gold fields where she takes shelter for the night with Jim Carmichael (Joel McCrea), a poetry lover who has spent two years on his claim. She lies to him about herself and returns to town. He later sees her at the Bella Donna and loses all his gold on her roulette wheel. The town becomes increasingly lawless and matters come to a head when Knuckles murders two others, one of whom is news-paperman Col. Cobb. Vigilantes hang Knuckles and then go after Chamalis. Mary attempts to make a getaway in a boat with Carmichael, who is shot. She pleads for his life with Chamalis, who lets her go at the end as the vigilantes have come for him. She joins her lover on the ship back to New York.

Making his Hollywood debut in a small role in *Barbary Coast* (1935), Donlevy made certain he was noticed by wearing black throughout. As a result, he was suddenly in demand and was given a contract by Sam Goldwyn. Left to right: Donlevy, Joel McCrea, Edward G. Robinson and Walter Brennan.

Inspired by Herbert Asbury's popular 1933 novel *The Barbary Coast*, the moviemakers were compelled to considerably tone down the "sordidness and … low-tone morality" of the original. Influential film censor and head of the Production Code Administration, Joseph Breen, especially objected to the first script he was shown. So much so that in the film, there is no mention of prostitution; it became instead a rather insipid love story between a "fine, clean girl and a sentimental young man." Breen was very satisfied with the result, which he called "the finest and most intelligent picture I have seen in many months."[3] One wonders if Asbury felt the same.

Donlevy had little to do; he had few lines and was only a subordinate of Robinson, constantly doing his bidding. The character was not allowed to emerge as anything other than a heartless heavy. Nevertheless, the young actor managed somehow to be noticed. He knew he had one chance to be seen and was determined to stand out in some way. The others were dressed in flowery costumes and he asked the head of the wardrobe for something plain; he passed him a black shirt that Clark Gable had worn in *The Call of the Wild*. This gave him an idea, and, very effectively, he wore black throughout. He was careful that every item of his clothing was black. This ensured that he was noticeable in all group shots even when he was in the background, and compensated for his lack of dialogue. It also enhanced his sense of menace. Also, as he is escorted to his hanging by the vigilantes, it made the fear in his face more noticeable in the fog. This was one of the most memorable scenes in the film in its economy and intent. Actually the scene was almost too real when an extra pulled on the wrong rope and nearly strangled him.[4] Afterwards Donlevy kept the shirt as a lucky charm.[5]

In everyday life, he also wore plain suits. The idea came to him when he was an Annapolis midshipman. One Sunday, he noticed a visiting clergyman giving a sermon, wearing a long black robe. He was fascinated by the way he was dressed: "I couldn't take my eyes off his face," he said.[6]

Donlevy was noticed after his first role and offers came thick and fast for the handsome new tough guy. Most called for the same vein of villainy. He was next seen as another hoodlum's right hand man in *Mary Burns, Fugitive* (1935). The story centered on Mary (Sylvia Sidney), a law-abiding café owner madly in love with "Babe" Wilson (Alan Baxter), who she soon learns is a ruthless gangster. During her trial as an accomplice, she is accused of withholding evidence and aiding a felon. The jury refuses to believe that she knew nothing about him. She is sentenced to 15 years and placed in a cell with Kate (Esther Dale) a stool pigeon, as the authorities expect she will try to escape and lead them to Wilson. When with

Kate's aid, she does escape, the G-men are aware of her every move. Mary finds work at a hospital, where she meets patient Barton Powell (Melvyn Douglas), who cannot see her because his eyes are bandaged. He falls for her voice and the way she makes coffee. Wilson and his cohorts rob a football stadium during a big match. Wilson later sends his aide Spike (Donlevy) to find Mary and bring her to him. With Kate's help, Mary gives Spike the slip, and he is shot by the Feds. Wilson meets up with Mary at a church. When the Feds move in, he kidnaps her and threatens the congregation with a grenade. Eventually the long arm of the law catches up with him and there is the expected happy ending.

Sidney, giving an excellent, emotional performance as always, was the main attraction of the film, which was described by a contemporary commentator as "a swift-moving, soul-stirring drama."[7] A later reviewer called it "a good typical wish-fulfillment melodrama of the '30s."[8] Donlevy was again noticed by critics, one of whom called him "a frozen pan gent of considerable versatility and vogue."[9] He was decidedly striking as Wilson's assistant; although the role was fairly small, it was many-shaded. The soft-spoken Spike's motivations were ambiguous. At times he waxed lyrical to his companions on the nature of love, but was unpredictable, which added to his potency. He made a convincing menace, "too convincing for comfort" according to *Modern Screen,* which gave the film four stars.[10] The scene of the attempted arrest in the church caused the most problems with the censors and in some countries it was taken out altogether.[11] Some of the most effective scenes took place in the tenement building where Mary hides out. This set was specially built on stilts.[12] The trade papers remarked that Donlevy, in only his second (Hollywood) film, was already proving popular.

Another Face (1936) was a briskly told but incredibly far-fetched gangster tale. In New York, things have become so hot for ugly hoodlum "Broken Nose" Dawson (Donlevy) that he arranges for a doctor to perform plastic surgery on his face so that he can evade the law. Pleased with the results, he takes the advice of his hapless sidekick Muggsie to try his luck in the movies. Before he leaves for his new life, he ensures that the doctor, a nurse and Muggsie are wiped out so they cannot talk. But he fails to reckon on another nurse who was a witness, and she also goes to Los Angeles. Passing himself off as rich playboy Spencer Dutro III, he finagles his way into a movie although he cannot act. Re-enter the nurse, who recognizes him immediately and tries to convince fanciful press agent Joe Haynes (Wallace Ford) about Dutro's real identity. After many shenanigans, Dutro is unmasked and caught by the cops.

The film strains credulity a little too much and was too comedic to be scary and yet not quite a comedy. "It was all sheer hokum," commented one reviewer, "but audiences hungry for a peek behind the cameras made it a respectable hit."[13] It might almost have been a sprightly precursor to *Dark Passage* (1947), but somehow could not quite decide whether it wanted to be thriller or satire, although it would have worked better as the latter. Donlevy, who was becoming known, had second billing behind Ford, at that time a far more established actor. The normally reliable Ford appeared rather shrill at times, but there was great support from the redoubtable Alan Hale. The plot would stand no scrutiny. The central premise was shaky enough, but the idea that the nurse who was present during the surgery would immediately go to Los Angeles was just one of many hard-to-swallow coincidences. Also, although she was not present when his bandages were removed, she had no trouble recognizing him at the studios. But such plot contrivances were not allowed to get in the way. There was ample opportunity for Donlevy to display his comedic talents, as some critics noted: "Donlevy provides not only thrills … but a large measure of the comedy. His attempt to perform like a ham actor is magnificent and supplies several of the best laughs in the film."[14]

It's surprising that more comedy roles did not come his way on the strength of *Another Face*, because at this stage of his career he seemed most suited to them. Here is a glimpse of the Broadway actor-comedian. He did especially well in scenes with Ethel Wales as eccentric spinster Aunt Hattie, whom he reluctantly accompanies on a walk at the beach. He said a great deal with sidelong glances and in his delivery of asides, and it was at such times that a future career in satiric roles seemed likely. It must have given the young actor some satisfaction to be directed by Christy Cabanne, the man who had dashed his dreams at the age of 21 when he (Cabanne) told him flatly that he would never make it in the movies.

Donlevy next turned up as another gangster in the jolly Eddie Cantor comedy *Strike Me Pink,* (1936), originally titled *Shoot the Chutes.* This time Donlevy was the head of a gang that menaces Eddie Pink (Cantor), timid new manager of the Dreamland amusement park. The gang discovers that Eddie is wild about glamorous singer Joyce Lennox (Ethel Merman), the wife of a gang member, and has her trick him into installing crooked slot machines. This pleasant but overlong movie ended on a high point with an inventive chase on a rollercoaster as Eddie is pursued by cops. (The Dreamland scenes were filmed at the Nu Pike Amusement Park at Long Beach, California.) The young Merman sang a few songs, but

Donlevy had little scope beyond the heavy's usual duties. *Strike Me Pink* was the fourth of five planned films in Cantor's Goldwyn contract, but it did not perform as well as the others at the box office, and the fifth was never made.[15]

The 1930s was the decade when aviation came into its own, and Mitchell Leisen's *Thirteen Hours by Air* (1936) was a typical adventure set aboard a Boeing 247. Donlevy's friend Fred MacMurray starred as pilot Jack Gordon. Among the assorted passengers traveling from New York to San Francisco are a nine-year-old heir to a fortune and his governess, a spoiled socialite (Joan Bennett) suspected of being a jewel thief, and Everts (Donlevy) who calls himself a doctor but seems to know little about medicine. Everts turns out to be a federal agent in pursuit of the dangerous criminal Palmer (Alan Baxter). During an altercation, Palmer shoots Everts and the co-pilot and tries to hijack the plane. He is stopped by Gordon, who flies them to safety.

The movie employed 500 extras and featured footage from airports all across the country. Airline executives who viewed the first rushes objected to the scenes of an emergency landing, so these scenes were altered accordingly.[16] Although the formula seemed overfamiliar, even in 1936, Donlevy caught the attention of Twentieth Century–Fox production boss Darryl F. Zanuck, who on the strength of this film offered him a contract.

His first assignment *Human Cargo* (1936) dealt with the human trafficking. The movie gave Donlevy a good lead role as Packy Campbell, an ace reporter assigned to cover the story. He must compete with beautiful debutante Bonnie Brewster (Claire Trevor), who works for a rival newspaper in order to see some real action. The gang they are investigating not only smuggles the migrants into the U.S. but makes them work as virtual slaves and then demands extortion money. Campbell discovers that nightclub singer Carmen Zoro (Rita Hayworth) knows more than is good for her about the gang. He secretes her at his apartment where he gains her trust and persuades her to tell him the whole story. Bonnie suddenly barges in with the police. Carmen is taken to police headquarters, but is shot through a door before she can speak. Bonnie teams up with Campbell to pursue the gang responsible. They eventually track the gang to Vancouver and join a boat of illegal migrants crossing into the U.S. With a little ingenuity the two reporters manage to save the day.

An entertaining adventure, *Human Cargo* was one of the few films of the decade to deal with the thorny subject of illegal migrants and proves that the misery of people-smuggling is hardly a new phenomenon. This

Human Cargo (1936) starred Donlevy as an ace reporter who exposes a people-smuggling racket. His co-star was Claire Trevor, but among the cast Rita Cansino (above right), caught the eye. The following year she changed her name to Rita Hayworth, and the rest, as they say, is history.

marked the first teaming of Donlevy and Trevor, who did remarkably well with their quick-fire repartee. Donlevy was singled out by one reviewer for his "restrained and believable" performance.[17] Impressed, Zanuck promised to promote the two leads to real star status, but neither really benefitted.[18] The movie is perhaps most notable as containing one of the early appearances by "Rita Cansino," who changed her name to Rita Hayworth the following year.

In *Half Angel* (1936), Alison Lang (the beautiful Frances Dee) is accused of poisoning her father. At the trial, all the evidence seems to be against her, but a "not guilty" verdict is returned by the jury. Duffy Giles (Donlevy) a reporter, goes straight up to Alison hoping to get her life story. Before he can interview her, she is spirited away by Mrs. Hargraves, whose house contains an assortment of ex-criminals and other down-on-their-luck individuals. Her husband disapproves strongly of her work, but cannot change her mind. Duffy arranges to meet Alison at the front gate one night. When she returns to the house, she finds Mrs. Hargraves dead and Prof. Hargraves apparently dying as a result of poisoning. Alison is arrested for their murder. Duffy, convinced of her innocence, sets out to trap the real culprit.

Another engaging comedy thriller, *Half Angel* showed Donlevy to advantage once again as a lively newspaperman who is the only one who believes in Dee. There was a decided air of mystery in some of the settings, especially the eerie house and its sinister inhabitants. The script was co-written by Gene Fowler from a story by English author and criminologist F. Tennyson Jesse, great-niece of poet laureate Alfred, Lord Tennyson. The combination of mystery and comedy put this in the tradition of such films as *The Cat and the Canary,* and it was enhanced by the presence of Charles Butterworth as Donlevy's assistant.

Human Cargo director Allan Dwan next cast Donlevy in *Trouble-makers,* which was later retitled *High Tension* (1936), an energetic comedy in which he starred as Steve Reardon, an underwater telephone cable-layer in the Pacific.[19] A larger-than-life character and one of the best in

Playing another crusading reporter in *Half Angel* (1936), Donlevy is the only one who believes in the luminous Frances Dee, accused of poisoning her father.

the business, Reardon is a popular figure at the company run by the irascible Willard Stone. Steve is the fiancé of Edith McNeil (Glenda Farrell), whom he calls Mac. She writes comic book stories, and he delights in reading them because they are written about him and his daring exploits. His romance with Mac is on again off again, and in one of the off times he gets drunk and goes to a bar where he sings "That Woman Made a Monkey Out of Me" and gets into a brawl with Ward Bond, who wants to get his hands on the cash Steve is flashing around.

Steve wakes up the next day and finds that pianist Eddie Mitchell (Norman Foster) has taken care of him and saved his money. He repays Mitchell, an out-of-work engineer, by training him to be a cable-layer and finding a job for him. Soon Mitchell is sent to Honolulu to take over as chief engineer. His decision to dynamite a section of coral is met with opposition from another engineer. Steve comes to Honolulu and makes a play for Mitchell's attractive secretary Brenda Burke (Helen Wood), who Eddie is also sweet on. Mac follows Steve to Honolulu and they decide to get married. Steve and Eddie fall out, then settle their differences when Eddie is trapped at the bottom of the ocean and Steve saves his life. Naturally, everything ends happily for all.

Short on running time (a little over an hour), *High Tension* was a boisterous knockabout comedy that also had several satiric aspects. Rich businessmen angrily berate the switchboard girls because their cables from overseas are ten minutes late arriving, meanwhile the cable-layers have to dive to great depths and undergo many hazards to repair them. There was some snappy dialogue amidst the rough-and-tumble humor. Donlevy seemed hyperactive, but the frenetic pace was par for the course of many other 1930s movies, which were often played at fever pitch. This was a great showcase for him and proved beyond a doubt that he had no trouble carrying a film. He was a very likable, fast-talking would-be big shot, full of hot air and very easy to see through. His character is typified by a scene when he is put in jail and boasts to the other inmates that he is indispensable to his boss, who will soon see him released. His boss never turns up, but Mac bails him out. All the other inmates call after him mockingly as he leaves: "Good night, Stevie."

He engages in a lot of physical comedy which he handles well. There is the memorable sight of him on a child's bicycle riding around the office, and a farcical run-in with a prizefighter which at one stage involves an improbable set-to with a grand piano. In one scene, Donlevy was required to walk 15 miles underwater in a diving suit. Somehow his air hose was fouled and he was unconscious when he was dragged out by technicians.[20]

He was next added to the cast of Jack London's *White Fang* but was missing from the final cut.[21] He was then announced as the lead in *Across the Aisle* opposite Gloria Stuart, which was retitled *36 Hours to Kill* (1936). This was the best so far, a decent story with appealing actors and a fine atmosphere. It gave Donlevy a first-class opportunity to shine as a bona fide leading man who actually gets the girl. The story concerned wanted criminal Duke Benson (Douglas Fowley), who hops a train to collect his winning sweepstakes ticket in Kansas. Donlevy is Frank Evers, the G-man on his trail posing as a reporter. He falls for fellow passenger Anne Marvis (Stuart), who is trying to escape a California subpoena by crossing the border to Arizona. Benson realizes he is being shadowed and knocks out the other G-man on the train, making his getaway at Topeka and taking Anne as hostage. They make for a hideout at Borden's Sanitarium where the gang meets. Evers traps Benson and the gang by placing an article in

Donlevy made a wonderfully breezy G-man in *36 Hours to Kill* (1936) and was seen to great effect opposite romantic screen partner Gloria Stuart. This underrated gem was one of the finest of the films he made during his time at Twentieth Century–Fox.

the newspaper claiming that a couple has come forward to claim the winning ticket. The gang's crooked lawyer takes him out to the sanitarium where Benson is waiting with a bandaged face. The quick-thinking Evers saves the day and the gal.

Well-received at the time, *36 Hours to Kill* got a glowing notice from *The Times* of London, which praised the two leading actors for

> the exceeding naturalness of their manner, the gaiety with which they replace the tension of the hunted, and the unusual charm with which they invest the stock characters.... As films go, this is remarkably unpretentious, depending for its success on a comparatively simple story, and instead of on the doubtful glamor of stars, on intelligent and sometimes moving acting.[22]

Stuart was perhaps the best co-star Donlevy had in this period, and all the other minor actors contributed enormously. Especially noticeable was James Burke as a constantly outwitted man trying to serve Gloria with a subpoena, and Stepin Fetchit as a lackadaisical porter. The story by veteran W.R. Burnett was solid, and the scenes on the train were especially effective. Director Eugene Forde, famous for the popular *Charlie Chan* series, handled the actors very well. The script kept things moving, and the only drawback was the short running time; perhaps more could have been done on the train. The momentum tended to slow down once they reached Topeka. However, the movie boded well for Donlevy's immediate future at Fox and he seemed at this point to be moving in the right direction. He even joined Stuart in a rendition of "Row, Row, Row the Boat" while sitting in the observation car during one of the most romantic scenes he had so far enjoyed on screen.

Donlevy was due to start in the romantic comedy *Ladies in Love* (1936), starring Janet Gaynor and Loretta Young, but was replaced by Alan Mowbray.[23] He was switched to *Crack-Up* (1936), an above-average adventure, lifted immeasurably by the presence of Peter Lorre. Donlevy's "Ace" Martin is assigned to fly the experimental airplane the *Wild Goose*, designed by John Fleming (Ralph Morgan), on transatlantic flights. Martin is actually an agent paid by a foreign government to steal top secret aviation plans. He convinces his roommate and co-pilot Joe Randall (Thomas Beck) to obtain them from the office. Martin tells him that the plans are for a new type of propeller that he invented and that someone stole. Col. Gimpy (Lorre), an eccentric who hangs around the airport, is in reality the head of an international spy ring. Fleming is keen to leave in pursuit of his wife, who has left him, and the *Wild Goose* makes a swift nighttime getaway. Martin has the plans with him. There is a stowaway on board, Col. Gimpy. The weather is poor and Martin ends up a long way off course.

Via a radio message from his girlfriend, Randall learns the truth about Martin and takes the controls. In his panic he crashes the plane into the sea, and Martin is blinded in the process. There is only one life jacket which is given to Randall, who escapes; the other three are doomed.

Director Malcolm St. Clair made several pre–Code features including an early version of *Gentlemen Prefer Blondes* (1928) and *Dangerous Nan McGrew* (1930). He went on to direct Laurel and Hardy in three of their later films. *Crack-Up* had some appealing noir elements, such as the double life of Col. Gimpy who moves from a busy street scene as a harmless idiot, enters a house, goes through to a backroom and is revealed as a mastermind. The film was peopled by several familiar faces and plenty of shady characters, including J. Carrol Naish. The best part is at the end, when the protagonists are trapped in the sinking plane. "You're a strange fellow, Martin," observes Gimpy, after having been shot by him. "Under other circumstances, we could have been good friends." Lorre was a natural; even in this type of undemanding fare, he made the admission fee worthwhile. He was aided by Donlevy, who thought the movie was "swell" and was effusive in his praise for Lorre's great skill as a comedian.[24] The *Inde-*

Malcolm St. Clair's espionage adventure *Crack-Up* (1937) was a typical Fox film of the era. It was decidedly lifted out of the commonplace by the presence of Peter Lorre (center) and Donlevy (right), seen here with Thomas Beck (left).

pendent Exhibitor's Film Bulletin commented: "Except for a surprise twist at the end, *Crack-Up* is not particularly fresh, yet these two players contrive, between them, to make it constantly engrossing."[25]

Midnight Taxi (1937) was a reasonable second feature about G-man Chick Gardner (Donlevy), who infiltrates a counterfeiting ring. He poses as a taxi driver to discover the identity of the top man. He is taken into the organization by Philip Strickland (Alan Dinehart), but not trusted by his deputy Flash Dillon (Gilbert Roland). From fellow gang member Gilda Lee (Frances Drake) he discovers that there is a plan to smuggle a big consignment of counterfeit bills at a distant wharf that night. He makes contact with federal agents, who attempt to foil the landing, but they are discovered and the gang makes a getaway. He is shot by his own men trying to escape. Having discovered Gardner's true identity, Dillon tells Lee to get rid of him. Instead she shoots Dillon and agrees to help Gardner in return for immunity from prosecution. Gardner joins up with his fellow agents while Lee goes with Strickland to the yacht of John Rudd, secret head of the organization. Then the feds close in.

The film moved swiftly (only 73 minutes) but it was well-realized overall, and Donlevy practically carried the proceedings. He was strikingly believable despite all the seemingly impossible situations he gets in and out of. One critic commented: "Brian Donlevy, a most convincing and natural actor, provides a piece of excellent portraiture."[26] Originally, *Midnight Taxi* was to have been a tale of narcotic smugglers, but the Production Code Administration's Joseph Breen objected, and the subject was changed to counterfeit money.[27]

Next came *This Is My Affair* (1937), a generally good vehicle for Robert Taylor and Barbara Stanwyck. Donlevy had only a few scenes and was shot in the second reel, so his character had no time to develop. The scenario began well with Lt. Perry (Taylor) being asked by President McKinley (Frank Conroy) to infiltrate a gang of bank robbers who are well-connected, and to report his findings only to himself, not even to the Secret Service. Perry easily locates the gang which consists of Batiste Duryea (Donlevy) and Jock Ramsay (Victor McLaglen), then falls in love with Duryea's sister Lil (Stanwyck) a nightclub singer. Duryea is killed while taking part in a robbery; Ramsay is wounded but escapes. Although Perry is successful in his mission, by the time he is able to report back, President McKinley has been assassinated. A new president, Theodore Roosevelt, is in office and knows nothing about the case. Accused of being a spy, Perry is imprisoned, but his life is saved by the intervention of a trusted secretary.

This Is My Affair is something of a curiosity for fans of Stanwyck. Although the premise is intriguing, it does seem odd that a president would approach a Navy lieutenant to go undercover and bypass the Secret Service. However, the story was said to be based on fact and is perhaps bizarre enough to be true in essence. The screenplay often evoked a distinct sense of its time and seemed imbued with nostalgia for the *fin de siècle*, which was then within the memory of many viewers. In the scene where Taylor and Stanwyck go boating on the lake to the accompaniment of "On the Banks of the Wabash Far Away," this nostalgia for a seemingly simpler time is very apparent. After one world war, the Depression and the looming political crisis in Europe, the time of McKinley and Roosevelt must have seemed a far more hopeful one in retrospect. The film, seldom mentioned today, was well received at the time and director William Seiter was nominated for the Mussolini Cup at the Venice Film Festival in 1937. British writer Graham Greene commented that the movie was "the best American melodrama of the year [with] admirable acting, quick and cunning direction [and] a sense of doom, of almost classic suspense."[28]

In *Born Reckless* (1937), Donlevy played Bob Kane, a champion race-car driver. He goes to work for a struggling taxi firm run by his friends the Martins, who are being literally bounced off the road by a rival company owned by Jim Barnes (Barton MacLane). Barnes' cars are made of reinforced steel, and he offers Kane $200 a week to drive for him. Kane intentionally wrecks some of Barnes' cars. Meanwhile, he falls for Barnes' girl Sybil (Rochelle Hudson). After a driver is killed by one of Barnes' men, Martin attempts to involve the district attorney to prosecute Barnes; however, realizing there is not enough evidence to convict him, Kane changes his testimony. This is a ploy by the Martins in order to let Kane infiltrate the gang and insure a conviction. In time, Kane, with help from Sybil, manages to trap Barnes, and also saves the Martins' garage from being blown up by a gasoline truck.

An entertaining movie, *Born Reckless* had many of the same elements that the other 1930s Fox product had: comedy, romance, thrills, a fast-moving story and snappy dialogue. Generally light-hearted in tone, this was as undemanding as the others, but no less successful. It did not move Donlevy's career forward greatly, but showed that he had no difficulty carrying a film, and could play a romantic and dashing hero as easily as he could a heel. Kane is an archetypal period character; a ladies' man who is never at a loss for words and often fond of a punch-up. This persona was a long way removed from the off-screen Donlevy. In yet another accident during a barroom scene, he had to smash a bottle, which nearly sliced off his finger. Afterwards he spent ten days in the hospital with an infected finger.[29]

Among all the movies Donlevy made at Fox in this period, *In Old Chicago* (1937) was one of the most prestigious, made at a cost of $2 million in direct competition with MGM's *San Francisco*. One of the few musical disaster movies, it starred Alice Faye as nightclub singer Belle Fawcett. The narrative begins with the O'Leary family in a covered wagon bound for a new life in Chicago. When they are within sight of the city, the father tries to race with a train; the horses bolt and he is dragged to his death. His wife and their three sons go on to the city. Immediately the mother finds work taking in people's laundry, living in an area known as "the Patch."

Years pass and the sons grow up. Dion (Tyrone Power) is a gambler, Jack (Don Ameche) is a lawyer with political ambitions and the third brother looks after the family cow. In the laundry, they find a tablecloth with a drawing by businessman Gil Warren (Donlevy). They realize it is a plan to run a tramline along a street and buy up the land cheaply. Dion bribes politicians to build a saloon on the street and run it himself. He tricks Warren into thinking he will support his bid to be mayor, but in truth he is working for Jack to become mayor. When Jack is successful, Dion expects him to do his bidding. Jack refuses and starts to target corruption in the Patch. The brothers are at loggerheads from then on and fight even more when Dion marries Fawcett to prevent her from testifying. When a cow upsets an oil lamp in the O'Leary barn, the fire spreads quickly. There is an attempt to construct a firewall by using dynamite to prevent the blaze from reaching the gasworks. Jack is shot and crushed to death by a falling building. Shortly afterwards, Warren is trampled to death by stampeding cattle. Dion, Belle, Mrs. O'Leary and the others escape.

There was something sadly lacking in the conception of this film and many of the characters are badly written. The fire scenes are among the best and most memorable parts and the story was mere background. Donlevy, his hair curiously styled in a kiss-curl, replete with impressive handlebar moustache and fancy waistcoat, seemed to be aiming at satire in his performance. This made him seem far less of a bad guy, especially when compared to the nominal hero of the film, Dion. Not only does Dion take Warren's money and ruin his chances of becoming mayor, but becomes a political fixer of the most devious kind, tricking his brother and marrying Belle to prevent her from testifying against him. In comparison, Warren seems merely a roguish but gullible chancer.

At the climax Donlevy was asked by director Henry King to "run up to Ameche's 'corpse' and step on his face."[30] He refused, but King insisted. The studio heads later deemed the scene "too brutal" and it was deleted. Donlevy later spoke of his feelings about the role: "The only part I never liked—the nastiest dog I ever played—was in *In Old Chicago.* There just wasn't any reason for his being so rotten."[31] This role was the template for many of the parts he was required to play in the following years, but he was getting well paid for his villainy and was averaging $100,000 per picture and rising."[32]

The fire scenes were well-handled, from the knocking-over of the oil lamp by Mrs. O'Leary's cow to the primitive fire engines rushing to fight the blaze, and the speed with which it spreads. Over two-thirds of the buildings in the Patch were made of wood, and there had been a three-month drought.

Whenever the film began to flag, it was enhanced by some of the bit-part players of the era. Especially noticeable was Eddie Collins as a diminutive drunk and Joe Twerp as a stuttering clerk with whom Donlevy played a wonderful scene at the judge's offices.

The amiable knockabout comedy *Battle of Broadway* (1937) reteamed Donlevy and Victor McLaglen as likable toughs on the loose in New York during a noisy Legionnaire's convention, both vying for the same gal (Louise Hovick, better known as Gypsy Rose Lee). The comedy is too loud at some stages, and many scenes end in a near-riot, but such was the approach in many comedies in that era. Donlevy was often called on to play such roistering roles at this stage of his career, and proved adept at the physical comedy required. But he was seen to good advantage during the less frenetic moments. There is a café scene at the beginning where he chats up a knowing waitress and he handles it with great charm and assurance.

So successful was the Donlevy-MacLaglen double act that they were paired a third time in *We're Going to Be Rich* (1938), the beginning of an American attempt to market singer Gracie Fields, then one of Britain's most popular stars. She was invited to Hollywood by Darryl F. Zanuck and signed a contract for four films. She even persuaded the makers to move production to England.[33] Filming commenced in October 1937 and finished just before Christmas.

The story begins in Melbourne in the 1880s, where Kit (Fields), husband Dobby (McLaglen) and foster son Tim set sail to return to England. On the boat, Dobby confesses, to Kit's anger, that he has a stake in a Cape Town gold mine, so they are going there instead. Dobby is a brawler and keeps getting into fights. Kit sings in a saloon owned by Yanky (Donlevy), who falls for her. Yanky's other singer Pearl becomes very jealous, but despite all their many trials and tribulations Kit stays true to Dobby.

We're Going to Be Rich was an enjoyable roustabout adventure with some wonderful oldtime songs. The South African setting made for a variation on the usual Western theme, and there was some attention to period detail. However, Gracie was a very English comedienne; what American audiences made of "Ee By Gum" and "Walter, Walter, Lead Me to the Altar" was never recorded. The strength of the film lies in the songs and Gracie's central performance, but the venture was not a success. The juxtaposition of American and English sensibilities was piquant in small exchanges such as when Gracie sings the sentimental ballad "The Sweetest Song in the World." Brian watches proudly, but Pearl has arranged with the conductor to play the music all wrong and the audience starts to jeer the singer. Donlevy throws a hambone at the violinist, telling him to play the music right, and addresses the noisy crowd: "You monkeys—listen!" He turns to Gracie, "All right, sister, now go ahead."

Donlevy had married singer Marjorie Lane the previous year, and she accompanied him on his trip. He called it "a sort of belated honeymoon."[34] She came well prepared, bringing with her 60 pairs of stockings—one for every day of their stay. At $2 apiece, the total cost was $120. At the time, not so long after the Depression years, that was the equivalent to about four weeks' salary for the average man.[35]

Donlevy's next movie was *Sharpshooters* (1938), a lively B-movie set in Metavania, a comic opera central European kingdom (probably somewhere east of Freedonia). Newsreel cameraman Steve Mitchell (Donlevy) and his assistant Waldo (Wally Vernon) are sent to cover the coronation of a new king, who is promptly assassinated. Under suspicion, they are pursued by the sinister prince regent Baron Orloff (Sidney Blackmer) and his supporters. After numerous adventures, they thwart three attempts to dethrone the rightful heir, Prince Michael. A contemporary critic wrote:

> It is enough for the average man and makes for swiftly developing, wisecracking and hard-punching thrills, replete with hilarious improbabilities, exaggerated portraiture verging on caricature, and not a little broad comedy. It … should be accepted in the enthusiastic spirit in which it was conceived.[36]

Fox announced the film as the first in a series dedicated to the exploits of the Daredevil Cameramen, but only one other was made, *Chasing Danger* (1939) which starred Preston Foster in the Donlevy role.

After making *Sharpshooters*, Donlevy asked for his release from his contract at Fox, which acceded to his request and also allowed him to contract with other studios.[37] As a result, he missed out on several scheduled projects: *International Settlement* was set in Shanghai with Dolores del Rio as his co-star, but his role passed down to George Sanders.[38] *Island in the Sky* would have teamed him once more with Gloria Stuart; the part was given to Michael Whalen.[39] *Big Town Girl* was designed as a joint starring vehicle with Claire Trevor, but his role was assigned to Donald Woods, who also replaced him in *Charlie Chan on Broadway* (1937).[40] When Donlevy was switched to *Midnight Taxi*, he was one of several actors who missed out on the role of Father Chevilon in *Seventh Heaven* (1937).[41]

4

Beau Geste and Beyond

"They wanted to make me a leading man at first. Gee, I would have liked that, but I didn't photograph so well. My eyebrows sort of hid my eyes. After that they tried plucking them out, but I looked worse than ever. Guess I'll always be a meanie now."
—"On location with *Beau Geste*," interview with
Viola Macdonald, *The Advertiser*, June 3, 1939, 3

Nineteen thirty-nine was a truly remarkable year in Hollywood. The art of moviemaking and the studio system was in full flower; the actors, directors, cinematographers, composers and technical staff were seemingly of one accord. This was the year of *Gone with the Wind, The Wizard of Oz, Stagecoach* and *Mr. Smith Goes to Washington.* Donlevy appeared in several of the other most notable films of 1939, *Jesse James, Union Pacific* and *Destry Rides Again.* He had his greatest role to date in one of the biggest of the year, *Beau Geste,* which he stole from Gary Cooper, one of the major stars of the era. At the end of the year, he was nominated for an Academy Award and his name was known.

The year began on a sad note for him personally, with the sudden death of his mother at Sheboygan Falls at the age of 67. She had been found dead at her home in Giddings Avenue by a neighbor. She had followed his career with interest from the very beginning, and had always been his biggest supporter. As soon as he started to receive big paychecks in movies, he regularly sent money home for her. Although she did not live to see his later successes, she was secure in the knowledge that he was on the rise. Donlevy traveled to Sheboygan Falls in January 1939 to attend her funeral and the melancholy task of settling her estate.[1]

His first role of the year was in Henry Hathaway's colorful *Jesse James* (1939). Donlevy essayed the role of the hateful Barsee, a railroad agent who offers landowners $1 an acre for their land on behalf of the railroad company which intends to run a line right across the territory. He and his heavies get tough if owners don't agree right away. When Ma James (Jane Darwell) refuses to sign without consulting a lawyer, Barsee tangles with the James brothers Frank and Jesse (Henry Fonda and Tyrone Power). After being shot in the hand and run off their land, Barsee returns with his cronies. He is told that they have gone and that only Ma is at home, sick in bed, but he doesn't believe it and calls to them to come out. Then he throws a bomb through the window and the house explodes, killing Ma.

Jesse goes into town to deal with Barsee; the agent pleads for his life, but Jesse guns him down. Wanted for murder, James flees, and so begins the brothers' all-too-familiar story of outlawry, which plays out in this action-packed but highly fictionalized version of events. The movie was full of the great Fox stock players of the era with especially good turns from Henry Hull and John Carradine. This was Donlevy's last for Fox.

Cecil B. DeMille's epic *Union Pacific* (1939) told the stirring tale of the spanning of America by rail. Among the fine supporting cast, Donlevy stood as out as Campeau, in the pay of a shady banker to delay the progress of the railroad. From left to right: Anthony Quinn, Lon Chaney, Jr., Donlevy and Lynne Overman.

Although he had played a few heels in his time, murdering Jane Darwell was too much to forgive!

Donlevy had an accident during the shooting of the saloon scene where Jesse kills Barsee. The wadding from a blank cartridge fired by Power hit him just below the right eye, badly burning his face.[2]

In his next film, Donlevy was at it again: He played yet another unscrupulous villain, working on the sly for the Central Pacific railroad in Cecil B. DeMille's *Union Pacific.* Although almost three hours in length, the movie rattled along and sustained interest throughout, thanks in no small part to the genuinely exciting nature of the story and the appealing performances of Barbara Stanwyck, Joel McCrea and Robert Preston. The supporting cast was no less impressive. Donlevy was a smart and surly saloonkeeper and partner of Dick Allen (Preston). As soon as he is introduced dipping his cigar in his whiskey and smugly surveying his domain, a girl on his knee, it is obvious that Campeau is not to be trusted. He has a clandestine meeting with shady banker Asa M. Barrows (Henry Kolker), who hires him to delay the construction of the Union Pacific railroad. Capt. Jeff Butler (McCrea) is equally determined the company will complete on schedule. Against all odds, including marauding Indians, mountains, long months of ice and snow, and all Campeau's attempts to halt the Union Pacific's progress, the two railroads eventually meet. The spanning of the continent by rail is a truly historic moment. This was one of DeMille's best but often overlooked epics and a great testament to those who built the railroad.

The role of Sid Campeau had been rejected by Charles Bickford, who objected to being flogged with a 25-foot rawhide whip; it was then offered to J. Carrol Naish, who also declined.[3] The perfectionist DeMille needed to see some tangible insight into the character that defined him instantly as a villain, whereas the scriptwriter Jesse Lasky insisted that the inner character was key:

> "Business is what the actors do that I can photograph!" DeMille yelled at Lasky during a story conference. "I can't photograph what they think or feel! What does Donlevy do with his hands?" DeMille kept after Lasky, finally calling him in the wee small hours of the morning. In desperation the groggy writer came up with the quirk of dipping a cigar end in a glass of whiskey. "Good, Jesse," said DeMille. "Put it in the script at once."[4]

Donlevy received two offers more or less simultaneously, one for *Beau Geste* and the other for *Jamaica Inn,* a project made by the British Mayflower Pictures, for a fee of $25,000. Mayflower made few films and Alfred Hitchcock's *Jamaica Inn* was the most notable. Donlevy chose to do *Beau Geste.*[5]

English writer P.C. Wren wrote his famous adventure tale *Beau Geste* in 1924 and two years later Hollywood released a highly regarded film version starring Ronald Colman and Noah Beery. In 1939 a sound version was commissioned and Henry Hathaway assigned to direct in Technicolor. Hathaway dropped out and the project was given over to William A. Wellman in monochrome. Filming took place at Buttercup Valley in Yuma, Arizona, the same location as the 1926 film which it followed closely. The only major change was the character of the sadistic sergeant who was altered from the French Lejeune of the novel to the Russian Markoff so as not to offend a French audience; presumably it was fine to upset the Russians.

The story begins as a relief column of Legionnaires arrives at Fort Zinderneuf in the North African desert and discovers that everyone is dead. When a shot is heard, bugler Digby (Robert Preston) is sent to investigate. Time passes and the bugler does not return so the commander goes to see for himself. Inside the fort there is apparently no one alive and no sign of the bugler. Soon the fort is mysteriously set alight and the Legionnaires flee to safety.

The scene fades to 15 years earlier and the three Geste brothers who have been brought up by their aunt Pat at Brandon Hall in England. All the inherited wealth of the family has been gambled away by their uncle and only the priceless Blue Water sapphire remains hidden in a secret chamber. The children play with boats on the lake and enact a Viking funeral according to legend; a figure is laid on the deck with a dog at his feet and the boat is set ablaze. Later they play Knights of the Round Table and Beau gets inside a suit of armor in the hall; the others hide when a visitor arrives, a foreign gentleman wearing a turban. The scene moves on to the grown-up brothers; Beau asks to see the Blue Water and it is brought out. The lights go out and the sapphire is gone when they go back on again. Their aunt asks the thief to put it back. He doesn't. As a matter of honor, Beau goes off to join the Foreign Legion; Digby and John follow.

In the North African desert, the brothers undergo a harsh regime under the tyrannical Sgt. Markoff. From an informer, Markoff learns about the sapphire the brothers have allegedly stolen. Markoff treats all the soldiers like dogs and calls them scum; he sends two deserters back out into the hot desert without provisions. Matters come to a head when there is a mutiny which Markoff almost foils; but at a crucial moment, the fort is attacked. The garrison is outnumbered, but Markoff marshals their forces well and even props up dead Legionnaires to give the illusion that the fort is fully manned. In time the force is dwindling; Beau is killed and John kills Markoff. Digby arrives with the relief column just after John escapes; he gives Beau a Viking funeral with the dog Markoff at his feet. He too escapes and joins up with John and they meet other comrades, but Digby is killed. John makes it back to Brandon Hall and the mystery is explained at the end. Beau stole the jewel (which he knew to be a fake) to save Aunt Pat from recriminations by their uncle because she had sold the original sapphire long ago, the night the mysterious visitor came to the house and Beau (in the suit of armor) overheard everything.

An old-fashioned, rollicking adventure tale, *Beau Geste* encapsulated many of the values of manly derring-do that were the stuff of *Boy's Own* and written by and for the Empire builders of the era. Wren, a lifelong soldier and physical instructor, may have spent some time in the Foreign Legion after the death of his first wife. The story represents a set of values which seem diminished by time and circumstance. Honor is now almost an unknown word in every sphere of life, but is surely still a thing of inordinate value. The story remained popular for a long time; there was another movie version in 1966 and a television series in 1982. The theme was always ripe for parody ever since the days of Laurel and Hardy's wonderful *Beau Hunks* and, much later, *The Last Remake of Beau Geste* (1977). Once colonialism faded as an ideology, and the sun finally set on the British and French empires, such adventures seemed jaded, but *Beau Geste* retains its appeal because of the central story of loyalty and honor-bound virtues, the performances, the fine cinematography and the timeless image of Sgt. Markoff shouting "Fight, you scum!" Above all, the sight of Fort Zinderneuf in the lonely desert lingers in the mind; the bodies propped up against the ramparts while the flag is flying and no soul is alive.

Making the movie was something of an arduous task in the Arizona desert and according to Wellman the atmosphere on set was made worse by Donlevy who, he said, began to think he *was* Markoff, constantly throwing his weight around and alienating the cast and crew. Wellman claimed that Ray Milland "hated him the worst" and that on several occasions he had to "step in to stop him slugging Donlevy." He continued: "As a matter of fact, no one liked the son of a bitch. His three tent mates left him. Donlevy was even nasty when asleep."[6]

When Milland was called on to bayonet the martinet sergeant at the end of the film, the scene was not entirely acting. Donlevy was supposed to be padded up, but Milland apparently wounded him intentionally, according to Wellman. Donlevy promptly fainted at the sight of his own blood and was only revived by a bottle of whiskey which cast member Albert Dekker had gone across the desert to fetch. Donlevy went to the hospital

Donlevy as *Beau Geste*'s sadistic Sgt. Markoff. His performance garnered him a Best Supporting Actor Oscar nomination, no mean feat in the outstanding cinematic year of 1939.

and was stitched up; Milland later apologized profusely.[7]

Despite the opprobrium that Donlevy apparently aroused, Wellman also commented that he "was giving a sensational performance, so much so that it improved all the other performances."[8] It seemed as though he really had to psych himself up to get into this role, which appears to run contrary to the other reports of his natural demeanor.

Donlevy's is the portrayal that everyone remembers long after seeing the film and the only one to be nominated for an Academy Award. He lost out to Thomas Mitchell for *Stagecoach*. Nevertheless, Donlevy had come a long way in a short time. "Donlevy shines as the outstanding actor of the piece," said the *New York Daily Mirror*.[9]

Donlevy later spoke about Markoff: "We all have something of the Markoff in us," he observed. "It's the part we suppress or live down in order to enjoy the much richer, less destructive benefits of civilization."[10]

Wellman's negative experiences did not stop him seeking out Donlevy for *The Great Man's Lady* (1942); it was stated categorically that "neither man held a grudge."[11] Milland went on to work with Donlevy twice after this, in *I Wanted Wings* (1941) and *The Trouble with Women* (1947).

The negativity that his role engendered made him very upset. He once outlined the effect of his performance on his public perception. As he described the scenario in an interview with Malcolm Oettinger of *Screenland* magazine, he was sitting in the tap room of the Brown Palace in Denver drinking with some friends:

> After half an hour a tall, distinguished looking guy ... came over, shook his finger at me and said, "I hate your face, I'll never forget it after *Beau Geste*." Then he walked out. Everybody laughed, but I was hurt. I didn't like it a bit. And I don't like it when kids yell at me on the street.[12]

After *Beau Geste*, Donlevy made sure he had a clause in his contract to always end a picture "with a clean bill of health instead of the stigma of 'heavy.'"[13] He also had some ideas of his own, and hoped one day to play the lead in a film version of the Broadway hit comedy *The Front Page*.[14] In the short term, he was offered more villainy in the shape of King Richard III in Universal's *Tower of London*, but this went to the more suitable Basil Rathbone.[15]

His next was a crime drama for Columbia, *Behind Prison Gates,* known at one time as *Escape from Alcatraz*. This engaging yarn gave Donlevy the perfect role as Craig, a quick-thinking G-man who assumes the identity of a dead bank robber in order to root out a gang responsible for a big robbery. During a break-out attempt, his partner is killed by a rifle bullet. At great risk, Craig works his way into the confidence of all the suspects. In time, he is recognized and he has to work fast to find the money and unravel the mystery of his partner's murder.

A wonderful minor noir gem, *Behind Prison Gates* wastes no time in telling its story and has great atmosphere. The prison scenes are effective, the prisoners constantly talking in low voices so as not to be overheard by the "screws" or even fellow prisoners. The way Craig manages to play both sides against the middle by causing the two convict "partners" to mistrust each other was very clever. The dialogue had much of the appeal of crime films of the era: smart, hardboiled and funny. "What's this?" Donlevy snaps when the cook slaps some slop on his plate at mealtime. "I just dish it out," replies the cook dryly, "I don't describe it." The throwaway lines are the salt of the whole thing, like the bit players who deliver them with such aplomb. Co-star Jacqueline Wells did not feature greatly, this was essentially a prison film, and although some plot elements strained credulity, this was immaterial to the overall enjoyment of a well-made period charmer. Director Charles Barton made a number of snappy little crime dramas and even some Westerns, but he was most famous for his Abbott and Costello comedies. He later worked in television and directed Donlevy toward the end of both their careers in an episode of *Family Affair.*

RKO's *Allegheny Uprising* was one of the weaker entries among the Westerns that Donlevy made at this time, despite the strong cast headed by John Wayne and Claire Trevor. Again, Donlevy was an out-and-out baddie, selling trade goods including rifles and rum to the Indians and the white settlers in 1750s Delaware. He even had the effrontery to murder a man and attempt to pin the blame on Big John. Donlevy took a good whipping for his trouble along the way, whining as the whipper drew near that he was just a driver and knew nothing about it. During the making of the movie, he became firm friends with Wayne and Glen Tryon. They spent so much time together that the Indians working on the lot dubbed them blood brothers—whereupon the three buddies "cut their thumbs with a bottle top and mixed their blood," swearing eternal allegiance to each other.[16]

The film was not well received in Britain, where it was re-titled *The First Rebel*. The depiction of the British as tyrannical colonial masters was not a popular one in wartime. As a consequence, the movie was not seen there for two years and had limited release.

In common with other films of the era, there was a big publicity drive for *Allegheny Uprising*. In the days before the electronic age this relied very much on personal appearances and special events. A huge parade followed the route from Allegheny to the stage of the Penn Theater in Pittsburgh, Pennsylvania, for the October 1939 premiere, timed to coincide

Destry Rides Again (1939), a much-loved comedy Western to this day, featured great performances from a marvelous cast. Prominent among them were Donlevy (left) as a saloon owner, Charles Winninger (center) as a drunken sheriff and star James Stewart as the man who tames the town.

with the centenary of Allegheny's incorporation as a city. Amidst much ballyhoo, the 12-block-long parade featured covered wagons, ox carts and period floats. Some of the film's stars were interviewed in a live radio broadcast from the theater.[17] Donlevy was set to be teamed once more with Wayne and Claire Trevor in Raoul Walsh's *Dark Command* (1940); he was to have played Cantrell, loosely based on Col. Quantrill, but his part went to Walter Pidgeon.[18]

Way ahead of all the other Westerns of the time was George Marshall's bona fide classic *Destry Rides Again* (1939), which took the lighthearted approach generally and got the tricky balance of drama and comedy just right. With a fine cast headed by James Stewart and Marlene Dietrich, the movie had a lively atmosphere and great character actors to enhance the proceedings. Donlevy embellished his by now familiar turn as a curiously appealing bad guy: prosperous-looking, sly, slippery as an eel. No wonder cinema audiences took to him; he had a presence and showed to advantage in all his scenes here. Crucially, he was never outshone by the glamorous leads. As always he had that knowing smile and his eyes were so expressive, especially when he sees that Destry has no gun. His eyes frantically scan the tall stranger, then he bursts into a boisterous laugh when he sees the humor of the situation in a flash. All the background characters contributed to this movie, which remains a favorite today.

This rollicking, ever-popular film also features the inimitable Marlene singing "The Boys in the Backroom" which became one of her most popular hits, and a lively rendition of the old favorite "Little Joe the Wrangler." There was great support from a host of familiar faces, especially the wonderful Charles Winninger as a drunken sheriff. Often imitated but never bettered, *Destry Rides Again* had brio and a kind of class that could not be replicated. This high-profile film raised Donlevy's profile. He was creating a niche for himself as an oddly likable villain bringing curious sympathy to a role many actors disdained. After *Beau Geste,* he was careful never to play such an out-and-out meanie ever again. Henceforward he was never all bad, and even the meanest of his characterizations never completely lost sight of the characters' humanity.

5

The Great Donlevy

"You're a tough guy, McGinty, you're not a wrong guy."
—Catherine McGinty, *The Great McGinty.*

It was Donlevy's misfortune that he did not look like the archetypal leading man of his time. He was around 5'9", slightly taller than Humphrey Bogart and four inches taller than James Cagney. However, Donlevy had broad shoulders and was often described as thickset and barrel-chested. This effect was exaggerated on screen. Although he had the compensation of being handsome in a rugged way, he seemed more naturally suited to being a screen heavy. This presented a cul-de-sac in acting terms so that most casting directors did not really *see* him. To them, he was pigeonholed as a heavy with all the onerous duties that entailed. It took a director of vision to see that there was far more to Donlevy than met the eye. Such a man was Preston Sturges.

Sturges had moderate success with his Broadway plays and made his way to Hollywood, working as a screenwriter on *The Power and the Glory* (1933). As a Hollywood director he came into his own with a string of films beginning with *The Great McGinty* (1940), also known as *Down Went McGinty*. His later films included *Christmas in July* (1940), *The Lady Eve* and *Sullivan's Travels* (1941). He was one of the most imaginative and idiosyncratic directors and his reputation has grown steadily since his death.

The Great McGinty begins in a bar in a banana republic when Daniel McGinty prevents depressed bank clerk Tommy Thompson (Louis Jean Heydt) from committing suicide. McGinty recounts the tale of his rise and fall to Thompson and a dancing girl (Steffi Duna). McGinty starts out as a hobo who is told by a politician (William Demarest) how he can make $2: All he has to do is vote for Mayor Tillinghurst on behalf of those voters who cannot make it to the polls because most of them are dead. McGinty takes the politician at his word and does the rounds of all the polling stations. He votes 37 times and demands his $74. Impressed by his enterprise, the Boss

(Akim Tamiroff) gives him a job as a collector of protection money. Pretty soon he makes him an alderman, and in time convinces him to run for mayor. The only proviso is that he needs to be married. Secretary Catherine (Muriel Angelus) suggests she can be his wife—in name only, of course. McGinty agrees, and does so well as mayor that the Boss makes him governor of the state. McGinty and Catherine fall for each other and he begins to question everything the Boss tells him. When he tries to do good, his political career unravels and he is soon back where he started.

A searing political satire, *The Great McGinty* was the first time Sturges directed from one of his own scripts. "He and we put our hearts into it," commented Angelus, who brought remarkable sensitivity and refinement to her role as Catherine.[1] Angelus was a British stage actress who made only occasional films. This was cinema's great loss because she was a fine and natural actress who could have had an excellent film career. But she said that stardom did not suit her. *The Great McGinty* was her last movie.

Preston Sturges' political satire *The Great McGinty* (1940) showed Donlevy to his best advantage as a down-and-outer elevated to governor. Left to right: Donnie Kerr, Donlevy, Mary Thomas and Muriel Angelus.

Sturges initially considered Spencer Tracy for the lead role. But passing Donlevy on the stairs one day on the Paramount lot, he suddenly realized he had found the one he was looking for. "My God," he said, "there's my man. There's the *Great McGinty*."[2] As Sturges' biographer observed: "Preston ... saw a vulnerability in Donlevy's muscular all American looks that had yet to be exploited."[3] This vulnerability is the key to the character of both McGinty and the actor.

The reviews were full of compliments. "A great show," commented *Time*, "*The Great McGinty* is shrewd, salty, adroit.... It is also an actor's dream. Brian Donlevy makes that dream come true."[4] Even the hard-to-please critics were won over: Bosley Crowther opined: "Much praise must be bestowed on Brian Donlevy for his masterful comprehension of McGinty, who starts out as a plain dumb palooka and grows into a thoughtful man."[5] The supporting cast of character players, headed by Demarest, was faultless and added to the shrewd humor of the piece. The early scenes when the hobo McGinty blithely casts his many votes are quite magical. Typical is the scene where McGinty enters to cast his vote as Dr. Heinrich Schutsendorf and an elderly lady becomes suspicious. "I could have sworn Dr. Schutsendorf was dead." McGinty says with a smile, "Not yet, lady."

Once the movie was released, the star embarked on a three-week tour of key cities to promote it.[6] He was guest of honor at several premieres including one in Philadelphia during which there was a civic luncheon and organized festivities.[7] In those days, Hollywood PR men had to be inventive. The opening at L.A.'s Westwood Village Theater tried to recreate an oldtime voting scene "with booths, torches and banners."[8] Audience members were asked to vote on several questions such as whether fans preferred the "tender brute" type lover *a la* Clark Gable. At the time, Paramount was trying to groom Donlevy as a romantic lead in a similar mode. A stellar audience helped things along with several cast members and others such as Ernst Lubitsch, Susan Hayward and Paramount head Y. Frank Freeman.

The Great McGinty certainly found its mark among some of the big civic operators of the era. The movie was famously banned from being shown in Jersey City by sitting mayor Frank Hague, who objected to its "rough and tumbling handling of politicians."[9] Hague was once called a "legendary political thief ... a crook with a bit of panache," which is presumably how he managed to be mayor for such a surprisingly long time (30 years, from 1917 to 1947).[10] It was all grist to the mill for Sturges, whose screenplay won an Academy Award. The movie, described by one critic as "Capra with the gloves off," did steady business and was a favorite for many years.[11] Unlike many of the era, it retains its breezy charm and sharp satire today. If anything, its relevance increases rather than diminishes with the years. The ragged coat Donlevy wore at the beginning of *The Great McGinty* was the same one as worn by Emil Jannings in *The Way of All Flesh* (1926) and later by Joel McCrea in Sturges' *Sullivan's Travels* (1941).[12]

Donlevy (left) with Akim Tamiroff record one of the numerous radio versions of *The Great McGinty*.

Donlevy reprised his role on radio a number of times and there was also a television version in 1955. Both Tamiroff and Donlevy appeared in a brief scene in *The Miracle of Morgan Creek* (1944) as a favor to Sturges. This was a social satire about a girl (Betty Hutton), who loves soldiers and after a wild drunken party marries a young soldier whose name she cannot remember. When it is discovered that she is pregnant, her long-time admirer Norval offers to be the replacement father. When sextuplets are born, the matter reaches the governor and the Boss, who sort everything out with a phone call.

Henry Hathaway's *Brigham Young—Frontiersman* (1940) was a rather long and over-pious account of the Mormons' fight for religious freedom and their long trek to Utah. The story begins in dramatic fashion at Nauvoo, Illinois, with a furious mob attacking a homestead where Jonathan Kent (Tyrone Power) and his family are entertaining. The men are stripped, tied to a tree and beaten to death; Jonathan is left unconscious; the women and children flee to the fields as the mob burns the house. At a meeting, Joseph Smith (Vincent Price) and others decide that the time has come to fight back. Angus Duncan (Donlevy) argues for compromise as a way to live in peace with their neighbors, but is labeled a coward for so doing. In time there is a trial of Smith at Carthage, where Brigham Young (Dean Jagger) speaks eloquently in his defense and the defense of the Mormons invoking the wider cause of religious freedom on which the nation was founded. Before the sentence can be carried out, a torch-carrying mob with painted faces bursts in and shoots Smith; he falls backwards out of the window.

Leaving Nauvoo and Carthage behind, the rest of the Mormons flee in their wagons. Thus begins their long trek, without any real destination in mind. Young tells them that they will go to Mexico if they cannot worship God as they choose in their own country. They suffer numerous hardships and become weary with constant travel; there is much sickness and hunger, and some die en route. Duncan hears that there is gold in California and tries to persuade the others to go there. But after crossing the Rockies, they arrive at a place which Young claims to have seen in a vision; this place is Utah, which looks like a desert to some of them, Duncan included. Life is hard in the "Promised Land" with heavy snow in long winters and drought and pestilence in the summers. The people become disillusioned. The last straw is when a plague of crickets descends and starts eating their crops. Everyone is pressed into service to combat the insect peril, but all is in vain. Young has to concede defeat and is about to tell his people that he had no mission from God after all, when flocks of seagulls arrive and begin eating the insects.

The early part of the film, culminating in the dramatic death of Joseph Smith, was well realized; then it settled into a humorless account of suffering on what seemed an interminable trail to Utah. Dean Jagger in the title role lacked the charisma to be a convincing leader of the chosen to the Promised Land, especially considering all the hardships he expected his people to endure in his name. Mary Astor did her best in the thankless role of his wife. (Young's other 54 wives were signally absent from the proceedings.)

Donlevy as Angus Duncan was the lone voice of dissent throughout and although everything he said made sense, he was treated first as a coward when he suggested compromise to live in peace with their neighbors, and later as a heretic because he disagreed with Young. Twice he claimed to have had his own conversation with God, but unlike Young is never believed, even though Young, by his own admission, only met with silence when he talked to the divine. In reality there were several factions of Mormons and some stayed in Illinois. Their own history is controversial and bloody; for instance, their militia murdered 120 emigrants from south Utah in the 1857 Mountain Meadows Massacre, which they blamed on the Indians.[13] Nor was it specifically stated in the movie why the Latter Day Saints were persecuted so violently and made to leave Missouri, Ohio and Illinois. Often the reasons were political, something only hinted at here. It is interesting to compare this movie to John Ford's *Wagon Master* (1950) which has everything *Brigham Young—Frontiersman* lacks: humor, pathos and humanity. Ford eschewed the pious approach and made his characters entirely believable, which Hathaway never quite managed to do.

Nonetheless, *Brigham Young* is a very well-made film and does not deserve its obscurity. Donlevy was praised by some reviewers as outstanding. There are some wonderful set-piece scenes such as when the crickets swarm, which took days to achieve because they did not arrive on schedule. The seagulls provided a rousing miracle end which seemed entirely in keeping with the director's too-literal approach to his subject.

When the Daltons Rode, a rousing adventure with a fine ensemble cast and a fast-moving story, built up incredible momentum to a predictable but entirely satisfying conclusion. Based on the novelization by Emmett Dalton, the only surviving member of the gang, the movie was full of action and well directed by the sometimes underrated George Marshall. Broderick Crawford played the lead role of Ben Dalton and Randolph Scott played his friend, who ends up taking his girl (Kay Francis) from him. Donlevy appeared as Grat, by far the most hotheaded of the brothers, and as usual he comes a-cropper—but then the outcome was already known to students of history.

The story begins with the arrival in town of lawyer Todd Jackson (Scott), an old friend of the Daltons. After initially mistaking him for an ornery stranger, they realize who he is and invite him to Ma's birthday party. They tell him about Rigby and his gang of surveyors who run people off their own land in some kind of land grab scheme. Todd agrees to help and they set up an association to investigate; but soon the Daltons are threatened on their farm by Rigby and his men. When a surveyor hits his head on a rock in a scuffle, Grat and Ben are put on trial for murder. Convinced that the rather farcical trial is going against them, the brothers escape and begin a rampage of robbery of stagecoaches and trains which leads to their predictable demise in a shoot-out.

Universal was adept at this kind of entertainment and one has to hand it to them that they knew what the public wanted and gave it to them. The film is well made and appealing; the action sequences are excellent and the elements of humor meant that it remained generally light-hearted but that the moments of tragedy were not diminished. The robbery of the train as the gang flees a small town with a posse in hot pursuit is pure theatrical Hollywood at its boldest. The stunt men involved most certainly earned their salaries, especially so considering that few of the principal players could even ride horses. It was a standing joke on the set that Donlevy needed a ladder to mount his steed, and many of the cast played the ladder joke on each other. The character players again proved their immeasurable value to the fabric of the movie. Especially memorable was Mary Gordon as Ma Dalton, who fights for her boys even when everything is against them. When the townspeople become a furious mob and attempt to hang her son, she shouts, "Is it a pack of wild animals you are now?" They will not be placated and she is pushed aside and falls to the ground; the sight of her vulnerable form in the dirt wrapped in her shawl is curiously touching.

Donlevy handled all his scenes well, he is entirely believable, from the opening, near-slapstick routine of becoming entangled in the back-cloth and bringing the scenery down while the family are having their photograph taken, to getting punched into a horse trough, to almost strangling a hostile witness in the courtroom. A somewhat improbable sequel, unimaginatively entitled *The Daltons Ride Again,* was made a few years later and had an entirely different cast.[14]

After his success in *The Great McGinty,* Donlevy received many offers, and was next announced as a replacement for Walter Brennan as

Al Jennings in *The American Vagabond,* based on the life of Western writer O. Henry.[15] Jennings was a bandit who robbed and stole stamps for Henry so that he could send his stories. Originally Douglas Fairbanks Jr. was to have played Henry but he backed out, after which the project stalled. Finally it was postponed indefinitely.[16] Although Mae West was keen to have Donlevy as her leading man in *My Little Chickadee* (1940), he was in such demand at the time that he could not oblige.[17] Donlevy's old friend Louis Sobol co-wrote with Quentin Reynolds *The Life of Floyd Gibbons,* a biography of the adventurous reporter. Sobol sought Donlevy for the title role. Donlevy approached Paramount head Y. Frank Freeman with the idea. Freeman was reportedly enthusiastic, but the film was never made.[18] Donlevy was also considered for the lead in *The Night of January 16th* (1941), the screen adaptation of Ayn Rand's stage play, but the role went to Robert Preston.[19]

One of the most enticing prospects was *Power House,* from a story by A.I. Bezzerides. Paramount bought the story, which he had co-authored with Meyer Levin, for $10,000, with the intention of casting Donlevy opposite Dorothy Lamour.[20] It involved workers on high tension power lines in the desert. *Power House* languished at the studio and never came to fruition.[21] Bezzerides later wrote the novel *Thieves' Highway,* which was made into a terrific noir movie by director Jules Dassin, and scripted the classics *On Dangerous Ground* (1951) and *Kiss Me Deadly* (1955).

Donlevy's first film for the war effort was *I Wanted Wings* (1941), made in the summer of 1940 and released when America was still neutral. It proved to be one of the most popular of the year and arguably one of the most successful of all war films made during the conflict. The story centered on three would-be Army Air Corps pilots: the privileged Jeff Young (Ray Milland), working-class hero Al Ludlow (William Holden) and sporty Tom Cassidy (Wayne Morris). They are all instructed to fly by Capt. Mercer (Donlevy). The film follows the trials and tribulations of their training as well as their romances and tragedies. The sensitive Ludlow is constantly assailed by doubts that he is good enough to make the grade as a pilot. However, Mercer recognizes that he is a natural pilot and just needs coaxing to achieve all he can in the service. His belief in Ludlow is confirmed when he makes an emergency landing under difficult conditions. Later, when a plane crashes and Mercer is severely wounded, he tells them to stay where they are until help arrives, but the recruits override his decision and Ludlow transports them all to safety and Mercer to the hospital, saving his life. They return to face a court martial, but the result is predictably positive.

Essentially a recruiting poster for the USAAF, *I Wanted Wings* was an appealing and not too heavy-handed movie which benefitted from the presence of the leading actors. The film only dragged about two-thirds of the way into its 135-minute running time, and picked up again during the dramatic climax. Donlevy had a good, sympathetic role in support and his belief in Ludlow is crucial in molding a good pilot and giving him the confidence to succeed. *I Wanted Wings* was a cheerful movie, and one of which the screenwriter Richard Maibaum was most proud. Donlevy was among those who also appeared briefly in the romantic Charles Boyer–Olivia de Havilland drama *Hold Back the Dawn.* In a subtle way for Paramount to advertise its own product, director Leisen was shown directing Donlevy and Veronica Lake in an *I Wanted Wings* scene.

In 1940 Paramount announced that Donlevy would go to England to take the title role in *The Life of Barney Barnato,* based on the exploits of the South African diamond king and rival to Cecil Rhodes. The film never

Although effectively a propaganda exercise, *I Wanted Wings* (1941) was released before America entered the war. This unpretentious movie seemed far less self-conscious than some in the genre and featured attractive performances from an excellent cast. Left to right: Harlan Warde, William Holden, Constance Moore, Donlevy.

materialized.[22] Instead his next assignment was MGM's *Billy the Kid* (1941), the first Technicolor version of an oft-repeated tale, and almost a direct remake of the 1930 version. Filming took place at John Ford's favored terrain, the iconic Monument Valley, Utah, and also at Oak Creek Canyon, south of Flagstaff near Sedona, Arizona. At times the magnificent scenery in glorious color overshadowed the story. At the outset, Bill Bonney (Robert Taylor) rides with the unscrupulous Hickey gang in an all-out cattle war. But he becomes influenced by benevolent English rancher Eric Keating (Ian Hunter), his sister Edith (Mary Howard) and ranch foreman and childhood friend Jim Sherwood (Donlevy), who all encourage him to go straight. When Keating is killed by the Hickeys, Billy sets off to track them down. In the inevitable showdown, Billy has to challenge his old friend Sherwood, who is faster on the draw and shoots him down. Sherwood realizes afterwards that Billy let him win, because the southpaw used his right hand to draw instead of his left.

The film recorded a modest profit, but despite its cast and the sumptuous color, it was rather a low-key affair and seemingly less popular than the previous version and Howard Hawks' rival movie *The Outlaw,* which was made around the same time but not released until 1946. Donlevy did his usual sterling job, and in some ways was the strongest character of all. Essentially the Pat Garrett of legend, he was renamed Sherwood for no apparent reason. Although this time he was a friend of the hero, it was typical of Donlevy's luck that he was still required to seem like the bad guy and had the task of shooting romantic favorite Robert Taylor.

The two actors got on well and swapped gifts. Donlevy gave Taylor an elaborately carved Finnish hunting knife that the latter described as one of his favorite gifts.[23] Knowing that Donlevy collected odd-shaped bottles, Taylor gave him a curious bottle shaped like a penguin which Donlevy considered turning into a lamp.[24] While Taylor arrived for the location shooting in his private plane, Donlevy drove a two-ton truck. At the time he was remodeling his Brentwood home and told reporters that his hope was to "bring back enough volcanic rock to put in an outdoor barbecue oven and garden wall."[25]

Victor Schertzinger's *Birth of the Blues* (1941) was a popular but entirely subjective Hollywood version of the history of jazz. Inspired by the rise of the first all-white group, the Original Dixieland Jazz Band, the story followed a group of musicians, the Basin Street Hot-Shots, who try to play their "hot" music in the face of much opposition. The cast was headed by Bing Crosby with Mary Martin as singer Betty Lou Cobb and Donlevy as happy-go-lucky, girl-crazy cornet player Memphis. Donlevy was tutored in the instrument by "Pokey" Carriere, who is actually heard playing. Donlevy's skill with the bugle meant that he really looked as though he was playing. Among the old favorites in the film, the appealing song "The Waiter and the Porter and the Upstairs Maid" was introduced, performed by Crosby, Martin and legendary trombonist and bandleader Jack Teagarden. Eddie "Rochester" Anderson was particularly effective in support, providing droll humor throughout. There was also some authentic feeling of the real blues supplied by the little-known but mesmeric opera singer Ruby Elzy in one of her few film appearances before her tragic early death.

Even in such an innocuous movie as *Birth of the Blues,* Donlevy was very conscious of his image and determined not to do anything to make himself appear as the eternal heel. He invoked the non-violent clause in his contract, as he recalled in a letter:

> I refused to do a scene which called for me to slap Miss Martin. Mary slaps me in the scene, and I am supposed to slap her back. Now, instead, Mary will not only slap me, but will heave me out of her apartment with the flat's furnishings on the way out.[26]

Donlevy fit easily into *Birth of the Blues,* working well with Crosby and Martin. There was an appealing scene near the beginning when the nascent band plays an impromptu set in front of the prison where Donlevy is incarcerated, and he joins in. Although he is the love rival for the affections of Martin throughout, he nonchalantly admits defeat to Crosby at the end; "I've been thinking—it's too unfair on all those other girls, I don't want them to miss out." Donlevy could have done more musicals; he displayed a lightness of touch and added much-needed acting credence to the proceedings. Composer-director Schertzinger had been making films since 1916; his highlights included *Paramount on Parade* (1930), the first two Hope-Crosby-Lamour "Road" films, and many songs including "Tangerine" and "I Remember You." *Birth of the Blues* was his penultimate film: He died suddenly in 1941 of a heart attack at the age of 53.

Donlevy enjoyed making the movie, which was a refreshing change from the previous fare he was offered. When filming ended in August 1941, he took a vacation hunting trip with Richard Webb, a bit part player he had met while making *I Wanted Wings.*[27] The two flew to British Columbia to indulge their passion for outdoor photography, taking with them both still and movie cameras.

Donlevy starred in *South of Tahiti* (1941), joining Broderick Crawford and Andy Devine as brawling pearl divers who become shipwrecked on a South Sea island. While Messrs. Crawford and Devine remained intent on getting their hands on the pearls which the natives use in their sacred ceremonies, Donlevy vies for the affections of lovely Maria Montez. The movie offered little new, but there was one unusual sequence in which a shark chased Montez, and the young prince of the island saved her by cutting his arm and drawing the shark away from her. All eyes were on Montez, however, which was just as well, as the scenery was so obviously fake and somewhere west of Pasadena on the Universal back lot. The well-spoken Englishman H.B. Warner played the native chief. The result was dismissed as "penny-pinching hokum without even the color to make it watchable."[28] Color would certainly have helped. Brian had fun with the beautiful Maria, especially when the two went swimming together. The antics of cohorts Crawford and Devine became rather tedious after a while and Donlevy could have handled the assignment better alone. The reviewers were surprisingly kind: "an exploitable mixture of action and satire," opined one, who praised Donlevy's tongue-in-cheek approach.[29] A number of trained animals were used in the film. They appeared when summoned by a gong and chase away an invading gang of white men. Although they seemed quite tame on screen and come and go at Maria's bidding, in reality they were somewhat less easy to handle, and Donlevy was reportedly badly injured on set by a leaping leopard.[30]

In a similar vein of broad humor, Donlevy was penciled in as the star of *Butch Minds the Baby* (1942), from a story by Damon Runyon, but ultimately the part went to Broderick Crawford. Instead Donlevy appeared for Columbia in *Two Yanks in Trinidad* (1941) with long-time buddy Pat O'Brien. They played a couple of racketeers who fall out over a woman. Independently of each other, they enlist in the army. While stationed in Trinidad they settle their differences and work together to thwart a group of Nazi agents who are attempting to smuggle oil from the island. This undemanding fare was a pleasant diversion for audiences at the time of its March 1942 release; it jived with the mood of patriotic feeling. A good-natured roustabout yarn, it proved popular. O'Brien and Donlevy had been friends since their Broadway days and worked seamlessly together as a double-act. One critic commented that Donlevy and O'Brien "put a world of speed and punch into proceedings."[31] Janet Blair replaced Claire Trevor as the girl they are both in love with. Donlevy even wrote his own sequel, but the studio failed to take him up on the idea.[32]

Around this time, Donlevy was touted as the possible star of the British Warner Brothers movie *Flying Fortress* but the role was assigned to Richard Greene instead.[33] Also, when his Paramount contract was renewed, Donlevy was announced as the lead in the light comedy *Twin Beds* for producer Edward Small, but George Brent got the role instead.[34]

Donlevy had always longed to play George Washington; he never got the chance but he came close when he portrayed the seventh president, Andrew Jackson, albeit in ghostly form, in *The Remarkable Andrew* (1942), based on the satiric novel by Dalton Trumbo. There was some reluctance on the part of Paramount to handle the material at all without significant changes and it was after much discussion that the movie was finally given the go-ahead. As late as January 1941 the makers announced that the film would not be made for the duration of the war. The reasons given were that the foreign market was "too precarious," it was "impossible to find the right people," and that "a fantasy of this sort is not what people want right now."[35] Against all the odds, the movie was made, but even then there were many problems. At one stage, Holden and Donlevy argued with the director Stuart Heisler about certain aspects of the screenplay. After the third day of filming, they appealed for Trumbo to take over, but he refused.[36]

In the small town of Shale City, Colorado, scrupulous young accountant clerk Andrew Long (William Holden) discovers a shortage of $1240. He shows this to his boss, who tells him not to worry about it and put it under miscellaneous outgoings. Long is not placated, even when the matter is referred to the city treasurer who assures him that the sum can be overlooked. Eventually this overriding need to go by the book leads to Long's dismissal. All his heroes are the founding fathers of America; he loves to read about history and has a huge picture of Gen. Andrew Jackson over his bed. That night he is visited by the ghost of Jackson (Donlevy), who promptly calls for a quart of whiskey. Jackson says there is corruption afoot at City Hall and vows to help Andrew root it out. When Andrew's girlfriend Peggy (Ellen Drew) arrives, she cannot see the president and, noticing the bottle of whiskey, believes her fiancé has turned to drink. In time, the bank shortage is blamed on Andrew, who is promptly sent to jail. Realizing that drastic measures are called for, reinforcements arrive in the ghostly shape of Gen. George Washington, Thomas Jefferson and Benjamin Franklin. They are accompanied by Jesse James and a lively but totally unknown historical character, Private Henry Bartholomew Smith. With the aid of a phonograph recording and the great memory of Franklin, plus a rousing patriotic speech by Andrew invoking the memory of his heroes, matters are resolved: Andrew is reinstated and gets his girl.

A wonderfully whimsical and simultaneously profound film, *The Remarkable Andrew* was aptly called a "refreshing fantasy" by *Time* magazine.[37] *The Film Daily* said it was "human and real," adding,

Donlevy (left) had great fun as the ghost of President Andrew Jackson in *The Remarkable Andrew* (1942). He's seen here with co-stars Ellen Drew and William Holden. When Holden eloped to Las Vegas with Brenda Marshall during filming, Donlevy was his best man.

> Every so often, but not often enough, a picture emerges from the lesser budget brackets with true, dramatic distinction. *The Remarkable Andrew* attains such status, because of the sincere and eloquent manner in which it combines entertainment and a reaffirmation of the fundamental truths of our democracy.[38]

The movie was undoubtedly one of Donlevy's best because it was so unexpected at this point in his career and allowed him to show his range. Donlevy spent years on Broadway in comedies, musicals and revues playing scenes with experts such as Bert Lahr, so it was no surprise that he could handle the humor with ease. Holden was perfectly keyed as the earnest dreamer and worked especially well in his scenes with Donlevy, which had an appealing naturalness. Despite the age difference, the two became great friends. One night when Holden was passing Donlevy's dressing room, he called him in and poured him a drink. "Don't let these monkeys push you around. I'll help you all I can," Donlevy told him.[39] During filming, the young star and Brenda Marshall eloped to Las Vegas with Brian and Marjorie as witnesses. The wedding, an adventure in itself, was conducted after many shenanigans in a hotel room "by a one-armed man who held the book with his hand and turned the pages with his chin."[40]

The Remarkable Andrew is well served by an array of familiar faces that people the small town, including the ubiquitous but always welcome Tom Fadden as an incredulous drugstore assistant: "Two quarts of whiskey and he's still standing," he exclaims as he sees Andrew walking down the street. The basis of the town in the original novel was Grand Junction, Colorado, where Trumbo lived for most of his early life. Much of the novel's isolationist stance was toned done to appease the British in particular, but this was not to its detriment. Trumbo's witty script won an Academy Award; it is surprising that this charming and telling satire is not more widely known and valued. Perhaps with the success of the biopic *Trumbo* (2015), his name will become known to a new generation who may reevaluate his life and work.

Donlevy, who seemed to be on a roll, was next handed the lead in *A Gentleman After Dark,* which had originally been offered to Rex Harrison.[41] The Richard Washburn Child story "A Whiff of Heliotrope" had been filmed twice before, as *Heliotrope* (1920) and *Forgotten Faces* (1936). The female star was Miriam Hopkins, who replaced Ilona Massey. It was a measure of Donlevy's rising status that he was given top billing: He had come a long way since *Barbary Coast* six years earlier, when Hopkins had been the star and he had been very much in the background.

Gentleman thief Harry Melton (Donlevy) becomes a changed man when his daughter is born on New Year's Eve 1923. Harry's friend from childhood, Detective Gaynor (Preston Foster), believes him to be essentially decent at heart and tries to convince him to go straight. Harry's wife Flo (Hopkins) is eager for him to return to a life of crime. He agrees to one last job, but is double-crossed by Flo and "partner" Eddie Smith. When Harry finds out, he loses his head and kills Eddie. For the sake of his daughter Diana, he appeals to Gaynor to bring her up as his own. He agrees and adopts the girl, marrying the child's nurse.

Gaynor becomes a State Supreme Court justice while Harry is serving his life sentence. Years pass and Diana is engaged to marry one of the socially well-connected Rutherford clan. Flo re-enters with her lawyer intent on getting a cash settlement from Gaynor. Believing that Flo will ruin Diana's life, Harry crashes out of prison. He meets Diana, who does not know who he is. He traces Flo and the lawyer to a hotel apartment where he tricks his way past the police guard. "How did you get in here? There's a police guard outside!" says a startled Flo. "I know," replies Harry nonchalantly. "Nice guy." In an altercation, the guard shoots the lawyer by mistake. The frightened Flo flees from one hotel to another with Harry in pursuit, always leaving a bunch of heliotrope flowers on the bed. In time he tracks her down and in her frightened state she falls from the hotel balcony. Harry returns to prison and Diana marries her fiancé.

Donlevy played very effectively as a gentleman crook, and he was so tender and attentive to the baby that it was not difficult to imagine him as the doting father which he was in real life. There was excellent support, especially from Foster as the good guy and Harold Huber as the loyal chauffeur and right-hand man.

His next project was announced as *Thunder Rock.* By this point, Britain had been at war for two years, and MGM was keen to begin making films in the country once again. This was an anti-isolationist parable about a man who seeks to escape from the troubles of the world by taking a job as a lighthouse keeper off the coast of Newfoundland. He hopes to write his book while secreted there, but is visited by the ghosts of those who died in a shipwreck a hun-

dred years before. All were trying to escape persecution in one form or another in Europe and start again in the New World. The man comes to realize that "No man is an island entire unto himself."

When the film was first conceived, it was considered politically divisive because there was still great resistance to America entering the war. Donlevy was an interesting choice, and an American actor in the lead would have given this movie greater resonance in the U.S. In the end, the role went to Michael Redgrave who was very effective but incredibly British, thus diluting the *raison d'etre* of the project and

Donlevy was thoroughly charming as Heliotrope Harry in *A Gentleman After Dark* (1942). Standing under the lamppost, he bears a striking resemblance to his character in the opening titles of his later TV series *Dangerous Assignment*.

ensuring that it was not so immediate to the audience for which it was intended.[42] In any case, it was immaterial because by the time it was released, America was at war. Donlevy was also sought for the lead in the Boris Morros production *Wings for Democracy,* based on a story by H.C. Potter about ferrying airplanes to England. That film was never made.[43]

The Great Man's Lady sounded promising, re-teaming three of the stars of *Union Pacific.* However, the result was rather disappointing, largely due to the thin premise. The starting point was Vina Delmar's short story "The Human Side" which had first appeared in *Cosmopolitan.* The incoherent tale appeared to move backwards and forwards. The deliberate screenplay did not help matters; although the movie was only 90 minutes long, it felt longer and seemed to take an age to begin. But Donlevy had a good, sensitive role (as the other great man in Barbara Stanwyck's life) even if he was not given enough screen time.

An old woman, Hannah Sempler (Stanwyck), is besieged by reporters on the day of the unveiling of a statue of Senator Ethan Hoyt (McCrea), one of the founders of Hoyt City. The press wants to know why Ethan died at her house and whether they were ever married. A young woman biographer (Katherine Stevens) shames them into leaving the old lady in peace. Hannah begins to recount her life story to the biographer...

The young Hannah first met Ethan when she was 20; defying her disciplinarian father, she eloped with him. They were married during a terrific thunderstorm. Ethan has dreams of building a great city, and takes Hannah to the place where it will be—at that time, there is only a rough-hewn log cabin. Ethan is offered a deal by a businessman to invest money in his scheme, if he accepts 25 percent of the profits only. Hannah gets rid of the businessman. Ethan decides to try his luck in the gold fields, but drunkenly gambles away his initial investment along with his house and livestock when he meets professional gambler Steely Edwards (Donlevy). Hannah manages to get everything back from Steely, who falls for her at first sight. Ethan and Hannah move to Sacramento where she runs a boarding house and he goes to the gold fields. He has no luck finding gold, but inadvertently discovers silver. There follows a silver rush, but in order to buy more mines, Ethan needs money. Hannah easily persuades Steely to give her the money. Ethan goes to Virginia City to be near the silver mines, and Hannah stays in Sacramento as she is going to have a baby, but does not tell Ethan. She has twins and, during a severe rainstorm, decides to go to San Francisco with Steely. Steely buys her a ticket to Virginia City instead. The river is flooded and the stagecoach washed away. The children are killed and Hannah is believed dead. Steely goes to Virginia City to tell Ethan, who promptly shoots him. Steely recovers and returns to Sacramento and discovers that Hannah is alive, and they go into the gambling business together. Ethan marries another woman and Hannah divorces him. Ethan later becomes a "great man" and reconciles with Hannah.

The plot seemed too contrived to hold the attention, and it was never really shown how the "great man" became great, or how he managed to build a city. McCrea appeared uncomfortable in a role that was ill-suited to his straight-as-a-dye persona. Stanwyck made a convincing 100-year-old lady, the makeup artists did a terrific job, and the actress managed to make the role live as she always did. Donlevy played an interesting character. Most certainly it was a sympathetic part—far more so than that of Ethan, who seemed a simpleton one minute and a bully the next. The screenplay would have been more successful had it focused on a dissection of what greatness means, and shown how Steely was arguably greater as a person because he was selfless and helped others. At the end, Hannah says that Steely died in the San Francisco fire helping others to escape, true to his nature.

Far from being the great gambler in real life, Donlevy had to have lessons from Major McBride on how to handle cards. McBride instructed many actors in the art, and his hands often appeared on screen. At the behest of director William A. Wellman, he began instructing Donlevy on the set of *Billy the Kid* at MGM the week before the actor moved to Paramount. McBride praised Donlevy as a good pupil, and the critics widely praised his acting.[44] Stanwyck and Donlevy had first become friends during the making of *This Is My Affair*. He was an actor she admired and they always enjoyed working together.[45]

According to Wellman, he and Stanwyck considered the movie to be among their finest work, and were disappointed with the poor reception it received.[46] Short stories have provided the basis for many successful works on screen, allowing more scope for the director's imagination. Unfortunately, *The Great Man's Lady* highlighted the problem of using a short story of insufficient depth as the basis for a film.

On the plus side, Donlevy was getting plenty of attention and was in demand at this time. For instance, his was one of many names considered for the part of El Sordo in Ernest Hemingway's *For Whom the Bell Tolls*—a list that included the author.[47] Donlevy was also in the frame for leading roles in *Across the Pacific* and *Dance Hall*.[48] In comedy *The Mayor of Forty-Fifth Street* he was to have co-starred with George Raft and Jackie Cooper, but the project was never realized.[49]Nor was *Let the Eagle Scream*, the story of a gangster who becomes president of a bank, also starring Claire Trevor.[50]

The Great McGinty and the war years put him in the spotlight as never before and he was seen as one of the greatest assets at Paramount. These years were the best of his career and a just reward for his earlier struggles and hard work.

6

The War Years:
Riding High at Paramount

"You have to be convincing in the movies because the people get so close to you. The people are smart and don't let anyone kid you into believing otherwise."
—"Mr. America," by Liza, *Screenland,* October 1944, 46

In the collective consciousness, one of the most indelible images of the Donlevy of the war years was as Major Caton in *Wake Island.* The epitome of the tough, undaunted leader, he exhorts his Marines to fight despite the odds. His calm authority made him seem inspirational. This was one of his finest roles and the war years were his best. After *The Great McGinty,* filmmakers finally realized that he could play any role. Around this time, he was seen in the most positive light of his entire career.

The isolated Wake Island lies in the middle of the Pacific, about 600 miles from the nearest inhabited settlement, and 6000 from the American mainland. This barren place was the setting for one of the first battles of the Second World War shortly after the December 7, 1941, fall of Pearl Harbor. Director John Farrow's *Wake Island* was released in August 1942, when the fate of many of those involved was still unknown; all the names were changed.

Major Caton (Donlevy) is assigned to the island and makes the trip from Pearl Harbor in the same aircraft as surly mining engineer Shad McClosky (Albert Dekker). The island is very flat and fairly barren save for a few trees, and it is easy to see why the Spanish and the British gave it the go-by over the preceding 400 years. McClosky is antagonistic towards the Marines and refuses to order his men into shelters during an air raid drill. After news of the Pearl Harbor attack arrives, he becomes cooperative. The Japanese fire from several ships; two are sunk, and the initial invasion is repelled. The island is pounded for some time, and there are frequent air raids; with so little ground cover, it becomes difficult to hide airplanes, and only two remain. Soon the enemy advance cannot be stopped and the island is overrun.

Wake Island was intended as an entertaining propaganda exercise, and on that level it succeeds. There is excellent footage of bombing raids, and the futility of defending a barren island in the middle of nowhere is very apparent. Naturally there are many historical inaccuracies, but in retrospect they seem unimportant. Although the defenders of the island successfully repelled the invaders for 12 days, they did not in reality fight to the last man, but surrendered and spent the war years in captivity either

Donlevy gave a measured performance as *Wake Island*'s (1942) Major Caton, leader of a besieged battalion on a Pacific island in the early days of the war.

there or in other parts of the Japanese empire. There were many more civilians billeted there than Marines.

At the end of the film, there was also a special short segment which showed Donlevy appealing for War Bonds. He spent much time promoting the Bonds and made several personal appearances across the country, often popping up on Pathe newsreels in such shows as *The Four Freedoms Show* at Portland, Oregon.[1]

The ideal hero, Major Caton was the image of calm authority, allied to real compassion for his men. Donlevy received uniform praise for his performance. Bosley Crowther wrote that he was "a credit to the corps, not to mention the acting profession."[2] Unsurprisingly, the film was "one of the year's most potent successes."[3] It was nominated for four Oscars, including Best Picture. Donlevy was placed third by the hard-to-satisfy New York Film Critics Circle Award in the Best Actor category.[4]

Paramount immediately bought O.O. Dull's story *One Man's War* and intended as a Donlevy vehicle; it was never made.[5] He was also interested in other projects of his own, including the adventure tale *The King of the Khyber Rifles,* intending to co-star with his pal Victor McLaglen. A film version was made some years later, after Donlevy had sold the rights to the story.[6] Paramount was keen to re-team Donlevy, Akim Tamiroff and Preston Sturges in the satire *Buy Me That Town* (1941), but all three men were busy with other projects.[7] Donlevy might also have featured in Maxwell Anderson's talky war drama *The Eve of St. Mark* (1944).[8] He, Albert Dekker and William Bendix were announced as the stars of *Advance Agents to Africa,* but the project was dropped.[9]

Donlevy was to have had the starring role in *Three Sheets to the Wind,* an independent feature for director Tay Garnett starring John Wayne. The idea of making a film version was shelved, but it was adapted into a 26-episode radio series which featured the same stars.[10] Donlevy planned to film a story he had written, *Dutch Treat,* with Garnett directing, but this also did not come about.[11] He was penciled to play a commanding officer in *Seek! Strike! Destroy!,* a film about the American Army Tank destroyers, pending approval from the War Department, which was never given.[12] Renowned British producer Michael Balcon wanted Donlevy to star in *San Demetrio, London* (1943), a stirring true story of heroism displayed by the merchant navy. Donlevy was enthusiastic, and would have been well suited to this Ealing Studios production. Alas, he was so busy that year that it was impossible for him to get sufficient time off.[13]

Donlevy followed *Wake Island* with the starring role as a flashy political operator in Dashiell Hammett's *The Glass Key.* Paramount was keen to push new hero Alan Ladd to the fore, so the writers weighted his part accordingly. This was the second version of the tale to reach the screen. The first had starred George Raft in 1935.

Ed Beaumont (Ladd) is the chief aide to political boss Paul Madvig (Donlevy), who supports Senator Henry's reform ticket in the upcoming election. Madvig is engaged to Henry's daughter Janet (Veronica Lake). Beaumont believes the Henrys are merely using Paul to gain political advantage. The reformers also wish to crack down on gambling houses, which arouses the ire of dangerous racketeer Nick Varna (Joseph Calleia). Henry's no-good son Taylor is having an affair with Paul's sister Opal. Paul finds out and a short time later Beaumont discovers Taylor's body outside the Henry mansion. Most people conclude that Paul has killed him, and in time he is indicted for murder. In truth he is covering for the real murderer, who is not revealed until the end. Of course, Beaumont and Janet fall in love. Madvig gives them their blessing and takes back the big diamond engagement ring from Janet.

The Glass Key (1942) was one of the most successful screen adaptations of a Dashiell Hammett work. Donlevy, playing a politically ambitious go-getter, was the nominal star but Paramount was keen to promote leading man Alan Ladd (left) and bolstered his role. Nevertheless, Donlevy shone in all his scenes.

Donlevy appears larger than life as Madvig, an ideal character to suit his screen persona: brash, flashy but curiously human and vulnerable underneath. None too bright, he is loyal and totally lacking in self-awareness. There is no real malice in him, and despite his past and shady connections, he comes across a jaunty, two-fisted bruiser. There were definite similarities between Madvig and Daniel McGinty. The politics of *The Glass Key* are far more cynical and complex than those of *The Great McGinty,* but the two characters are not a million miles apart.

Of the other actors, William Bendix stood out as a malicious thug. The two leads were their usual passive selves. Ladd and Lake suited the noir idiom perfectly. Not only did they look wonderful together, but their minimalist approach was ideal for lead actors in the genre: less was definitely more. However, this allowed the real actors around them to do their stuff. Donlevy and Bendix stand out all the more, and Donlevy in particular deserves plaudits for holding the viewer's interest when it might otherwise wane. For all its darkness, noir needs its counterpoints: for instance, the harassed district attorney and the nervous waiter attending to Bendix's potentially murderous room service. Despite the studio's best efforts for Ladd to outshine him in all their scenes together, Donlevy creates a lively portrait of another likable character and ends up stealing all his scenes.

This was the second time (after *I Wanted Wings*) that Donlevy worked with Veronica Lake. For some reason, she was convinced that he hated her, as she recalled in a *Time* magazine interview:

In the first scene ... the action called for me to hit him on the jaw. Well, I really hit him. I've said I could punch and I did.... But he just stood there and took it.... I saw his eyes glaze and I knew I'd really hit him. Right away I began to cry. I was terrified....[14]

He asked what was wrong and she replied that she did not know how to pull a punch. "I'll give you till the next take to learn," he said. Lake admitted at the time that Donlevy helped her a lot.[15] The studio intended to reunite Lake and Donlevy in *War Boom,* about mushrooming prosperity caused by an army draft camp.[16] *War Boom* may be the same as *War Town,* which was to have starred Fred MacMurray, Donlevy and Dorothy Lamour and based around a civilian conscription camp. Whether this was one movie or two, nothing came of it.

Donlevy had been considered for the role of Sam Spade in *The Maltese Falcon* (1941) although it is now impossible to imagine anyone else but Humphrey Bogart as Spade.[17] Paramount were keen to team him with Alan Ladd and Paulette Goddard in a version of Dashiell Hammett's 1927 novel *Red Harvest* which had previously been filmed as *Roadhouse Nights;*

this project was abandoned.[18] He was also lined up for the lead in United Artists' *Washington Correspondent,* which was never made.[19]

His next film was an "almost noir," the crime drama *Nightmare* (1942), a wartime flag-waver for Universal. The story begins during a blackout with starving gambler Daniel Shane (Donlevy) breaking into a house and fixing himself something to eat. Widow Leslie Stafford (Diana Barrymore) arrives and says that he can stay there if he helps her get rid of her husband, otherwise she will call the police. Shane eventually agrees and goes upstairs to her husband's room, only to find him already dead, slumped on his desk with a dagger in his back. She convinces the phlegmatic Shane to dispose of the body, which he reluctantly does. He hails a taxi and passes the corpse off as a drunken buddy. Near the docks he gets out and quietly slips the body out of sight while the night watchmen are preoccupied, then returns to the house. The next morning the body has returned. As

Nightmare (1942), a noirish thriller, starred Donlevy as a phlegmatic gambler in wartime England who gets tangled up with young widow Diana Barrymore and Nazi agents. Donlevy based his radio and TV series *Dangerous Assignment* on his *Nightmare* character.

the police arrive at the house, the couple makes a quick getaway and head to Scotland. Thereafter they have numerous adventures, along the way uncovering Nazi spies and a bizarre plot involving a whiskey distillery which is not what it seems.

Although set in Britain, this was the familiar, "pure Hollywood" version full of quaint villages with cozy pubs the size of ballrooms filled with jolly yokels sporting a bewildering array of accents from strange variants of Cockney via cod Scottish to genuine Irish. All the British actors on the lot were pressed into service and even Arthur Shields popped up, presumably because all cops must be Irish. It was certain that Ian Wolfe would put in an appearance as a sly butler at some stage. The plot strained credulity from the onset so that any passing resemblance to *The 39 Steps* was soon forgotten. However, the movie proved popular, and critics praised Donlevy, who "makes the best of his role ... underplaying his lines when necessary and bringing a certain lightness to the business at hand."[20] He later cited the film and role as his favorite. The studio was keen to film a sequel but that did not happen.[21] Barrymore's performance seemed hampered by her attempt at an English accent that made her appear rather stiff at times. This was perhaps her biggest role and her well-charted decline led to her suicide at the age of 38. She got on well with Brian and joined him for long lunches each day in his dressing room.[22]

Stand By for Action was to have been filmed in England with a mostly British cast, headed by Robert Donat. However, the war was at its height in the Atlantic, and so the action was switched to the U.S. Navy in the Pacific.[23] Donlevy played a lieutenant commander who has reached the top the hard way and resents the apparently privileged new man Robert Taylor, constantly making it tough for him. However, the war focuses their minds on the task in hand and all differences are forgotten.

Despite the cast (which included Charles Laughton), the film was not so well received. One called it "studio-bound war heroics, slurping into sentiment."[24] The *Times* of London critic summed it up neatly, saying this was "not the kind of film the American navy deserves."[25] Latter-day reviewers have been far kinder, but the setting is so false at times that it gets in the way of the action. The title is somewhat misleading because there is far more standing by than action, which only takes place in the last 15 minutes.

Donlevy was announced as the lead in *Sahara* (1943) but wanted to be around for the birth of his child, so the role went to Humphrey Bogart.[26] He was slated as Bogart's replacement in the fantasy *Our Friend Curley,* but the Columbia film was postponed after star Rita Hayworth walked out on production, an action for which she was suspended.[27] The movie was retitled *Once Upon a Time* (1944) and starred Cary Grant. Curiously, Donlevy turned down the lead in Metro's unusual romantic ghost drama *A Guy Named Joe,* and it was given to Spencer Tracy.[28] Donlevy was sought for the starring role in the screen version of Eugene O'Neill's allegorical play *The Hairy Ape,* but that memorably went to William Bendix.[29] Donlevy was also handed the lead in the romantic comedy *It Had to be You,* but his role went to Cornel Wilde.[30] Among other abandoned projects was *Storm,* based on the novel by George R. Stewart,[31] and *Everything Happens to Him,* based on the life of charismatic sports promoter Tex Rickard.[32] Donlevy replaced Fred MacMurray in *Caribbean Patrol,* an account of armed merchantmen, which was in the planning stage at Paramount for some time but never actually happened.[33]

In 1943 he was handed the co-starring role in George Marshall's musical *Incendiary Blonde* opposite Betty Hutton, based on the life of nightclub singer Texas Guinan. Donlevy felt the part was not suited to him and refused to play it. For this act of defiance, he was promptly suspended by his studio. His role was assigned to Barry Sullivan instead and later to the Mexican actor Arturo de Cordova.[34] This followed Donlevy's refusal to play the lead in *Double Indemnity.* The episode did not seem to harm his career in the long run and he was allowed to record five charity broadcasts on radio in New York soon afterwards. He also embarked on a USO tour of Alaska for the duration of his suspension.[35] Stars were becoming too choosy according to studio bosses who sought to make an example of some. Paramount famously sued Don Ameche for refusing to play a role. In order to punish Donlevy, they left him without a project for a while. Although *Two Years Before the Mast* was completed in 1944, it was not released until 1946.

During the war, Donlevy often visited Army and Navy hospitals, military bases and Marine depots, in addition to all his personal appearances for film promotion work. The visits to wounded servicemen always affected him, particularly when he met young men who had been blinded or maimed. Like many stars, he was often heard on the radio, took part enthusiastically in war bond drives and traveled all over the country doing morale-boosting USO camp shows. He received a royal welcome wherever he went. During a typical visit like that at Spokane, Washington, he met wounded servicemen at Baxter Hospital and toured Fort Wright. The girls in the administration block put up a big sign reading, "Brian Donlevy come and see us girls!"[36] At night they threw a party for him in the Officers' Club. At one such event, an October 1943 army show in at Chanute Field,

Rantoul, Illinois, he collapsed with a severe respiratory infection.[37] After two days in St. Luke's hospital in Chicago, he took a turn for the worse, but then over the course of the following week made a slow recovery.

Although Donlevy did not serve in the war, he was still listed on the Army Aviation reserve with which he held a commission. He had also passed exams in order to qualify.[38]

In 1943, Donlevy signed a two-picture-a-year deal with Paramount and began a four-year contract with MGM for one picture a year. The Metro deal allowed him script approval.[39] MGM bought *Dark of the Moon* by Margaret Bell Houston, a Texan who was a granddaughter of Sam Houston. This began as a magazine serial and was later published as a novel. It was intended as a vehicle for Donlevy, Macdonald Carey and Dorothy Lamour. The film was never made.[40]

Donlevy was next announced as the star of *Hostages,* a story of the Czech resistance, and sought Larraine Day as his co-star.[41] In the event, neither appeared in the film, and Donlevy was instead assigned to Fritz Lang's *Hangmen Also Die!* (1943), which covered similar subject matter.

Hangmen Also Die! was based very loosely on contemporary events in the Czech Republic, which was constituted as the German protectorate of Bohemia and Moravia during the war. The hangman of the title refers to Reinhard Heydrich, who was assassinated in 1942 by two British-trained paratroopers. A more accurate version of the story is related in *Operation Daybreak* (1982). In Lang's movie, scripted by fellow German exile Bertolt Brecht, Czech underground fighter Dr. Svoboda (Donlevy) is portrayed as the sole assassin. Heydrich is seen briefly at the beginning, but the assassination happens off camera, and no details are given. In attempting to escape, Svoboda is aided by Mascha (Anna Lee), and later seeks refuge at the house of her father Prof. Novotny (Walter Brennan). He stays with them for the night before the resistance can help him. He tries not to implicate them, but in her anger Mascha implicates herself when she insists on going to Gestapo headquarters. Inspector Gruber (Alexander Granach) is suspicious and, although he allows her to go home, her father is arrested with the other men of the city and imprisoned awaiting execution. Despite the reprisals, the underground remains determined not to give up the assassin. Svoboda argues that he ought to give himself up. As the hostages continue to be executed, the resistance discovers there is a traitor among them and frame him so that he is executed by the occupying power. Mascha and Svoboda try to convince the inspector that they are lovers, in an attempt to hide the wounded Dr. Pillar. Mascha's fiancé

ANCHE I BOIA MUOIONO

BRIAN DONLEVY-WALTER BRENNAN-ANNA LEE

Regia di FRITZ LANG

Donlevy and Anna Lee in an Italian poster for *Hangmen Also Die!* (1943). Donlevy had the lead role as a Czech doctor and assassin of Reinhard Heydrich in a highly fictionalized account of a true event. Director Fritz Lang's autocratic attitude made life difficult for many of the actors but the finished result has more merit than many thought at the time.

Jan tries to waylay the inspector, who by now realizes that Svoboda is the assassin and goes to the hospital to arrest him. Svoboda kills the inspector and the quisling is killed, but the fight goes on for the Czechs and the closing caption reads "This is not the end."

Some rehearsals took place at Donlevy's house, in theory to cut down on the amount of film used by 25 percent.[42] Lang was his usual autocratic self; neither Donlevy nor Anna Lee relished making the film. Lee cut her arm badly when Lang made her do several retakes of the scene in the cab when she smashes the glass; he demanded that real glass be used. He also insisted that everyone speak with American accents, but at one stage a tall Texan extra thought Lang was insulting his Southern accent and knocked him to the ground. None of the crew helped him up.[43]

A rather long-drawn out melodrama, *Hangmen Also Die!* contained many scenes typical of Lang, but made for only occasionally engaging viewing. Ostensibly the star of the picture, Donlevy is cool and convincing, but rather unemotional, and his part is badly underwritten. Although he goes through some soul-searching over the consequences of his actions, his fears are soon dismissed by another underground member. The writer was obviously more interested in the characters of the inspector and the quisling, who are both far more prominent. These two actors give the best performances on display. Brecht was clearly not interested in examining the motives and emotional responses of the assassin.

Because the assassination is not shown, there is a marked feeling of lack of involvement in the screenplay, which is reduced to some wonderful set piece scenes interspersed between the tedious parts. Although its subject was the war, and this was Lang's contribution to the propaganda effort, the film is essentially another exercise in noir. The scene involving the murder of the inspector seems so typical of Lang: the inspector's bowler hat rolling innocuously on the floor while his lifeless legs dangle over the side of the table. The film is worth the admission fee for such touches alone. It won a Special Mention at the Venice Film Festival in 1946.[44]

The Soviet government was so impressed by Donlevy in *Wake Island* that they requested him as the American narrator of the documentary *Stalingrad* (1943).[45] Directed by the acclaimed Russian filmmaker Leonid Varlamov, this was a stark record of the 162-day siege, shot by five different cinematographers.[46] The film incorporated German newsreel footage that had been captured by the Russians. One of the foremost propagandist documentary makers of the Soviet era, Varlamov won five Stalin Prizes for his films including *The Earth and Climatic Belts* (1933), *An Arctic Voyage* (1940) and *Moscow Strikes Back* (1942). *Stalingrad,* later retitled *The City That Stopped Hitler: Heroic Stalingrad,* was the first film recounting the battle which proved to be a decisive turning point of the war. *Stalingrad* received excellent notices. One critic called it "by far the most thrilling and exciting of all official war pictures."[47] A film historian labeled it "a film that caused global astonishment."[48] John Wexley, who wrote the script for the U.S. version, was working during the day, as was Donlevy, who recorded the narration at night.[49] He was widely praised for his skillful narration. Wexley was later denounced as a Communist and blacklisted by HUAC.

Donlevy was next announced for the British production *I Live in Grosvenor Square,* aka *A Yank in London,* with Anna Neagle, C. Aubrey

Smith and Flora Robson. At the last minute, Donlevy was replaced by Dean Jagger. Smith and Robson also missed out.[50]

In January 1944, Donlevy was one of numerous celebrity guests invited to the White House for the president's birthday celebrations. After lunch, the Hollywood stars were shown around the executive mansion by Mrs. Eleanor Roosevelt.[51] Donlevy reflected on his great advance since the days many years before when he had played with a stock company in Washington which had unexpectedly folded. With time on his hands, he went to see the White House and loitered near the gates. It was not long before a guard told him, "Move along, buddy."[52] Some years later, Donlevy met President Truman at a film premiere and acted in a play for him.

Donlevy was nominated as mayor of Malibu colony during the war, and served three terms in the post from 1944 to '46. It was a purely honorary position and he was never tempted to actually enter politics.[53]

In August 1944, he was guest of honor at the American Newspaper Guild's Annual Convention banquet, held at Milwaukee's Schroeder Hotel. At the North West Road station, he was greeted by several hundred fans. He said he hoped to visit Beaver Dam

An American Romance (1944) gave Donlevy a starring role as a European migrant who makes good in early twentieth century America. The film could have been a warm human story, but in post-production was badly edited and became instead a paean to American industrial strength. Donlevy and his co-star, Australian actress Ann Richards, both did remarkably well in what remains an overlooked and sublimely shot film.

and Sheboygan Falls while in Wisconsin, and reportedly had his eye on a dairy farm near Sheboygan and some other properties.[54] He met up with several old pals from the town, including Milford Wachter, with whom he was pictured in the local newspaper.

When Spencer Tracy prevaricated over whether to accept the role of Gen. Doolittle in *Thirty Seconds Over Tokyo* (1944), Donlevy was called in as a replacement by producer Sam Zimbalist. But it was said that Donlevy "had no box office clout." Then Tracy changed his mind and accepted the part as written.[55] Donlevy did replace Tracy in the next project. Eighteen years in the planning, 15 months in the making, and costing almost $3,000,000, King Vidor's *An American Romance* was called one of the most eagerly awaited and prestigious films of 1944. The result was not the success envisaged. But this underrated movie is not the monumental failure it was perceived to be at the time, and Donlevy made a great impression in the starring role.

Slovenian migrant Steve Dongas (Donlevy) arrives at Ellis Island in 1898 minus the full $25 entry fee. Understanding immigration officials recognize his keenness to work and allow him to enter the country. He walks a thousand miles to stay with his cousin Anton (John Qualen) in Mesabi, Minnesota, and works alongside him at the iron ore plant. Teacher Anna O'Rourke (Ann Richards) helps him to read and write. Instilled with ambition, he decides to hitch a train to Pittsburgh where he eventually becomes head of the steel-making operation. He writes to Anna and she joins him there, they are married and have five children. The boys are named after U.S. presidents. He finds a way to double steel production and then becomes interested in car-making. He moves to Detroit and, in partnership with Howard (Walter Abel), attempts to get some moneyed industrialists to invest in his plans for a new type of car. The money men merely wish to protect their own interest and offer to buy the plans but sit on them and avoid competition. Dangos and Howard decide to set up on their own plant with the help of Anton. The car plant becomes big business, but then Dangos encounters labor problems and finds himself in bitter opposition with his own board and his son Ted (Stephen McNally). Dangos retires to California, but with the coming of the war reunites with his son and partner in the production of aircraft.

Although overlong, *An American Romance* is a stirring film, beautifully shot in color. In an impromptu contemporary newspaper survey to determine the movie which "best typified American life," *An American Romance* was voted second just below *The Best Years of Our Life* and ahead of *State Fair*.[56] The publicist and lyricist Howard Dietz cooked up an idea to promote the movie and invoke a patriotic mood at the same time by inviting 45 of the world's best artists to contribute drawings and paintings directly inspired by the film. Instead of paying the artists, he promised to contribute substantially to the Society of Illustrators' Philanthropic Fund.[57] The results were exhibited at the Columbus Day premiere in Cincinnati and afterwards routed to various theaters across the country. *Life* magazine featured several of the finest works in a wonderfully inventive spread. Graham Kaye, Walter Early, Stevan Dohanos and many others contributed some excellent pieces, successfully evoking the theme and atmosphere of the film; many focused on its star, Donlevy. *Life*'s brief review noted: "[Vidor's] willingness to tackle the touchy problem of labor unions is, for the movies, both unprecedented and refreshing."[58]

There was the usual big build-up to the film's October world premiere in 132 cities simultaneously. It was promoted in every conceivable way: by car cards, taxi hire covers, dashboard cards and school posters.[59] Donlevy and other cast members took part in an exhaustive ten-day promotional tour of the middle and eastern states.[60] There were advance screenings in 48 state capitals. These were followed by parades in Louisville, Cincinnati and Indianapolis which involved the stars of the film each unveiling a new bomber purchased through war bonds and christened *An American Romance*.[61]

In spite of the fanfare, and the qualified backing of the bosses of the nation's steel industry, the box office returns were disappointing. When interviewed many years later, Vidor commented:

> I wrote *An American Romance* for a star cast consisting of Spencer Tracy, Ingrid Bergman and Joseph Cotten, and at one time the studio promised to let me have these people. When I finally came to do the film, I had none of them…. I compromised by taking Brian Donlevy and a girl [Richards] they wanted to develop, justifying myself on the grounds that I'd become a kind of "company man" at MGM and had been on salary for a year without making a picture. But neither Brian Donlevy nor the girl was very exciting, and that, combined with wartime conditions and studio cutting, spoiled the film. I cut a lot of it out to begin with, and then the studio cut more. I'd discovered, when taking it out on the road in the Middle West that it was too heavily loaded on the documentary side at the expense of the human side, and wanted to cut it accordingly. Well, the studio did the reverse: they cut out the human story and kept all the documentary stuff. Then, to avoid having to redub the music, they made further cuts according to where the music ended, which was of course nonsensical and ruinous to the film. That's when I became very annoyed and left MGM for good.[62]

The movie was essentially a patriotic paean to American industrial might. But despite Vidor's negativity, Donlevy and Richards are appealing and convincing leads. Some maintained that this was Donlevy's finest performance, and he was most certainly equal to all that was asked of him. He handled the comedy scenes as adroitly as the emotional moments, and maintained throughout a fine characterization of a simple-hearted but fiercely determined soul. One commentator noted that he looked "more handsome and rugged than ever," and was well-paired with the natural acting of attractive honey-blonde Australian Ann Richards.[63] One appealing sequence (the family's ride in the car to attend George's graduation) was especially well realized, Donlevy's penchant for comedy coming to the fore as the car breaks down. The movie was very well served by its supporting cast, especially John Qualen and Walter Abel. Donlevy's six-week-old daughter Judy appeared as the babe in arms.[64] Warm-hearted, humorous and moving by turns, Donlevy "never relaxes his hold on the part" and shows that he is an actor of unexpected range.[65]

An American Romance led to many other opportunities for its star. He was offered him $250,000 to star in a movie in Mexico. He negotiated with Paramount to allow him to do so, but the deal fell through.[66] He was considered for the role of Tony Angelo in the musical comedy *Nob Hill* (1944), but was replaced by George Raft.[67] Although touted as the favorite to play legendary prizefighter John L. Sullivan in the biopic *The Great John L* (1945), the role was handed to an unknown stage actor instead.[68] In addition, Donlevy bought the movie rights to *Desert Padre,* a *Saturday Evening Post* story, and hoped to produce it himself, but dropped the idea when he could not muster the necessary financial backing.[69] He was considered essential for the adult lead in *Boys' Ranch* with Skip Homeier and a gang of kids, but in the end he was replaced by James Craig.[70]

Donlevy popped up in *Duffy's Tavern* (1945), along with other famous stars, as himself. He and Sonny Tufts were featured in a sketch with Paulette Goddard in a bathtub. An unsuccessful big screen adaptation of a long-running and very popular radio show, this was essentially an exercise in star-spotting. It had a featherweight plot and was neatly summarized by one observer as "a million-dollar cast struggling with ten cents' worth of material."[71]

As the war drew to a close, it was announced that Donlevy had signed to record the ten most famous speeches of the war. Although this project never came to fruition, he did record two patriotic addresses, "Columbus," by Joaquin Miller and "The American Flag" by Joseph Redman Drake. Both were released on the Decca label in 1947. Some years later, the recordings appeared on an LP, *Our Common Heritage,* along with similar contributions from Walter Huston and Fredric March.

There was a time when children were scared by Donlevy, but once when he was in New York he was besieged by a crowd of kids fighting for his autograph. They were so excited, they inadvertently pushed him into the road and he was knocked over by a taxi, after which he spent some time recovering in a hospital.[72] As early as 1936 there was a Brian Donlevy Fan Club whose president Louise A. Baldwin contributed the column "Star Gazing" for her local newspaper the *Mount Vernon* (Indiana) *Democrat*.[73] He was very popular in the 1940s and during the war became the pin-up of choice of the Women's Marines Auxiliary at Hunter's College, New York.[74] It was reported that his "thousands of … fans … have begged Paramount to give him a romantic role" which, to their credit, the studio at least attempted.[75] At that time, it was also reported, "[T]he other day three gals tried to kiss him in a hotel lobby, he received 16 mash notes and at a nightclub an excited schoolgirl got away with his necktie."[76] He was flattered and not a little surprised by the female attention, but it didn't go to his head:

> The thing that I dread more than anything is that my lady customers might get to the point where they see things in me that don't exist. I've always wanted … to have a good male following because most men aren't fooled by other men. If a fellow is generally liked by … his own sex it means that he's at least partially succeeding at being on the level with himself and others.[77]

7

"Gentlemen,
this is my wife..."

"He really isn't a bad guy. He is easy to handle, not at all tem-peramental except when he's starting a picture with a strange director—that always worries him. He's a quick study, eats any-thing that's placed in front of him, sleeps nine hours a day and likes horses."
          —Marjorie Donlevy talks about her husband
          with Malcolm Oettinger, "I Hate Your
          Face," *Screenland,* March 1941, 84

When he first arrived in Hollywood in 1935, Donlevy established himself in a very short time. He was making good money and he had his long-dreamt-of house on one of Hollywood's highest hills. But the dream was bittersweet, and after his break up with Yvonne he was mostly alone and very soon bored for company. "I'd like to come home from work to more than a big house and a Filipino houseboy who never gets phone messages correct," he said.[1]

He went on dates with Lucille Ball and Broadway actress Jean Lewis, among others. Then, at a New Year's Eve party at the Trocadero nightclub, he met singer Marjorie Lane.[2] He asked her out, but the petite redhead told him she already had a date with Robert Taylor. Night after night he haunted the club just to catch sight of her.[3] Their on-off romance played out over the spring and summer; at one stage he indicated in a newspaper interview that they were practically engaged.[4] This annoyed Marjorie, who retorted that she would not marry for at least two years, not until she could be sure what her future in motion pictures would be.[5]

Downhearted, Donlevy was nothing if not determined. He kept chasing her, and often called her up at the studio, but she was usually away singing for Eleanor Powell. Brian and Marjorie met for dinner one night, he asked her to marry him, she said maybe; but he had set his mind on the outcome and was not to be denied. She later admitted she didn't take to him at first, found him "too bossy," and resented the way he "took things too much for granted."[6] But this reluctance on her part only increased his ardor. "I think she will say 'yes' one of these times," he said, "and then we'll run away to Arizona and get it over with."[7] He made marriage sound as inviting as a visit to the dentist and she was fairly ambivalent, so it did not sound like the most auspicious start to a relationship. But Marjorie weighed up her options and finally said yes. They didn't run away to Arizona, but to Ensenada, Mexico, where they were married on December 22, 1936. As though marriage in another country seemed unreal and was somehow of uncertain legality, they went through a second ceremony on New Year's Eve at the Wilshire Episcopalian Chapel in Los Angeles, just to make sure.[8] Not that marriage in Hollywood was any more real; however this time they did it her way, "California style," surrounded by friends, and with Eleanor Powell as the matron of honor.

Marjorie was 24 when they married, but only admitted to 22; she had been born in Kansas, the daughter of a public relations man, and arrived in Hollywood with her mother. She had no musical training, but did have ambition and was soon singing in nightclubs, especially the Trocadero on Sunset Boulevard where she hoped to catch the eye of passing studio executives. She succeeded: MGM boss Louis B. Mayer put her under contract.[9] She was lucratively employed as a singer specializing in dubbing actresses who couldn't hold down a note, including Jean Harlow, Isabel Jeans and Ann Dvorak.[10] Despite her success, she really wanted to be an actress. "Only drama can get the acting desire out of the system," she said.[11] For all that, her career was exclusively behind the scenes; she was heard but never seen. However, she was certainly noticed by many men, among them the famous artist-illustrator James Montgomery Flagg, who called her "the most attractive girl in Hollywood's younger set."[12]

Soon after their marriage, she began to discard the things about her Briny that she didn't like. First to go were the scarves, of which he had a great many, often multicolored in silk or satin; they spoke of a streak of pure flamboyance in his nature which she did not wish to encourage. He was always sartorially elegant and enjoyed smart clothes which were often the most expensive. He used to wear suits with padded shoulders in his early movie days; she gave them away "to a couple of guys who hung around, cluttering up Brian's life—and then got rid of them." From now on, they should only know "nice people," she asserted.[13] Next to go was the ostentatious car which was several blocks long; it was so big, he had to have an extension built on the garage, which already housed three others. Finally she persuaded him to leave his cherished house on the hill; she objected to the location, the 20 spacious rooms and the decor. They moved to a smaller place (one visitor described it as an "atrocious shingled bungalow") which she set about decorating.[14]

They moved to the new place in Brentwood in 1940 and transformed it into a "charming and gracious farmhouse in the early American style."[15]

Donlevy with his second wife, singer Marjorie Lane, at their Brentwood home. Four years after the 1943 birth of their daughter, the Donlevys went through a bitter and very public divorce.

It had several acres of land with rolling lawns, swimming pools, flower and vegetable gardens, orange, lemon, avocado and grapefruit trees, and a huge workshop. They also kept dogs; both Brian and his pet dachshund were very fond of avocados.[16] There was also a massive playroom that covered the back of the house entirely. He loved to get his hands dirty and was a keen gardener; he took pride in growing his own produce and also kept chickens. In the early years of their marriage, she used to help out in the garden. They once spent an entire day planting 11 rows of potatoes in a 200-foot-long patch.[17] When he was not knocking down walls or fixing up his massive bar, he was building walls, mixing cement, chopping down trees, fixing his wine cellar or assembling small items of furniture such as a table or a bed tray in his workshop. He bought an old railroad car that had once belonged to a millionaire with the intention of setting it up in the backyard as a study.[18] He relished the luxury of living in a lovely house after a succession of apartments, hotels, shared rooms and friends' couches during his Broadway years. Villa Donlevy was described as "part modern, part Cape Cod, with burnished copper kettles, iron-grill work and tooled leather," replete with Dresden china, Dickens pieces and Royal Doulton mugs. His romanticism was noticeable, and there were numerous love seats and window seats. To complete the ensemble, the well-stocked bar was a "replica of a New York speakeasy."[19]

Brian first developed an interest in mining in 1937, when his buddy Victor McLaglen persuaded him to grubstake a prospector.[20] From then on, he became obsessed with it; he read every book he could find and subscribed to journals on the subject. He began with a gold mine in Death Valley's Panamint springs, but this failed to yield the expected results. In time he had extensive interests in several properties including a ten-acre hill of the graphite ore antimony in which the government took an active interest. Apparently antimony was a rare and "deadly poisonous element used in alloys in coating the projectile ends of large caliber artillery shells." He later donated the mine to the nation.[21] He also owned mica, silver and tungsten mines, the latter proving very profitable. At one time he considered going into partnership with an oldtimer who had spent 30 years on a claim. Donlevy had several close shaves; it was a hazardous hobby and cave-ins were regular occurrences. Once he claimed he was trapped overnight by a landslide "on a three-foot ledge over a 750-foot chasm."[22] But there was something in mining that seemed to bring out his true nature; it was physical hard work which he thrived on, allied to a sense of adventure, the joy of discovery and the added possibility of actually striking it rich. At this point he was conservatively estimated to be making about $150,000 a year so in a sense he had already struck the mother lode. But there was something honest about earning from the sweat of one's brow that undoubtedly appealed to him.

He seemed to need something happening all the time and relished almost schoolboy adventures such as the time he went searching for Jean Lafitte's sunken treasure off the coast of Cuba in June 1941. The story was that documents were found in one of four ancient cannons by a fisherman near Batabano during a record low tide. Donlevy asked Paramount for three months' leave of absence to devote himself to the search. Not someone to do things by half, he wrote to Cuba's minister of the Interior Dr. Jose Manuel Cortina seeking (and receiving) permission to import a diving bell and suits. He even took along his buddy Claude Wilson, an ex–Marine, to help. It was never stated if his studio gave their approval but it seems unlikely. No treasure was ever found.[23]

He spent less and less time with his wife, who did not share his enthusiasm for mines, etc. "I'm a desert man myself," he boasted cheerily; "You can have it!" was his wife's retort.[24] He had a physical restlessness and needed to be constantly moving or doing something. Each morning he went for a five-mile run. At the gym six times a week, he played handball or squash. He was, as one observer commented, "hysterically athletic." According to him, he just liked to keep in condition, but she joked that he did it on purpose "so he'll be too tired to have to go dancing sometime."[25] He also bought works of art and built up an enviable collection.[26] In addition, he was an avid collector of pipes and had some rare and unusual items.[27] Marjorie collected antiques, especially clocks of which she had many in several rooms in the house, all showing different times.[28] He was a decided romantic, always buying her flowers, often orchids with little heartfelt notes attached. He was generous to a fault and frequently bought her clothes and jewelry which reflected his slightly ostentatious taste, for instance "a gold bracelet embossed with a heart fashioned in rubies."[29]

In February 1943, their daughter Judith Ann was born. He had no say in the name, which was his wife's idea; he could not indulge his superstition about initials and didn't think JAD was sufficiently lucky. Rather than bringing Brian and Marjorie together, the birth of their daughter seemed to drive them further apart. He claimed that she showed no interest in their home or in him; "She showed me no love and affection," he said, adding that it was almost impossible for him to get a date with her over a two-year period. Nor did she like California or the life they were living, and she accused him of not taking her out enough. Somewhat incongruously, he was asked in court what he did when he found out his wife was going out with other men: "I talked to her about it. Several times … it looked like a brawl … it wasn't…. She said I was too suspicious. Then she called me names." At this, "the audience sighed."[30] Used to the tough guy image of Donlevy on screen, it was difficult for them to equate with it the mild-mannered, soft-spoken man testifying before them.

In essence their characters were incompatible; Donlevy was a shy homebody who was generous with money; his wife loved socializing, but was financially astute. "I want a wife who gets as much pleasure out of a home as I do," he had once remarked. "She can't be much of a gadabout because I'd rather stay at home than go out and paint the town red every night."[31]

Brian and Marjorie separated for a while after Christmas 1945 and then attempted a reconciliation the following spring.[32] But she claimed he told her he was too tired and she became increasingly bored with him. They began to quarrel over minor things and she once complained that he was just "lying around … doing nothing but read magazines."[33] She later claimed he retorted that she should "go to New York and get things out of [her] system."[34] Furthermore he told her to "go and do anything you want to do."[35] In court there were many claims and counter-claims, as is always the case in divorces, and the truth is usually somewhere in between. She said he "encouraged her to go out with other men, tapped her telephone lines … and once tried to run over her in his automobile."[36] He admitted to spending $15,000 on hiring detectives to shadow her.[37] Things came to a head on December 15, 1946, at which time he followed her to a hotel room in New York accompanied by detectives and several respectable friends such as pediatrician Milton Tobias. They entered the room where she was naked in bed with James Hannan, a socially prominent businessman and sportsman. The whole thing seemed like a total set-up, the scene as described in court was pure Hollywood and Donlevy sounded exactly like one of the characters he played so often on screen:

> As flashbulbs popped and Hannan fell out of bed…. Mrs. Donlevy screamed: "Brian, darling, you can't do this to Jimmy." [Donlevy replied,] "Whom are you calling darling—look what you've done to me." He turned to the assembled company; "Gentlemen, this is my wife."[38]

He said she took no interest in her daughter, something which the child's nurse appeared to confirm. Under oath, Kathryn Brown said, "Mrs. Donlevy ignored the child to go to parties with other men and left liquor within the reach of the girl, who was once found drinking a glass of gin."[39] Among the seven items on the affidavit, he also claimed she had "associations" with James L. Stack, Jr., playboy brother of actor Robert Stack, which claims were successfully refuted.[40]

The first divorce suit in February 1947 was set aside because Marjorie claimed with good reason that she "was tricked into divorce by fraud and duress."[41] Donlevy went against the advice of his attorney S.S. Hahn, who advised that he should not produce photographic evidence in court or attempt to discredit her. But Marjorie had been denied her day in court and demanded $250,000 and custody of their four-year-old daughter.[42]

The final divorce settlement in November 1947 awarded shared custody of Judy and a complicated-sounding financial deal. Brian was instructed to pay Marjorie $125,000 over the next five years beginning with "$50,000 immediately, $25,000 next year and alimony of $10,000 a year for five years ... thereafter she will receive $3000 a year for six years."[43] These figures changed in July 1952 when she married Dr. Bob Fick. This also ended in divorce in 1966. Her third marriage, to millionaire ice cream manufacturer Sumner Bates, was a happy one. Marjorie never resumed her career, which effectively ended in 1937. She lived out the remainder of her life away from the glare of the spotlight and died at the age of 100 in 2012.

8

The Postwar Years

"Any consideration of the American 'film noir' of the 1940s would be incomplete without him. He was as much a part of the genre as the low-key lighting and the terse dialogue."
—"Brian Donlevy—A Famous Film Tough Guy,"
The Times, April 7, 1972, 16

Donlevy played equally well in dramas, musicals and lighthearted comedies. Although by the mid-1940s he was beginning to slip down the batting order, he nonetheless enjoyed a pleasing variety of roles.

Richard Henry Dana's *Two Years Before the Mast* was an account of the author's service in the merchant navy between 1834 and 1836. The memoir described in matter-of-fact detail the harsh conditions aboard ship during long and hazardous voyages. It became a classic of its kind and highly influential in improving the lot of the merchant seaman. Hollywood producers were keen to bring the stirring tale to the screen. Producer Edward Small acquired the movie rights and in 1939 made a deal with United Artists. But with the declaration of war, these plans were dropped. In 1943, Paramount bought the rights from Small. It was announced that John Farrow would be director and Alan Ladd the star.

Charles Stewart (Ladd), the spoiled son of a ship owner, is shanghaied and forced aboard the *Pilgrim,* one of his father's ships. The crew suffers terribly under the harsh Capt. Thompson (Howard da Silva) and his first mate Amazeen (William Bendix). Also aboard is Richard Henry Dana (Donlevy), an aspiring writer who keeps a journal of the voyage, and a young stowaway, Sammy (Darryl Hickman), who desperately wants to be a sailor. During the trip from Boston to Monterey via Cape Horn, crew members undergo numerous privations including floggings, short rations and lack of fresh food, which leads to scurvy. The captain refuses to ever go into port to replenish provisions because he is only concerned with the schedule. In time his actions lead to mutiny. The men then decide to

Donlevy (left) turned down the role of the ruthless captain in *Two Years Before the Mast* **(1946); he was far happier playing author Richard Henry Dana, whose novel formed the basis of the screenplay. He's seen here with Esther Fernandez and Alan Ladd.**

return to Boston and face the consequences of their actions so that Dana has a chance to publish his book and make a real difference to the lives of all seamen.

In common with the usual Hollywood approach, the screenplay took great liberties with Dana's original. The makers introduced a woman into the proceedings, but her half-hearted romance with Ladd only served to slow the pace and was an unnecessary addition. The ending also appeared rushed: Rather than the expected trial of the mutineers, there are just a few short scenes in which Dana and Stewart state the case for reform.

Taken on its own terms, *Two Years Before the Mast* is an engrossing, well-acted movie which gave Donlevy a good sympathetic role for a change. Initially he was offered the part of the sadistic captain; he declined, having tired of such roles. Most of the action takes place aboard ship, and the set is very authentically drawn. Farrow took pains to have the crew speak in the language of the era and made the principal players and supporting actors familiar with early nineteenth century parlance and all aspects of maritime life. There is a claustrophobic feel to the ship which heightens the sense of unease. Ships of that era must have been fairly cramped and it is easy to understand how tempers could fray when there is really no space for privacy except in one's own thoughts. Although Ladd is rather too deadpan, he is so ably supported by the other actors that any deficiencies are soon forgotten. Donlevy seemed so benevolent and tender in his scenes when young Sammy falls ill that it was impossible to imagine the same actor as Markoff. Indeed, from accounts of those who knew him, he was far more akin to the sensitive writer concerned for the welfare of his fellow man. Undoubtedly, he would also love to have been a famous writer in real life, and often wrote the kind of adventure stories which had always appealed to him.

Although the movie was completed in 1944, it was two years before the release (in 1946); for some reason it was held back by the studio. It proved very popular. One reviewer noted, "Donlevy manages to make Dana's own generous humanity warm and sincere."[1] Donlevy again teamed with Ladd in *Wild Harvest* but although he began filming on location, he was replaced by Lloyd Nolan.[2] There was also the prospect of reuniting with Bendix in George J. Schaeffer's independent feature *Scruffy*, but this failed to get the necessary funding.[3]

Brian had a regular stand-in and dresser, Byron "Sugar" Fitzpatrick. "Sugar" had been shell-shocked during World War I and spoke with a high, soft voice. There was a suggestion that he had once saved Donlevy's life in an on-set accident, which is very likely because he had many. "Sugar" worked on *Birth of the Blues, Wake Island* and *An American Romance,* among others. He became a semi-permanent member of the Donlevy household, and Donlevy said he was better than a nurse with his daughter. "Sugar" was said to have "struck more than one person he heard making disparaging remarks about his boss."[4] When Donlevy moved to Universal, "Sugar" stayed on at Paramount and with Brian's blessing shifted his allegiance to William Holden.[5]

After a gap of several years, Donlevy returned to the Western genre in *The Virginian* (1946). By then the formula was becoming very stale, and this was probably the weakest of all the Westerns he ever made. A Vermont schoolteacher travels to Medicine Bend, Wyoming, and falls in love with cowboy Joel McCrea. Once again Donlevy was the black-clad villain of the piece, this time a ruthless cattle rustler. He had a distinct presence and did what he could in the confines of the role, putting his sly smile and smart delivery of lines to good use. However, some of the dialogue was risible, and at one stage he actually tells the erstwhile McCrea to get out of town by sundown. The Californian scenery looked fine in color and the supporting players all did their best to enliven proceedings, but the formulaic story won out. Even so, the movie did quite good business at the box office.

Canyon Passage, French director Jacques Tourneur's debut Western and his first film in color, was a horse of a very different color. This was a beautiful, well-crafted and haunting adventure set among the early settlers of Oregon.

General store owner Logan Stuart (Dana Andrews) escorts a friend's fiancée, Lucy Overmore (Susan Hayward), from Portland to a Jacksonville, Oregon, mining settlement. In the course of the journey he falls in love with her. He delivers Overmore to his friend George Camrose (Donlevy), who begins to steal from the miners' gold deposits to feed his gambling addiction. When a local miner is found dead, Camrose is accused. Johnny

One of Donlevy's best postwar roles was that of George Camrose in *Canyon Passage* (1946), a beautiful, haunting Western set in Oregon and shot in Technicolor. Camrose is a weak and restless character, and his friendship with the film's protagonist Dana Andrews is both touching and convincing. Donlevy is seen here with Susan Hayward.

Steel (Lloyd Bridges) agitates the other miners to hang Camrose, but Stuart intervenes on his behalf. Word arrives that the outlying homesteads are under attack by Indians; they were incensed by the murder of an Indian girl by the brutal Honey Bragg (Ward Bond). During the melee, Stuart helps Camrose escape, but Camrose is later killed and Stuart's general store is burned to the ground.

Tourneur made his name with a couple of effective low-budget horror films, *Cat People* (1942) and *I Walked with a Zombie* (1943). His use of lighting and cinematography made these psychological horrors incredibly influential. Among his later movies was the underrated and intriguing Western *Stars in My Crown* (1950) and the British-made chiller *Night of the Demon* (1957), arguably one of his best. *Canyon Passage* had many of the hallmarks of the director and seemed to transcend the limitations of genre.

The characters are interesting and varied, presenting a wide scope of humanity, from the stoic, good-humored homesteaders to the nasty inhuman Honey Bragg, by far the worst of all. Donlevy played a many-shaded character. Although George Camrose was essentially weak, there was something in him that made him seem likable despite everything. Donlevy was always a much better actor whenever he let his guard down and allowed himself to be vulnerable. Camrose feels trapped by the town and by his own weakness; he constantly gambles even though he is in debt and starts to take gold from the bags in his keeping. He uses some gold belonging to McIver, who has been away for some time. McIver suddenly shows up one night and surprises Camrose. The scene is during twilight when Camrose sees McIver go down to a river. In those split seconds that he decides to follow him is reflected all the weakness of the character; his need to gamble outweighs everything else in his life, and he is essentially lost. The use of music in this scene, a piano tinkling in the background, is especially piquant, and the songs of Hoagy Carmichael are utilized remarkably well, including "Ole Buttermilk Sky" and "Rogue River Valley." Especially effective is "Silver Saddle," the refrain of which recurs at some of the quietest dramatic moments. The audience secretly hopes that Camrose will not follow McIver down to the river, but of course he does.

Although Camrose is engaged to Lucy, they are never especially passionate. He seems ambivalent about her, and it is obvious that the attraction between Stuart and Lucy is the main story. But Camrose has an unrequited love for the barkeeper's wife even though she gives him absolutely no encouragement. Camrose is a restless character who seems to take little direct interest in the community despite the fact that he han-

dles all their gold. When the others are helping to build a house for a
newly married young couple, Camrose spends the afternoon under a tree
with Lucy. He wears fine clothes when others are clad in buckskins, and
trusts his intended bride from the East with his best friend. His restlessness
is mirrored by that of Stuart, who is in many ways his counterpoint. At
no time do they fall out, even over Lucy. After his death and considering
all Camrose has done, Stuart speaks only words of kindness about him:
"There was a lot of good in George," he reflects at the end. "In some other
line of country, he might have made the grade." He understands his innate
difference because they are both essentially outsiders in the settlement.
This was one of Andrews' finest roles; Stuart has a real humanity and generosity of spirit that is seldom encountered. Tourneur's beautiful Western
has a deeper resonance because the characters are so well understood that
the drama unfolds itself naturally and leaves a haunting impression encapsulated by the soundtrack, which poignantly underscores this very human
tale.

Donlevy teamed with William Demarest again, this time playing
bootleggers in the light comedy *Our Hearts Were Growing Up* (1947). This
was a sequel to *Our Hearts Were Young and Gay* (1944), which was based
on Cornelia Otis Skinner's autobiographical novel. The second film followed the adventures of Cornelia (Gail Russell) and Emily (Diana Lynn)
during their days at Princeton College in the 1920s. En route to a house
party, they evade their chaperone by adopting Tony Minetti (Donlevy) as
their uncle. They end up in Greenwich Village and get into several entan-
glements and misunderstandings in this light-as-a-feather confection. The
charming, old-fashioned atmosphere of the original was retained and the
character actors enhanced the film a great deal. Donlevy was perfectly
keyed as a gentlemanly gangster and his near double-act with Demarest
was always good value. Skinner had tried to prevent the studio from filming a sequel to her novel, but Paramount won.[6]

Song of Scheherazade was a wonderfully enjoyable musical based
on the life of Russian composer Nicolai Rimsky-Korsakov (played by
acclaimed French actor Jean-Pierre Aumont) and his early years at sea.
Nicolai, a subaltern in the Imperial Russian Navy, longs to be a composer,
but is prevented from doing so by Navy regulations. During a stopover in
Tangiers, he works on his composition "Scheherazade" with the tacit
approval of his captain (Donlevy). While in Morocco, Nicolai falls in love
with exotic Spanish dancer Cara de Talavara (Yvonne De Carlo). He tries
to smuggle her on board ship, but is soon found out and forbidden from
writing another note of music while he is in the Navy. At the end he returns

Walter Reisch's *Song of Scheherazade* (1947) was a fun musical inspired by the early life of Russian composer Nikolai Rimsky-Korsakov. Donlevy effectively sent up his own screen "tough guy" image and scored a decided hit as the chain-smoking captain.

to Russia to see his ballet performed, and of course meets Cara again: She is one of the dancers.

The movie offers a colorful spectacle and contains most of the familiar Rimsky-Korsakov music including "Flight of the Bumblebee," "Capriccio Espagnol" and "The Song of India" from *Sadko.* It was beautifully real-ized by Austrian director Walter Reisch. Aumont was a very popular star who had been awarded the Legion d'Honneur and the Croix du Guerre for his war service. Unsurprisingly, *Song of Scheherazade* did very well at the box office in Europe, especially so in France. The muted pastel color, elaborate set designs and, above all, the music make for a charming, good-natured movie.

There was some alarm over the skimpiness of Yvonne's costume, but in the event the censors had more problems with that of Eve Arden who played her mother. The movie was, according to one reviewer, "a tutti frutti nightmare of wasted Technicolor and music."[7] The same critic remarked that Donlevy deserved "laurels for holding up at all under a trying role" as the bellowing captain.[8] He enjoyed himself in the film but admitted that he did not relish smoking two packs of king size Turkish cigarettes a day.

Song of Scheherazade has become something of a cult classic and for others almost the definition of kitsch. The whole thing is really great fun: for instance, the sultry De Carlo dancing and the whip duel between the two men fighting for her. The great comedienne Eve Arden adds much to the film with her witticisms. Donlevy as the macho captain, stripped to the waist, surveying his crew, warily smoking his cigarette on a holder the whole time, was a delight. During filming, his little daughter came to see him. "Isn't daddy silly," she observed dryly.[9] He was, and it was such fun to see him being so silly, sending up his own image in a perfectly suited role.

Around the same time, Donlevy's services were wanted for two Lon-don productions. He was due to play the lead in *Petticoat Lane* for Andrew Stone, but the project was dropped.[10] Donlevy was then announced as the replacement for Laurence Olivier in Charles Bennett's *The Trial of Madeleine Smith,* based on the sensational murder case of a nineteenth century Glasgow socialite.[11] Bennett was a British writer famous for his screenplays for Alfred Hitchcock. When Vivien Leigh was unavailable for the starring role, Ida Lupino was sought.[12] Bennett was forced to drop the project when he was handed another assignment, *Madness of the Heart* (1949). David Lean made a version of the Smith case, *Madeleine* (1950).

Donlevy also hoped to finance his own production *The Minister and the Safecracker,* but that too ran into the sand.[13] In 1946, *Variety* announced that producer Julie Pfeiffer hoped to have Donlevy and Otto Kruger in *The Front Page,* but that production never saw the light of day.[14]

The gestation of *The Beginning or the End* (1947) was rather torturous, which in a sense suited its difficult subject matter. Less than 18 months since its first detonation, the atom bomb was all too recent in the minds of everyone to appear to require the big-screen treatment. But the makers felt that they could tell the story behind the defining moment of the twentieth century and humanize something that is incomprehensible to most people even now. MGM producer Sam Marx first visited President Truman and obtained his approval for the movie in late 1945. The screenplay, written by journalist and onetime war correspondent Bob Considine and retired Naval Commander Frank Wead, was approved by the White House and the U.S. War Department. Eight technical advisers worked on the film (four atomic energy scientists and four representatives of the War Department). The authorities oversaw the work of the cast and camera crews at Oak Ridge, Tennessee, the University of Chicago, Columbia University and the atomic laboratories at Los Alamos, New Mexico, during the spring and summer of 1946. But then there was dissension. First, Mrs. Roosevelt objected to Lionel Barrymore portraying her late husband because he had been critical of FDR. Barrymore sent her a letter in which he claimed to have been misrepresented, but neither that nor a visit to Mrs. Roosevelt by Marx could placate her. As a consequence, the renowned British stage actor Godfrey Tearle was assigned the role. Then chief scientist Sir James Chadwick backed out when the producers would not permit him to use his own photographed sequences. German scientist Dr. Lisa Meitner was also uncooperative; in the movie, she had been portrayed by Agnes Moorhead, whose scenes had to be deleted. Other European scientists begged off so the decision was made to have an all–American cast. Dr. Niels Bohr took many months to finally say yes, but then said no; Albert Einstein, after "vacillating for months," reluctantly agreed to be portrayed by Ludwig Stossel. Finally the other doctors hesitatingly gave their assent.[15]

After Spencer Tracy turned down the central role of Gen. Groves, head of the Atomic Project, Clark Gable was suggested. The scientists balked at this, and were much relieved when Donlevy was assigned.[16] There were numerous conferences between studio head Louis B. Mayer and Bernard Baruch addressing the scientists' chief concern, that the subject had been trivialized by the producers. The scientists maintained that Hollywood "had treated the atomic bomb so frivolously that the world would think the U.S. did not take a serious view of the most devastating weapon of all time."[17] The resulting movie was a box office loser; its drama-documentary approach seemed to be its biggest drawback, and the attempt to create a romantic interest side story was particularly unsuccessful. The makers strove so hard to please everyone that they actually pleased no one. Donlevy was his usual authoritative self, and one critic observed that he "makes a pretty snappy spark-plug out of dynamic Gen. Groves."[18]

Brian, Van Heflin and Paulette Goddard were announced as the leads of *The Night Watch*, an adventure about the founding of the state of Israel. The movie was later renamed *Sword in the Desert* and featured none of these actors.[19]

In director Sidney Lanfield's *The Trouble with Women*, newspaper-man Joe McBride (Donlevy) runs a story about college professor of psychology, Gilbert Sedley (Ray Milland), who writes a work in which he appears to advocate wife-beating. Sedley sues the newspaper for $300,000. McBride sends his star reporter Kate Farrell (Teresa Wright), with whom he is in love, to persuade the professor to withdraw his suit. She enrolls in his class and of course promptly falls in love with him. She jilts McBride and marries the professor, at the same time convincing him to withdraw his suit. A slight movie, *The Trouble with Women* nonetheless contains pleasing performances from the three leads, and an interesting variation on the theme of the battle of the sexes in postwar America. It was set in

In Sidney Lanfield's light-hearted drama *The Trouble with Women* (1947), Don-levy played a hardboiled city newspaper editor in love with his star reporter Teresa Wright. It was typical of Donlevy's luck that he lost her to college professor Ray Milland.

Hollywood's version of a midwestern state, where all the college professors wear glasses, and all the city editors are tough customers with hats on the back of their head.

Donlevy had a decent role as a determined assistant district attorney in Henry Hathaway's hard-hitting *Kiss of Death* (1947), a classic noir. Richard Widmark made a memorable psychotic who pushes a wheelchair-bound woman down a flight of stairs. Victor Mature was the man in the middle whom Donlevy encourages to follow the straight path.

The story begins at Christmas with an out-of-work Nick Bianco (Victor Mature) and two others robbing a jewelry store. He is shot making his getaway, in a similar manner to the way his father died 20 years previously. Once he has recovered, he is taken to Assistant District Attorney Louis D'Angelo (Donlevy), who offers him a reduced sentence if he will name his accomplices. He refuses and is sent to prison. After a while his letters to his wife are returned unopened, and he tries to find out about her and

Assistant D.A. Louis D'Angelo (Donlevy, right) takes an important call at the 37th precinct, watched by Perc Launders (left) and George Smith in an atmospheric shot from *Kiss of Death* (1947). This excellent noir features a memorable performance from Richard Widmark as a giggling psychotic.

his children. He discovers that his wife killed herself by putting her head in a gas oven. He is visited by one-time neighbor Nettie (Coleen Gray), who tells him some of the details of his wife's affair with Rizzo, a gang member. Changing his mind about informing, Nick contacts D'Angelo, who protects him by implicating Rizzo as the stool pigeon. But Nick is forced to testify against killer Tommy Udo (Widmark), who is found not guilty thanks to crooked lawyer Howser (Taylor Holmes). Nick marries Nettie, but is worried that Udo will come after his family and packs them off to the country. He sets about finding Udo, determined to trap him into convicting himself.

Kiss of Death has a fine atmosphere and some memorable performances. The standout is Widmark's giggling psychotic. Mature also does well despite his apparent limitations. "I'm not an actor," he once joked, "and I have 64 films to prove it."[20] But this throwaway line conceals his real ability which he showed in *My Darling Clementine* (1946). He had something indefinable that made him seem thoughtful and he could convey a great deal of emotion when doing very little.

Donlevy played the assistant D.A. as though born to it. His very appearance instills confidence despite the fact that his department is not so efficient. He asks a great deal of Nick, and his department lets him down more than once. First they are outwitted by the sharp shyster lawyer; then the police tailing Udo lose him. Nick's motivation throughout is his children; he changes sides because of them; then goes after Udo to protect them. But D'Angelo is alongside him all the time.

This was a marvelous movie which repays many visits. The cinematographer's terrific use of angles is especially noticeable in scenes featuring staircases and corridors. In particular the staircases are used to highlight the light and dark of humanity. One set of stairs is lethal as the scene of the murder of the helpless woman bound to her wheelchair: the other is the scene of joy when Nick runs up the stairs to Nettie after his release from prison.

To obtain the documentary feel, *Kiss of Death* was partially shot at Sing Sing Penitentiary and in many other locations in New York including the Chrysler Building, the Criminal Courts Building and the Tombs. During filming in the latter, the company was assigned a section of the ninth floor covering about 100 feet of corridor and adjoining cells, and warned to stay within that area. One day Donlevy went wandering, and ended up in a side corridor where he was stopped by a zealous guard and tossed in a cell. Brian protested that he was an actor, and the guard went off to verify his story. Meanwhile Donlevy found himself sharing "a cell with a hold-up artist awaiting transference to Sing Sing for a 24-year stretch." In time, director Henry Hathaway came to confirm Donlevy's identity.[21] Donlevy was often accompanied on set by his four-year-old daughter Judy, who he took to the Central Park Zoo during breaks in filming.[22]

The whimsical drama *Heaven Only Knows* began in Heaven with the premise of a mistake in the Book of Life. Duke (Donlevy) has gone the wrong way in life because he has no soul. Instead of making good as a civic leader and marrying the preacher's daughter Drusilla Wainwright (Jorja Cartwright) as had been ordained, he has followed the wrong path. Saint Michael (Robert Cummings) is sent to Earth to straighten things out and see that he marries the right girl after all. Duke runs a gambling joint and is in a constant fight for superiority with Bill Plumber, his partner in a gold mine. Plumber's men set fire to Duke's saloon and Duke narrowly escapes with the help of Mike. As retaliation, Duke's man Treason (Gerald Mohr) sets fire to Plumber's place, but a young boy is trapped inside the building. Duke goes in to rescue him. Dynamite is stored in the cellar and

Heaven Only Knows (1948) was a whimsical religious allegory about an angel sent to Earth to see that gambler Duke (Donlevy) marries the preacher's daughter (Jorja Cartwright), as ordained.

the place explodes, but Duke emerges with the child. Plumber challenges Duke to a shootout, and against the odds Duke is the winner. He takes refuge in the church with Drusilla. There is a lynching party outside the church, but Mike and the reverend stall them. Duke escapes with Drusilla. Some time later, Mike is almost hanged, but Duke saves him and they go back to town. That evening, Mike heads out on the special night coach.

Heaven Only Knows had the background of a typical Western, but was essentially a religious fantasy. The censors had major problems with some scenes, mostly involving women's lingerie being discussed in an angel's presence, and objected to the overfamiliarity implied in calling Saint Michael "Mike." But such trifles aside, the film had much to commend it, not least the appealing central performances by Donlevy and Cummings. Although Cummings at times overplayed the pious innocent-at-large routine, the two worked well in all their scenes together, almost becoming a double act at one stage. The religious allegory is obvious, and one of the characters, Treason, is literally the devil at Duke's elbow. There is a telling scene in the schoolroom when Duke confesses to Drusilla that he always felt he was destined for better things, but what they are he is not able to articulate. Donlevy plays this scene in a very subtle way, but this felt like the crux of the matter, when he admits that he does not know himself at all. Here is the central premise of the screenplay: Beneath the comedy and Western trappings, this was about the fork in the road and the chance to go either way. Duke is not dissimilar to *Canyon Passage*'s George Camrose, and is encapsulated in the words his friend speaks about him after he is dead: "It's a fine line between what could be and what is." Donlevy continued his run of accidents on set; this time he lost a tooth during a fight sequence.[23]

Director Albert S. Rogell made a lot of B-movies since his debut in the early 1920s, among them *The Black Cat* (1941) and *In Old Oklahoma* (1943). He later moved to television and directed Donlevy again in *Double Trouble* (1956) for *Ford Television Theater*. *Heaven Only Knows* is among Rogell's most fondly remembered films.

Killer McCoy was a wonderful boxing drama with a great performance by Mickey Rooney in the title role. Fast-talking street kid Tommy McCoy reluctantly agrees to help his indigent father (James Dunn), a one-time vaudevillian, by appearing with him in a dance routine for the church social. There is also a boxing match that night, and McCoy sees a chance to get even with the kid who pushed him off his paper-selling beat. McCoy has no technique, but emerges victorious. The lightweight champion Johnny Martin (Mickey Knox) sees potential in the kid and agrees to train him. McCoy does well, but his father drinks away his money and does not send it home; then Mrs. McCoy dies suddenly. McCoy has to fight his old mentor Johnny, who has been out of the game for some time and isn't in shape. During the match, McCoy catches Johnny lightly and he falls to the mat. Despite all efforts to revive him, Johnny dies. McCoy wants to quit, but gambler Jim Kane (Donlevy) proposes that he should keep on fighting under his management, so long as no one else knows about it. McCoy is successful, but falls for Kane's daughter (Ann Blyth) whom Kane has tried to shield from his nefarious activities. Pop inadvertently spills the beans about everything to a rival gangster and is taken hostage along with Kane's daughter, forcing McCoy to go down in the eighth round. Pop overpowers his tormentors, saving the day for his son and fiancée.

A remake of *The Crowd Roars* (1928), *Killer McCoy* was Rooney's movie all the way, and he proved that he could act. He handled the ring scenes and those with his father equally well. James Dunn was a standout as Pop, a variation of the wayward father he played so memorably in *A Tree Grows in Brooklyn*. Donlevy was excellent as the gambler; tough and cool in his dealings with other big time operators. His underplaying emphasizes the menace and double meaning in their polite and circumventing conversations. He is fiercely protective of his daughter and determined to keep the "pug" away from her. But he is not really a bad guy, and at the end he accepts the situation and even admits to liking the kid. MGM announced that they intended to team the two actors in another movie.[24] In real life, Donlevy became friends with Rooney, and the two went to Oregon on a camping trip together after shooting ended in July 1947.[25]

At this stage of his career, Donlevy appeared in a number of mostly variable comedies. He was little more than a stooge in the Red Skelton vehicle *A Southern Yankee* (1948), loosely based on Buster Keaton's classic *The General* (1927). Although the great comedian Keaton was officially technical advisor on the movie, it was never his style to criticize anyone and, according to Arlene Dahl, he made a few observations to the director, but spent most of the time asleep.[26] The film was fairly well received and recorded a profit. Comedy is a very subjective thing and, seen today, it is difficult to raise a smile at the goofy antics of this once popular comedian. But there have been few comedies about the Civil War, especially one in which a hapless comic spies for both sides. Donlevy played a cigar-smoking Southern gentleman, a variation on the many other villains he usually essayed, and was the strongest member of the supporting cast.

In 1947 Fox planned to build a series of movies around Donlevy as a private detective.[27] Later in the year he was announced as one of the three stars of *Rogue's Regiment* (1948)—the others were Burt Lancaster and Edmond O'Brien. This was based on a Robert Buckner story about a group of Nazis who join the French Foreign Legion in Indo-China to escape the War Crimes Trials. None of these actors were in the finished movie, which starred Dick Powell, Vincent Price and Stephen McNally.[28] Donlevy might have had the starring role in *Strike it Rich* (1948), based on Texas oil millionaire Jack Wrather's own life story, but after lengthy discussions the part was assigned to Rod Cameron.[29]

Twice he had the chance to play baseball heroes. His was one of the names considered for the part of Lou Gehrig in *The Pride of the Yankees* (1942), which went to Gary Cooper.[30] He might also have had the lead in *The Babe Ruth Story* (1948), but his agents and the studio could not come to a deal, so William Bendix got the job.[31] Donlevy played the "Sultan of Swat" on radio in *Big Boy* the same year.

Sam Wood's *Command Decision* (1949) is lacking in spectacular action sequences but features excellent performances by an all-star cast. Standouts were Clark Gable (left) as head of Bomber Command and Donlevy as the man who replaces him.

Billed as one of the first big movies of the year, MGM's *Command Decision* boasted a stellar cast headed by Clark Gable. Based on a long-running Broadway play which had also been a bestselling novel, it was directed by the acclaimed veteran Sam Wood whose credits included *Kitty Foyle* (1940), *For Whom the Bell Tolls* (1943), two classic Marx Brothers films and 24 days' work on *Gone with the Wind* (1939). With such a pedigree, it would seem that the project could not fail, but this talky psychodrama of a worthy play makes rather dull cinematic fare. This is unfortunate, because beneath the seemingly static exterior, this is a quietly engrossing and devastating exposition of the pressures of leadership and the wearing human toll of conflict. There is no glory in any of it.

Gen. Dennis (Gable), in charge of the U.S. Air Force in England during World War II, is faced with growing criticism from superiors, Congressmen and the press. He has forced squadrons to go on repeated missions over Germany to attack vital military targets. He is determined to pursue Operation Stitch, a secret plan to destroy a new superfast aircraft that German engineers have developed in three production centers. He is eventually removed from his post because of the scale of losses. Gen. Garnet (Donlevy) is assigned in his place.

Although well-acted, *Command Decision* is hampered by its setbound staginess. There are three main sets: the general's office, the high-ceilinged map room and the observation platform. In one tense sequence, a bombing mission returns having lost two-thirds of those who set out, and Dennis talks an inexperienced pilot home, only to see his plane explode. Otherwise, this was a drama about the psychological and human cost of war and its political aspects. As such, it was highly successful. Gable won many plaudits for his performance, and conveys the heavy toll of responsibility ably. Donlevy's character is at first enthusiastic and keen to have his own command, but when he replaces Dennis he begins to see the nature of the task ahead of him. Everyone looks to him for all the answers immediately. Not only is he suddenly faced with questions of strategy and life-or-death decisions, but he has to take account of the weather, the political situation, the wider aims of the war, and square all his decisions with his conscience when potentially sending men to their deaths. "You've hated all of this from the beginning," he says to Dennis, who is about to leave, finally beginning to realize the psychological bruising Dennis has been through and the enormity of the task he faces. The dehumanizing effect of war is made suddenly apparent in these subtle scenes between Gable and Donlevy as Gable says good-

The only film produced by comedian Jack Benny, *The Lucky Stiff* had a good cast but a complicated plot. Nevertheless, the actors entered into the spirit, and Donlevy always worked seamlessly with the great Claire Trevor. This lobby card shows, left to right, Trevor, Donlevy and Dorothy Lamour.

bye. Sadly, the movie may have lost most of the more impatient members of the audience by this time, which is a great shame because for such moments *Command Decision* deserves its place as one of the better and more thoughtful war films. Gable and Donlevy were friends off-screen and the two once went fishing off Santa Monica with director Walter Lang.[32]

Donlevy returned to light-hearted fare in *The Lucky Stiff* with Dorothy Lamour and Claire Trevor. The plot was very complicated, but essentially concerned Anne Marie St. Clair (Lamour), a nightclub singer with whom Malone (Donlevy) is completely enchanted. He goes to see her each night at the Casino Club where he sits and makes cow eyes at her. She is the girlfriend of Childers, a shady operator, but really loves Britt, his right-hand man. Childers is killed, and members of a sinister protection racket believe that Anne has been executed in the electric chair. Malone concocts a plan to scare them into the open by having her appear as a ghost. Thereafter the plot goes sideways several times, but ends predictably enough with Malone realizing that his future lies with his faithful secretary (Claire Trevor) after all. The plot was far too complex and all three stars deserved much better material. However, they all played their parts well; Claire and Brian kept things ticking along. There were some good one-liners and appealing comedy, especially when Malone drives an old car in pursuit of a horse-drawn buggy and ends up blocking the path of a fire engine. Donlevy was ideal as Malone, ever-optimistic but hapless as a lawyer, who solves cases despite everything. Leading authors of the genre in recent years have called *The Lucky Stiff* one of the more interesting versions of the works by the rather neglected writer Craig Rice and praised Donlevy as "the best of the screen Malones."[33] This was the third of four movies that Brian and Claire Trevor made together; and a couple of years earlier he might also have appeared with her in a remake of the Western *Frontier Town.*[34]

Donlevy was considered for the role of the widowed father in Eagle-Lion's *Mickey,* about a tomboy, but Bill Goodwin was later assigned the part.[35] The industrialist Jay Gould wanted Donlevy for the title role in his intended production *Enter Mr. Webster,* based on a novel of the same name, but it was not made.[36] He was sought by producer Sam Engel as co-star of the forestry service adventure *Fire* along with Linda Darnell and Dana Andrews, but nothing came of the project.[37]

In the postwar years, Donlevy made several stage appearances. He took an interest in the Little Theater project in Malibu Beach colony, along with fellow actors Robert Walker, Dennis O'Keefe and Warner Baxter. Walker announced that he planned to direct A.A. Milne's short play *The Man in the Bowler Hat.*[38] In October 1947 he was invited to head the cast of a revival of *What Price Glory* at the Detroit Music Hall for their first winter season in a two-week run. This time he was elevated to the role of Capt. Flagg.[39] The show was well received and a near sell-out, making $13,200 in its first week alone.[40] The following month at Detroit, he played the Inquisitor in Maxwell Anderson's *Joan of Lorraine* with Luise Rainer. Although Donlevy was touted as a replacement for Paul Douglas in *Born Yesterday* on Broadway, the part went to a succession of less well-known names.

Donlevy made some interesting films in the immediate postwar years, but undoubtedly his divorce took its toll on him. It was not simply the financial loss (which was substantial), but he seemed to be losing his sense of direction. Shortly after his divorce, an interviewer provided a glimpse of the private Donlevy at home: "Brian, dressed in a tan shirt and a blue sailing cap, stared reflectively into his drink as he perched, stocky and muscular, on a stool behind the handsome bar in his den. "Kids," he said, "are the most wonderful thing in life. I wish I had 20."[41] Increasingly, his daughter was everything to him and he frankly admitted that she kept him together in the aftermath of his traumatic divorce.

9

Impact and
the Early 1950s

"If you turn the other cheek in this world, you get hit by a lug wrench."

—Walter Williams in *Impact*

Donlevy's career had been on an upward curve since his break-through year of 1939; but by the end of the 1940s he had reached a plateau. The negative publicity surrounding his divorce no doubt affected him personally and, more pertinently, harmed his public perception. Despite his best endeavors, he found it difficult to change course and play lighter or more varied roles. He did the best he could with the material offered and even tried to produce his own movies although this yielded no tangible results.

He had one of his best postwar roles in *Impact* (1949) which gave audiences a glimpse at what his career might have looked like had Hollywood producers been rather more adventurous and less lazy. Although the movie was a personal success for him, it was not a box office hit nor was it critically acclaimed. It would be almost a year before he worked again.

In *Impact* he plays San Francisco industrialist Walter Williams (Donlevy), who believes himself to be happily married to Irene (Helen Walker). However, Irene has a young lover, Jim Torrance, whom she passes off as her cousin Jim from Illinois. Walter and Irene planned to drive to Lake Tahoe for the weekend, but Irene pretends to be ill. She asks Walter to pick up her "Cousin Jim" and give him a lift to Denver, Colorado. She has already made reservations at a hotel in Oakland, California, in the name of Mr. and Mrs. Burns in preparation to meet up with Torrance later. Walter picks up "Cousin Jim," who attempts to murder him and then pushes him over the side of the mountain. Trying to make a quick escape in

117

Williams' car, Torrance is killed in a horrific head-on collision with a gasoline tanker. His body is burned beyond recognition and is presumed to be that of Williams. Unaware of all this, Williams revives and groggily makes his way onto the back of a truck. He awakes and finds himself in Larkspur, Idaho. Dazed and confused, he telephones Aunt Margaret to ask about "Cousin Jim" and is told that there is no such person. He meets war widow Marsha Peters (Ella Raines), who runs a garage, and agrees to stay on to help her. In time, they fall in love. He enters into the spirit of the place with gusto, and even joins the local volunteer fire department. In San Francisco, Irene is arrested for his murder. Marsha discovers the truth and persuades the reluctant Walter to go back to San Francisco and clear his wife. As he thought, he is charged with Torrance's murder, but is cleared with the help of the maid Su Lin (Anna May Wong) and dogged Police Lt. Quincy (Charles Coburn).

Impact was dismissed lightly at the time as a minor B-movie with a second-string cast. However, it has far more resonance than seen at first glance and gave Donlevy a chance to show another side of his persona. The character he plays is tough only in the boardroom; at home he is very romantic with his wife, always buying her things. Even when he is away from her, he sends her a dozen roses every morning with "love from Softy" on the card. He is so infatuated with her that it comes as too great a shock to him when he realizes the truth. He reaches his lowest ebb when he breaks down at the Larkspur railroad station and a kindly clerk shows concern. Donlevy handles all these scenes subtly.

The contrast between modern, streamlined San Francisco and quiet, rural Larkspur is profound. The big city is impersonal and reminds Walter of the false sentiment of his wife who he had loved too much. Larkspur puts him in mind of his distant past and gives him the sense that he can change his life, forget all that has happened and find happiness with Marsha. There is a palpable feeling that some of Donlevy the man is revealed in this movie. He is quiet and understated, and it is easy to believe he really is "Softy." As the film continues, Williams begins to find himself again. This is a story of redemption. After all that has befallen him, there is a tangible sense of release in the scene when he goes walking with Marsha by the river. The birds are singing and he says to her, "I hate to tell you how many years this Sunday takes me back." In other noirs, the countryside is also used for its contrast; for instance, at the end of *The Asphalt Jungle* (1950), Sterling Hayden's character feels a desperate need to return to the scenes of his early life on the farm. Similarly, the protagonists of *On Dangerous Ground* and *Out of the Past* attempt to escape from the

A kindly Larkspur railroad station clerk (Hans Herbert) is concerned for the dazed and confused Walter Williams (Donlevy) in *Impact* (1949). An undervalued noirish drama, this featured an excellent performance from Donlevy as a jaded industrialist whose world falls apart but who gets the chance to start again.

complications and dangers of their lives in the city to the apparent safety and tranquility of a rural idyll. In the world of noir, of course, it is never so simple and they always have to face the music at some point.

Ruth Hussey was initially announced as the lead for *Impact*, but was

Walter (Donlevy) agrees to stay in Larkspur and help beautiful war widow Marsha Peters (Ella Raines) run her garage in *Impact* (1949). The underlying theme of the film seemed to be one of disenchantment at the postwar world, the need to reconnect with oneself and to find a sense of belonging in the wider community.

later replaced by Helen Walker, a wonderful unsung actress who had a tragic life.[1] She brings exactly the right note of surface detachment covering emotional turmoil. During filming, Brian was stricken with what was described as a serious respiratory ailment and was confined to a hospital for some time.[2]

Director Arthur Lubin began his long career as an actor in the 1920s. He switched to directing and made his name with a succession of Abbott and Costello films. He made occasional ventures into other genres, notably with the horror remake *Phantom of the Opera* (1943), and spent over $1.6 million on the fantasy *Night in Paradise* (1946), which made a sizable loss. He had great success on television, helming episodes of *Bonanza, The Addams Family* and *Mr. Ed*. Screenwriter Jay Dratler wrote and co-wrote a number of noir thrillers including *Laura* (1944), *The Dark Corner* (1946) and *Call Northside 777* (1948). Dratler adapted *Impact* from his own short story.

Although in many ways it appears to be a noir, *Impact* has more in common with (say) George Orwell's novel *Coming Up for Air*. The protagonist of that story is a disenchanted middle-aged man who seeks to escape his humdrum life and unhappy marriage by returning to the scenes of his pastoral childhood. In the process he becomes completely disillusioned because he does not find the answers he is looking for. In *Impact,* Williams doesn't actively seek his lost happiness, but inadvertently discovers it.

An undervalued film, *Impact* encapsulates a kind of postwar malaise that seeks its relief in escaping the stifling falsity of the big city by returning to a rural idyll and the small-town values of a less complicated past. It addresses a human longing to connect with each other and rekindle the sense of community seemingly lost in the course of a fractured century.

Donlevy tried his hand at producing with few tangible results. He set up a company, New Colony Productions, with Tom Somyo and announced that his first movie would be *John Winton,* a California Gold Rush tale by gossip columnist Lloyd Shearer.[3] For his leading lady he pursued Jane Russell; filming was due to begin in Florida. The project never got off the ground.[4] Neither did a long–dreamt of movie about George Washington in which he would have had the starring role.[5] There were reports that his first production would finally come to fruition at the end of 1949. *Wild Sable Island* would be set on an island off Nova Scotia, famous as the scene of hundreds of shipwrecks. Donlevy sent a camera crew to shoot scenes of the hurricanes that hit the area every fall.[6] He hoped that the great Italian actress Anna Magnani would be his star, but the project fell through.[7]

In September 1949, Donlevy signed to make the movie *Midnight* in Ireland the following February for writer-producer Desmond Leslie's Leinster Films. Then Leslie, a second cousin of Winston Churchill, was beset by financial difficulties and the project was abandoned.[8] Donlevy was due to start as the father in Jean Renoir's *The River,* set in India, but the role was given to British actor Esmond Knight.[9]

After his divorce, Donlevy had many dates with a succession of actresses, which meant he was a regular subject of the gossip columnists. Over the early summer of 1949 he pursued Audrey Totter. The two had met during the making of *The Beginning or the End* in 1947, but they didn't have their first date until the night of the Friar's Frolic in May 1949 where they were photographed together. "He's a very sweet person," she remarked. "He courts beautifully."[10] Ever the romantic, he sent her three dozen red roses every Saturday, and in true Hollywood style when she was making *Tension* "he flew over in his own plane and dipped a wing at

her."[11] He showered her with gifts and once bought her the biggest television he could find.[12] At the time, such a TV set cost over $2000. In addition
he bought her a phonograph and recording machine.[13] She was surprised
that most nights he took her to the opera, which he loved. In June he
bought her a gold ankle bracelet inscribed with the words "No trespassing,"
which seemed to amuse her.[14] When asked if their romance was serious,
she replied, "I think he is a wonderful man, but who can tell about a thing
like that."[15] They became engaged, but somehow the relationship went
sour.[16] She surprised everyone in July when she entered Romanoff's arm
in arm with Paul Douglas, and was then seen at La Rue's with Greg
Bautzer.[17] After that, she returned his ring.[18] By April of the following year,
they "cut each other dead" in the café at Universal-International.[19]

Next he pursued Joan Crawford; in a familiar pattern, he haunted
the film set where she was working and sent her three dozen red roses
every Saturday.[20] Again, the romance petered out, but he still kept sending
the roses.[21] After Joan it was Eve Arden's turn. It's hard to know how serious
these "romances" were or if they were just designed to keep his name in
the public eye.[22] He was spotted with Eve at Ciro's two nights running,
which almost constituted an engagement.[23] In the early 1950s he turned
his attention to socialite Edith Eddy Ward, who owned the Western Hills
Hotel at Palm Desert. He often attended parties at her clubs and stayed
at her holiday villas.[24] His name was also linked to actresses Pamela Duncan, Marla Stevens and Rita Lynn.[25] Later he expressed a desire to meet
Nancy Sinatra, but admitted to be being "bashful."[26]

Donlevy was idle during most of 1949 and the early months of 1950.
Eventually he made his comeback in Universal's *The Magnificent Heel*, the
story of a ruthless cameraman by Nat Dillinger.[27] Directed by actor Joseph
Pevney, this was retitled *Shakedown* on its release. Donlevy had second
billing as gangster Nick Palmer. Howard Duff excelled as heel Jack Early,
who stops at nothing to get a great picture. He is aided by Palmer, who
gives him a tip-off about a planned robbery by a rival gang headed by
Colton (Lawrence Tierney). In return, Early sells Palmer out. He has
designs on Palmer's wife Lita (Anne Vernon). Palmer arranges to meet
Early one night, but Early is hiding in the underground car park, having
photographed Colton planting a bomb in Nick's car. He then watches as
Nick approaches the car and takes another picture of the bomb going off.
Afterwards he pursues Lita, who does not entirely trust him. Early get his
much-deserved comeuppance when he is crossed by Colton and Lita and
essentially trapped by his own cunning.

A good noir drama, *Shakedown* was a relentless expose of the life of a heel, and Early was possibly one of the most unscrupulous characters in the genre. Although most of his shooting is done with a camera, he is lethal to all those around him. Donlevy was the victim, and of the gangsters on display he was easily the most human. He trusts Early too readily, giving him the benefit of the doubt he should never have been had. It is a shock to lose Donlevy so soon in the piece, but when he is there, he is a reassuring presence and instantly believable as a gangster who just has to make a phone call to get things done. Although they represent the traditional bad guys, Tierney and Donlevy are clearly outdone by Duff, who is unstoppable and capable of anything.

It was announced that Donlevy was cast as the lead in the noir *Roadblock* opposite Marilyn Maxwell, but neither appeared in the eventual movie.[28] Donlevy was one of the names considered when Harry Cohn was casting the movie version of *Born Yesterday* (1950). After the Columbia president's first choices, Humphrey Bogart and James Cagney, proved unavailable, Donlevy was almost cast opposite Marie McDonald.[29] He was also sought for a biopic of early Western star William S. Hart, to whom he bore a resemblance, but the film was never made.[30] Donlevy was sought out to co-star with Dane Clark and renowned French actress Viviane Romance in *It Happened in Paris,* but none of those stars appeared in the final film.[31] An idea that emanated from Donlevy was for a version of the popular adventure *The Count of Monte Cristo* transferred to a Western setting, but he could get no backing.[32]

Donlevy played Col. Quantrill for the first time in *Kansas Raiders* (1950) starring Audie Murphy as the young Jesse James. Set towards the end of the Civil War, the story began with Jesse, brother Frank, the two Younger brothers and Kit Dalton (Tony Curtis) joining Quantrill's Raiders, who ride under the infamous black flag. Jesse is impressed by Quantrill, who recognizes an able successor in the youngster. Over drinks, the colonel outlines his military strategy to aid Gen. Lee in the greater struggle. However, Jesse begins to question his leader's tactics and finally is completely disillusioned after the notorious Lawrence, Kansas, massacre. Meanwhile, Jesse and Quantrill's fiancée Kate Clark (Marguerite Chapman) fall in love.

Circumstances begin to turn against Quantrill and his men leave him: there is a price on his head, $1000 dead or alive. In a confrontation with Union soldiers he is caught by gunfire and blinded. Jesse, Kate and the others take him to a cabin where they try to help, but the situation becomes hopeless as the Union troops surrounding the cabin begin to close in. Kate and the men manage to escape and Quantrill pushes Jesse out to safety. The blind colonel leaves the cabin, starts shooting and is gunned down.

Although historically inaccurate, *Kansas Raiders* was a well-shot color Western with an interesting take on the Quantrill saga. A contemporary critic brought attention to Donlevy's portrayal, calling it "the most creative characterization seen in Westerns for years."[33] The relationship between Jesse and the colonel made an intriguing dynamic. At first it is hero worship on the part of Jesse for someone he sees as a strong and resolute leader with a clear plan. This becomes bitter disillusionment after the behavior of his troops and the Kansas massacre. When the tide turns against Quantrill, his men desert him and he is blinded, Jesse feels a genuine sympathy for him and remains loyal to the end. Quantrill becomes a much more interesting figure once he is almost helpless, and there is an elusive bond between the two men throughout.

Filming took place at Idyllwild, California, between May and June 1950, and was a pleasurable experience for Donlevy, who became firm friends with young Murphy.[34] The two had been due to work together before on *Bad Boy* (1949), but at that time Brian's role of the tough but benevolent superintendent of the reform school was given to Lloyd Nolan.[35] Some of the *Kansas Raiders* footage was lifted from a previous Universal production, *Tap Roots* (1948). Neither overfamiliarity with the characters nor the glaring historical inaccuracies dented the film's popularity; it was one of the top ten box office hits of 1951.

Between movies and television work, Brian also appeared in summer stock whenever he could. He played Lob in a version of J.M. Barrie's *Dear Brutus* in 1950. The final performance at Olney, Maryland, was given for President and Mrs. Truman. This seldom-seen play, written in 1917, involved a man who invites several strangers to his country estate one midsummer's eve. A mysterious forest appears outside the mansion and they are all invited to enter and walk down the paths they might have taken in life. This allegory is one of Barrie's lesser-known works. In 1951, Donlevy considered joining his old friend James Cagney in a revival of *Broadway* on the New York stage, but this did not come to pass.[36]

Since 1790, the American Coast Guard has done sterling work saving lives, protecting the coasts, fighting during wartime, guarding against smuggling, keeping shipping lanes safe and latterly preserving wildlife habitats. It was something of a disappointment, then, that this noble service should have been short-changed by the cinema with a routine film like *Fighting Coast Guard* (1951).

Shortly after the Japanese attack on Pearl Harbor, Comdr. McFarland

Donlevy (right), and co-star Ella Raines meet President Harry Truman at the premiere of *Fighting Coast Guard* (1951). Despite the fanfare, the movie was a rather formulaic romance played out against the backdrop of the oldest service in America.

(Donlevy) appeals for volunteers to join the Coast Guard Officer's Academy. Welder Barney Walker (John Russell) is antagonistic towards the shipyard's foreman Bill Rourk (Forrest Tucker), and tricks him into joining the service. Rourk is posted overseas. Walker continues to needle Rourk, claiming that McFarland was instrumental in Rourk's posting. To complicate matters, both Rourk and McFarland are in love with the admiral's daughter, Louise Ryan (Ella Raines). Rourk breaks rules to see Ryan, but eventually proves himself a hero during his war service in the Far East. Far from hindering his career, McFarland has been helping Rourk all along and at the end even gives his blessing to his marriage to Ryan.

In this run-of-the-mill war film, the ostensible "hero" is an uncouth character who breaks the rules and nurses his grievances. He begins with a chip on his shoulder and ends with the chip intact. He is rewarded by marriage with beautiful Ella Raines. Rourk made a sharp contrast to Donlevy the selfless commander, who appears thoroughly admirable and maintains his graciousness in love and war. The actual war often seemed mere background to the machinations of the plot and the screenplay did not benefit from the use of stock footage. The movie was peopled by several familiar war "types," and it is easy to understand how such a film became lost in the morass of contemporary B-movie actioners.

Donlevy and his co-stars attended the premiere in front of President and Mrs. Truman amid great fanfare from the Navy, Marine and Coast Guard Drum and Bugle Corps.[37] While working on location at the Terminal Island Recreational Division in San Diego, Donlevy agreed to appear in a television drama for KFMB-TV. He insisted that his four-figure fee for playing the starring role be given to the Terminal Island Recreational Division Fund. This was not publicized at the time, but divulged later by a set worker.[38]

Slaughter Trail was already completed when Howard Hughes found out that Howard da Silva had been an unfriendly witness before the House Un-American Activities Committee. "He's a Commie," declared Hughes, who ordered that all footage of da Silva's Capt. Dempster be reshot with Donlevy as a replacement.[39]

Donlevy played the commander of a fort on the Arizona border. Three masked bandits rob a stagecoach with the secret help of one of the passengers. While making their escape, they shoot some Navajo braves and steal their horses; this puts the normally peaceable tribe and the white men at loggerheads. Lorabelle Larkin (Virginia Grey) arrives at the fort and is at first antagonistic towards Dempster. Ike Vaughan (Gig Young) seeks refuge at the fort, but is identified as the bandits' leader by one of the coach passengers, who recognizes his malicious laugh. Eventually the Indians attack the fort and get their revenge on Vaughan. Lorabelle looks after the captain's daughter and falls in love with the captain.

The action was helped along by catchy ballads and folk songs which effectively told the story. This new approach injected life into the hackneyed format and gave the movie a different feel to most other films in the Western genre. Toothy cowboy crooner Terry Gilkyson interjected at intervals with several songs, including some that he had penned himself such as "I Wish I Wuz" (which entered the hit parade) and "Everybody's Crazy Ceptin' Me." Donlevy seemed very comfortable in the starring role and he noticeably blossomed in the scenes with the child. He even danced well during a charming sequence just before the Indian attack. Virginia Grey talked about the film when interviewed years later: "We reshot virtually the whole film because Howard Hughes 'didn't want no Commies in his movies.' This made the picture a financial pleasure. It was way out in left field, a strange, offbeat picture, but one of my personal favorites."[40]

Donlevy's next for Republic was a good film noir, *Hoodlum Empire*, based on the Kefauver Senate investigation into organized crime. These hearings, held in several cities across the country, were often televised live, generating great public interest and high viewing figures. *Hoodlum Empire* was one of several films inspired by the hearings.

Joe Gray (John Russell), a former gangster who fought in the war, is now a changed man determined to lead a respectable life. He agrees to testify before Senator Stephens' (Donlevy). grand jury investigating big business crime. The target of the Congressional hearing is Gray's uncle, mobster Nick Mancani (Luther Adler), who raised Gray like a son. The mob is determined to stop Gray appearing, and Mancani's violent right-hand man Charlie (Forrest Tucker) constantly threatens Gray's life. The

Republic, mostly known for Westerns, made a decent stab at the noir genre with *Hoodlum Empire* (1952), based on the contemporary Kefauver Senate hearings. An excellent cast was headed by Donlevy (center), seen here with Damian O'Flynn (left) and Gene Lockhart.

stories of each character watching the hearings on TV is told in flashback as Gray tries to extricate himself from his former life.

Although the movie looks promising when considering the cast list alone, the film was arguably not as successful as it could have been. The actual format of televised hearings tended to make the screenplay too wordy at times, and the excessive use of flashback slowed things down, rendering the plot confusing. Director Joseph Kane was a prolific maker of B-Westerns and seemed less assured with contemporary dramas. Of all the actors, Claire Trevor, Adler and Tucker stood out. Donlevy was naturally convincing and made the steely determination of his character very apparent. He has a mission, but a level head, and none of the over-pious religious zeal of fellow Senator Gene Lockhart. Donlevy won admiration from a number of observers; one said he made Stephens "an impressive character ... [H]is impersonation ought to help the Kefauver campaign."[41] Another noted, "The scenes where Donlevy ... expresses his regret to Russell for having doubted him are extremely touching."[42]

Donlevy's next two Republics were Westerns. *Ride the Man Down* (1952), also directed by Kane, reunited him yet again with Ella Raines. This time they were on opposite sides of a bitter range war. Rod Cameron, a kind of poor man's Randolph Scott, was the ostensible star although distinctly lacking in charisma. Ella was beautiful as always and compensated for some of the grimness in the story. The premise was that a big landowner, Everts, has died and his ranch foreman Will Ballard (Cameron) is determined to see that the range is not broken up. Bide Marriner (Donlevy), the area's other big landowner, is equally determined that anyone should be able to take control now that the old man is out of the way. Ranch hand Sam (Forrest Tucker) is engaged to Celia Everts (Raines), but when she seems to prefer Will, he switches allegiance to Marriner. After Everts' brother is killed, the war escalates, but Will eventually emerges the victor.

Ride the Man Down was a decent Western, but it would have benefitted from some injections of humor and a more original story. At the time it was very well-received and the trade papers noted the great cachet of the cast which in their words gave the movie "big marquee value." The *Film Bulletin* was especially glowing in its praise, calling it an "unusually exciting Western," and further commented: "It is of major caliber in every respect and a credit to Republic."[43] Donlevy played another combative bad man, but one who ultimately has second thoughts about his chosen career path. By then it is too late of course and he is shot by J. Carrol Naish. Donlevy had encountered Naish many times in his career and it was about time that the other great Hollywood villain should get one over on him. After all, Donlevy had started out by shooting Naish in *Crack-Up,* and memorably sent him up into the lookout to certain death in *Beau Geste.*

Donlevy's next Republic Western, *Woman They Almost Lynched* (1953), was an appealing adventure yarn which featured Donlevy as the renegade Quantrill for the second time. The movie was interesting for focusing on the women characters: a "genu-wine lady," Sally Marris (Joan Leslie); the gun-toting Kate (Audrey Totter), moll of Quantrill, and the formidable mayor of the town, Delilah Courtney (Nina Valera). The male characters largely took a back seat and the screenplay held the interest because of this different approach. Even Quantrill and his men were kept in check by the mayor, who is decidedly not a woman to cross. The movie also benefitted from its sharp black and white photography. This likable B-film is oddly refreshing and deserves rediscovery, because it does not follow the predictable formula.

Woman They Almost Lynched (1953) was an unusual, little-known Civil War Western. Donlevy (left) was the renegade Col. Quantrill, with Audrey Totter (center) as Kate, his gun-toting moll, and Joan Leslie as Sally Marris, an Easterner. It was a refreshing change to see the women run rings around the men.

Around the same time, Major Speed Chandler, a retired USAAF chief pilot, sought out Donlevy to play opposite Wally Cox in *Cavalcade of the Air,* a biopic of the aviator Douglas "Wrong Way" Corrigan.[44] However, the financing was lacking and the film was never made.

On the so-called "straw hat" circuit, Donlevy appeared in *King of Hearts* in South Carolina. In February 1954, producer Paul Gregory announced that he wished to take a company to Chicago with *The Caine Mutiny Court Martial,* which had been a big Broadway success that season. His desired cast included Donlevy, Zachary Scott, Wendell Corey and Jonathan Hale[45] While this never eventuated, Donlevy led a very successful revival of Clifford Odets' *The Country Girl* on tour during that summer. He played the role of the once-great actor, now a washed-up, insecure alcoholic with a much younger wife. By all accounts he gave an honest and revealing portrayal. The production was well-attended and he garnered some of his best theatrical notices.

Donlevy had met Lillian Arch Lugosi in 1953. At the time she was seeking a divorce from her husband of 20 years, Bela Lugosi, the famous horror star. Brian and Lillian became inseparable from then on and seemed to be married in all but name, although they did not actually tie the knot until 1966.

For most of these years, the mainstay of his life was his daughter Judy, with whom he spent as much time as possible in the six months he was allowed with her each year. Mostly they stayed at his two-story home in Malibu Beach. In later years, she often accompanied him on trips to Europe. He also kept an apartment in Lower Manhattan which he had decorated in the style of 1775. It was warm and friendly, described as having "a rosy glow," with "rosy rugs, walls, white furniture ... and he put a ship in a tiny bottle."[46] In the Malibu house, he had two rooms made for her, "One for the little girl she was and the other for the young lady she would become."[47]

In the wake of two failed marriages, his very bitter divorce, dissatisfaction with his film roles allied to waning interest in his career and the realization that he would never be another Hemingway, it is not really so surprising that the loner Donlevy sought consolation in the bottle and the love of his daughter. He admitted he bought her too many toys and "more dresses than she wears," but just couldn't help himself. "I don't believe children are spoiled by love or too much love can be given them," he once observed. "She seems to know when I see a pretty dress I have to buy it just because it reminds me of her. Picking up things for her 'little girl' room has been my greatest happiness."[48]

10

Radio and Television

*"I get sent to a lot of places I can't pronounce. But they all spell
the same thing: trouble."*
 —Opening lines from *Dangerous Assignment*.

Throughout his career, Donlevy was heard on radio, and he enjoyed
an excellent television career beginning in the late 1940s. By far his most
successful series in both media was *Dangerous Assignment,* in which he
starred as a private detective sent to exotic locations. It ran first on radio
and proved still more popular on television. This presented the perfect
vehicle for his persona, playing to his strengths, and the success was just
reward for the hard-working veteran actor after so many years. He earned
a star on the Hollywood Walk of Fame not for his many roles on the silver
screen, but for all that he achieved on television.

As with other actors of his generation, he was very often heard on
radio in the early part of his career. Usually he reprised his most popular
movie roles such as *Wake Island* and made several versions of *The Great
McGinty.* In the 1930s he was often heard on *Eno's Crime Club* and *Hillbilly
Heart Throbs,* which used folk songs to tell stories and featured such popular country-western stars as Carson Robison and the Vass Family. Donlevy was also heard in episodes of the human interest drama series *The
Court of Human Relations.* He made numerous appearances on the long-
running *Cavalcade of America* playing an array of captains of industry,
naval heroes and men of principle in such documentary-dramas as "Joe
Palmer's Beard" and "Odyssey to Freedom"; he even played baseball legend
Babe Ruth in "Big Boy." He had a leading role in several episodes of the
classic series *Suspense* including "Lazarus Walks," which told the strange
tale of a man who returns from the dead and is compelled to speak the
truth with ultimately tragic consequences. He also played in a version of
Cornell Woolrich's famous novel "The Black Path of Fear."

One of his most popular roles at the time was as a sardonic Santa

Claus in Arch Oboler's thought-provoking *These Are Your Brothers,* broadcast at Christmas 1940. Described by one reviewer as "the best radio drama we've heard this year," it featured Donlevy as "a small-time racket man in a Santa suit, cadging dimes from passers-by. 'C'mon suckers, give,' [he] mutters as the coins clink into his cup."[1]

With his quiet authority, he was heard to good effect narrating Steven Vincent Benet's essay "Thanksgiving—November 1941." He also read director John Farrow's poem "Letter from His Commanding Officer" on a Memorial Day broadcast in 1943. Donlevy was one of several actors who played Dr. Benjamin Ordway, the title character of the series *Crime Doctor* from November 1942 to January 1943. He often took part in charity broadcasts and guested on variety shows such as *Burns and Allen* and *The Bing Crosby Show.* Fittingly, he was featured in a short recruiting drama for the National Guard, *Turnabout,* and co-starred with William Holden in *Boomer Jones,* a Labor Day broadcast directed by Mel Ferrer.

Donlevy was among those who made spoken appeals for the American Cancer Society at the Franz Lehar festival, along with Vivien Leigh, Laurence Olivier, Herman Wouk and Shirley Booth *et al.* He was often host, interviewer or interviewee and took part in discussion shows with his fellow actors in such shows as *Vox Pop* and *The Kate Smith Hour.* He was also heard in the adventure series *Three Sheets to the Wind* with John Wayne, which ran for 26 episodes.

In 1949, Donlevy approached NBC with an idea for a detective series. *Dangerous Assignment* was a mystery-adventure which had so many familiar elements that it could almost have been written by him. The noir atmosphere, humor and quick-fire dialogue were delivered in Donlevy's familiar rapid New York twang and the series proved popular. The show ended in the mid–1950s as radio itself began to decline in the public consciousness, by which time television had taken its place. Much of Donlevy's radio work is available today on CD and as MP3 downloads and gives a good insight into this wonderful medium. In the world of radio, there are some real gems which are often overlooked when considering the actors and actresses of the Golden Age, many of whom recorded extensively.

In Donlevy's television debut, *Chevrolet Tele-Theater's* "Weather Ahead" (1949), he played as the captain of a vessel in wartime faced with the difficult decision of whether to sail into a bad storm or stay in an enemy port. He made an impression the following year in *Pulitzer Prize Playhouse's* hour-long teleplay "The Pharmacist's Mate," scripted by Budd Schulberg and set aboard a submarine in wartime. While hunting the enemy, a crew member an appendicitis attack. There is no doctor on board, and the mate agrees to perform the operation. Donlevy played the skipper and his naturalism was very apparent; he had instant authority and seemed the ideal man in a crisis; fully aware of all the responsibilities of the position, but able to successfully choose and handle the men under his command in a balanced and decidedly humane way. It was really no wonder that regulars saluted him during the making of *I Wanted Wings* as he always appeared entirely convincing in uniform.

On TV, Donlevy was often given tough guy roles similar to those he had played on the big screen. The hard-driving construction boss in "Tunnel Job" is faced with making life-and-death decisions for his crew working on a tunnel project 1500 feet below river level. Even when cast as a man of the cloth in episodes of the ABC religious-based series *Crossroads*, Donlevy was still pretty tough. These stories were often based on true-life people and events. As the Reformed churchman Reverend Chambers in "God of Kandikur," he was faced with a giant cobra and other dangers in a remote Indian Mission post. In "Mr. Liberty Bell," he was head of the Silliman University in the Philippines at the time of the fall of Corregidor; he organizes local resistance against the Japanese and constructs a short-wave transmitter from purloined parts. In the episode "The Judge," he played a Presbyterian minister in a wild Kentucky town faced with so much lawlessness that he decides to take matters into his own hands.

His successful radio series *Dangerous Assignment* gave rise to a still more popular television series in 1952, his greatest TV success. Not only was he the star, but he produced the show and promoted it as well. Each week, Donlevy's detective Steve Mitchell was sent to some exotic location to investigate a mystery. The character was an extension of the one he had essayed in *Nightmare,* one of his favorite films. The series was typical of many in the Cold War era and each case involved international espionage. The air of mystery was maintained throughout and the series was well-realized, involving intriguing ideas. All 39 episodes are available on DVD.

Setting the tone for the series, the opening credits began with a misty gaslit street and the well-dressed, top-hatted figure of Donlevy walking towards the camera. Under a lamppost he lights a cigarette; suddenly a thrown dagger embeds itself in the post and he dashes away. Every episode began with distinctive Donlevy narration that immediately evoked the feel of noir: "Danger is my assignment. I get sent to a lot of places I can't pronounce. But they all spell the same thing: trouble."

From the beginning the character was established: Mitchell, a two-fisted adventurer, is phlegmatic, wryly humorous and far from infallible. He succeeds in the end often due to alertness, quick-thinking or sheer luck. The different locations maintained the interest and some familiar faces popped up at intervals among the guest stars including such old-timers as Percy Helton, Mabel Paige and Thurston Hall. Some stories were ideal for the 30-minute time allotment, but others had enough in them for an hour or more. At one point, MGM was eager to make a big-screen version of the show. Some years later, Brian made a movie in Brazil, *The Girl in Room 13* (1959), which was effectively the film of the series.[2]

Dangerous Assignment ran for 39 episodes and proved very popular. From the first, the show was well-received, one prominent publication commenting that Donlevy "underplays all the way, refusing to strike poses or adopt mugging tricks usually associated with cloak and dagger heroes."[3] The combination of fast pacing, excellent production and "a convincing thesping job by [the] star" ensured the show's popularity.[4] Donlevy promoted it well, taking out ads in a number of trade papers. However, the enterprise failed to become a financial success. Donlevy agreed to accept the producer's idea of taking a moderate salary in exchange for written assurance of future income and capital gains. But the promised income did not come his way. "I got nothing," he later remarked, "I was robbed."[5] After many years of trying to set up his own company, he finally achieved his goal with the Donlevy Development Corporation. However, he was not the head of the organization, but the vice-president.

Undoubtedly *Dangerous Assignment* could have run for much longer, but the problem of any long-running series is a decline in quality over time. In 1953, NBC was unsuccessfully sued for $150,000 by Joan Miller who claimed that her name had been used for that of a spy in an episode of the radio show. During the war, Miller "had performed highly confidential and restricted work for the Office of Information,"[6]

Many actors enjoyed working on the show and Brian always put them at their ease. Robert Easton was a very tall actor whose height sometimes irked shorter actors with ego problems. Easton commented that Donlevy "was the smartest actor I ever worked with, in terms of handling that problem. I didn't have to stand in gutters like with Charles Bronson, because [Donlevy] was smart, he established me at 7'4" so he must be 6'8""[7]

Donlevy hoped to produce another television series with the working title *Log of the Silver Shark*. Billed as a comedy-adventure, it featured a sailor, a Coast Guard man and a Marine.[8] He did not intend to star in the show. A pilot was made on location in the Bahamas, but the series was not taken up by the networks.[9]

Donlevy did admirably in the title role of the *Kraft Theater* presentation of the acclaimed Irish drama "Home Is the Hero" by Walter Macken. A hit play for the Abbey Theater, this was the tale of a man, wracked with guilt, who has a very difficult homecoming after five years in prison. The author adapted his own two-act play to fit the 50-minute running time. He noted that young cast member Anthony Perkins mumbled, but was impressed with Donlevy. According to Macken, the actor "did a remarkable job in one week—nice fellow to work with too."[10] Donlevy appeared in a familiar role in the sentimental comedy "At Ease" as a hard-as-nails army sergeant with the proverbial heart of gold who is made head of a military academy by mistake. He managed to inject life into such familiar material.

He was the likely star of *The Great Mouthpiece,* based on the Gene Fowler book about crusading district attorney William J. Fallon. It went into production in May 1956, but a series never materialized.[11] Over the years he also appeared in episodes of such popular series as *Rawhide, Wagon Train* and *Perry Mason* and was a guest on quiz and comedy shows. On one panel game show, *The Name's the Same,* he was the guest in a regular feature called "I'd like to be..." in which each week a celebrity was invited to say who they would most like to be. Donlevy chose the comic book character Tom Corbett, Space Cadet.

In December 1955, Donlevy took part in one of the earliest charity telethons for the Portland, Oregon, station KPTV. Along with other stars including Victor Jory and Magda Gabor, he raised over $65,000 to fight cerebral palsy.[12]

Donlevy also appeared in a TV version of *The Great McGinty* with Thomas Gomez in the Akim Tamiroff role. He did good work in the *Ford Theater* presentation "The Policy of Joe Aladdin." In the *Star Stage* production "Honest John and the 13 Uncle Sams," he played a political boss who hires a dozen men to parade around town dressed as Uncle Sam, but 13 show up. He was featured in the *Climax!* episode "The Pink Cloud," about a man, wrongly convicted of a crime, who seeks revenge on the man who landed him in prison. There was good support from Jay C. Flippen and Doris Dowling. In *Westinghouse Theater*'s "The Laughter of Giants," Donlevy essayed the role of a domineering, self-made man with a much younger wife (Rita Gam). He introduces her to a young artist (Patrick McVey) with unforeseen consequences. Donlevy was memorable in the excellent drama "Escape" as an injured escaped convict who takes refuge at the farm of Frank Lovejoy and his wife Sylvia Sidney, who turn out not to be quite as helpful as they first appear. *DuPont Show of the Week*'s "Beyond this Place" was directed by Sidney Lumet and based on an unusual A.J. Cronin story about a wronged man. It boasted a stellar cast including Donlevy, Peggy Ann Garner, Shelley Winters and Farley Granger.

By 1960 Donlevy's body of television work earned him a star on the Hollywood Walk of Fame. But he was never given a star for his more impressive film career.

In 1962 Donlevy had a small role in an episode of *Saints and Sinners,* a short-lived series about a city newspaper, the *New Star Bulletin.* In "Dear George, the Siamese Cat Is Missing," a woman's husband is kidnapped and only some of the newspaper staff members are let in on the story, for the sake of the man's safety. Donlevy played Preller, a recruit to the paper who is trying to make a new start. Soon a rival newspaper, the trashy *Globe,* gets hold of the story and splashes it all over the front page, putting the abducted man in grave danger. Suspicion falls on Preller, who had worked briefly at the *Globe.* The story ends happily for all concerned. Donlevy worked very well, especially in his scenes with the underrated Nick Adams. As one reviewer commented, "Old timer Brian Donlevy stole the show … as an alcoholic, weak, over-the-hill rewrite man suspected of tipping the scandal sheet, a man desperately trying to hold a job he knows is his last chance."[13]

Donlevy made his final television appearance in an episode of the popular sitcom *Family Affair.* In "Hard-Hat Jody" he played a man on a building project befriended by young Jody. He turns out to be someone her Uncle Bill has been trying to meet for years. Donlevy's portrayal drew praise: "[H]is scenes with the boy are full of warmth and charm," said one reviewer.[14] It was a suitably charming close to a successful television career.

11

Quatermass to the Rescue

"You took my job, you took my hotel. You thought you could push me right off the Earth."
— Joe McClure in *The Big Combo*

The mid–1950s were a difficult time for Donlevy and actors of his generation brought up in the studio system, which was then breaking down. He had mostly been a villain in A-pictures and a hero in B-pictures. He could not change pace in the way some actors could; he was very much stuck in the mold of 20 years before. Unmarried for the past decade, he had courted a succession of actresses to little avail. He looked noticeably older and heavier. His drinking became a big problem. In April 1955 he was fined for drunk driving after an incident in which he "jumped two curbs, rolled onto a parking lot and crashed into another car."[1] The judge fined him $150, ordered him not to drive for 90 days and to refrain from drinking for a year.[2] In addition, his interest in his work seemed to have diminished; hence his later years in movies mostly proved the law of diminishing returns. But there were some unexpected highlights, most notably a classic noir and two landmark science fiction films.

Joseph H. Lewis' *The Big Combo* has been described as "a wholly defined film noir."[3] Critics have celebrated it, and this time the praise is deserved. The story concerns Police Lt. Diamond (Cornel Wilde) and his obsession with bringing criminal mastermind Mr. Brown (Richard Conte) to book. Although Brown is a known racketeer (and possibly responsible for murder), the police cannot arrest him because he is careful not to leave evidence. Diamond is told to drop the case by a superior, but he is determined to arrest Brown.

From the opening titles, the jazz music of David Raksin immediately conjures up a suitably sleazy and downbeat atmosphere encapsulating the

137

Donlevy (left) as Joe McClure, with Richard Conte as his ruthless boss Mr. Brown in Joseph H. Lewis' dystopian noir *The Big Combo* (1955). Donlevy gave an excellent portrayal as the all-too-human henchman whose hearing aid Brown uses as a weapon of torture.

movie's fatalistic sense. The amazing John Alton photography, the sharp dialogue and the fine playing of an excellent cast combine to make this one of the most memorable and unsettling noirs.

Brown is ruthless and amoral. Donlevy's Joe McClure, like many of the other characters in the film, is weak. All are essentially trapped by their weaknesses and desires. One critic summarized it succinctly: "The striking contrasts between the black and white photography and Lewis' sexual overtones isolate *The Big Combo* in a dark, insular universe of unspoken repression and graphic violence."[4]

The Big Combo was the apotheosis of many noir roles for Donlevy; McClure, a small-timer who was once big, is usurped by Brown. McClure secretly dreams of making it big again and plots to get revenge on the big guys. He tries to enlist the help of Brown's henchmen, which is of course his fatal error. Their loyalty is to each other and Brown, in that order. As usual, Donlevy ends up dead, his end chillingly memorable at the hands of Richard Conte's callous gangster. The scene where Brown removes

McClure's hearing aid makes his demise one of the most chilling. His noiseless death is one of the starkest in noir; somehow seeing gun flashes but not hearing the expected sound is startling. The idea for this twist, wholly in keeping with a hugely influential movie, came not from the director, but from a key grip working on the picture.[5] But it fits into the pattern of the film, which is filled with darkness both literally and metaphorically; the remarkable use of light, sound and narrative results in one of the genre's most striking films. McClure is an essentially human character: When faced with certain death, he begs to live. When Brown ends up in the same situation, he begs to die.

It was impossible not to feel for McClure as his simmering resentment is directed at Brown, on whom he longs to exact his revenge; "You took my job, you took my hotel. You thought you could push me right off the Earth...." Naturally the tables are so easily turned and the expected counter-revenge is dragged out by Brown as he taunts his victim: "I feel sorry for you, Joe," Brown says, "so I'm gonna do you a favor. You won't hear the bullets." Brown uses the hearing aid as a weapon of torture. He taunts Diamond with it, while Donlevy looks on and flinches, reflecting in his expression that he suddenly feels empathy for Diamond. The hearing aid is a symbol of human physical weakness; Brown effectively turns this weakness on McClure, which sums up the whole ethos of this remarkable noir.

Science fiction was popular in the 1950s and Donlevy signed up for the starring role in *The Gamma People,* which was due to be filmed in the summer of 1951 in Vienna, where he was staying with his daughter. There were delays and the film was not made until 1955. What would have been Donlevy's role in this artless entry in the fantasy canon went to Paul Douglas, to the detriment of the final film in the opinion of many genre aficionados.[6]

Then he was offered the lead in a movie by Britain's Hammer Films. *The Quatermass Experiment* was a popular science fiction series on British television which aired in July 1953, starring Reginald Tate as Prof. Bernard Quatermass. It was a critical success. It was two years before a second Quatermass series appeared, by which time Tate had died and another actor had taken the role. Hammer was keen to make a film version based on the original; they titled it *The Quatermass Xperiment,* the "X" because they consciously pursued an "X" certificate, which at that time meant that audience members had to be over 16. The producers cast around for a name to play the lead and, with an eye on the American market, went for Donlevy, much to the chagrin of the creator of the franchise, Nigel Kneale.

Donlevy (left) as Prof. Quatermass eyes the unfortunate Caroon (Richard Wordsworth) in Hammer's *The Quatermass Xperiment* (1955).

The film begins with the return to Earth of a rocket, part of Prof. Quatermass' experiments to probe outer space; it crashes in a field. Two of the three crew members are missing; the third, Victor Caroon, is taken to the hospital. Quatermass and Inspector Lomax (Jack Warner) examine the rocket to find out what went wrong. The in-flight filmed record of events is sent to a laboratory to be restored. At the hospital, Caroon regains consciousness, delirious and sweating profusely. He knocks over a plant and hurts his hand. Soon, he manages to escape from the hospital and a search is mounted; it becomes apparent that he is seriously deranged and deformed by something from the rocket which infected him. The trail leads to Chessington Zoo where several animals are attacked and drained of blood. By now Caroon has become subsumed by the thing which possesses him; he is a dangerous monster and is tracked down to Westminster Abbey. Quatermass and his team think fast and electrocute the monster in the gantry. "What now?" asks one of the scientist's assistants. "We start again," says Quatermass as he strides off into the night.

Filming of the low-budget enterprise began in October 1954 and ended in December, which helps to explain the cold feeling of the finished result, heightened by night shooting. The unfortunate Caroon was portrayed by stage actor Richard Wordsworth, great-grandson of the Romantic poet William Wordsworth; in later years, he toured with a one-man show in which he played his illustrious ancestor. The special effects were generally good despite the lack of finance, although the finale in a mock-up of Westminster Abbey was effectively an exercise in bathos; the blob-like creature made the whole thing seem risible. The unwritten law of such movies is that the monster should never be seen. It was during the lesser moments that Donlevy's worth could be judged overall and he delivered the often trite lines with conviction which helped to ground the movie. *The London Times* critic wrote that he was "a little brusque in his treatment of British institutions, but he is clearly a man who knows what he is doing."[7] It could easily be argued that most British institutions need to be dealt with brusquely in order to see any action.

While staying in London, Donlevy was invited to a royal gala function at which other Hollywood stars were present including Jane Russell. He met the queen and other members of the Royal Family, who asked him about his stay in London and the part he was playing.[8] He happened to mention to Prince Philip that he was filming near the village of Bray in Berkshire. "Pop in at the Hind's Head," remarked the prince, "and give my regards to Mrs. Williams the landlady."[9] Donlevy often visited the Plough at Elstree village in his lunch hour during filming.

The show's creator, Nigel Kneale, disliked Donlevy intensely from the onset; he referred to him disparagingly as "a former Hollywood heavy gone to seed."[10] His initial problem was with the American's portrayal of his beloved character. He had envisioned Quatermass as an erudite scientist with a questing spirit, whereas Donlevy, he said, played him as "a mechanic with a closed mind."[11] He described Donlevy as "paralytic drunk" and maintained that he was only in it for the money, but with such a small budget that cannot have amounted to a hill of beans. No matter what difficulties the makers encountered with their star, they nonetheless invited him back for the sequel *Quatermass 2,* released in the U.S., two years later as *Enemy from Space.* According to Kneale, when he visited the set of that film,

> (Donlevy) was so full of whiskey he could hardly stand up. He staggered over to the set and looked dazedly around. They held up an idiot board with his lines on, and he said "What's this movie called?" And they said, well, it's called *Quatermass 2.* He said, "I've got to say all that? There's too much talk. Cut down some of the talk." He tried to read it and he had go after go, so crippled with drink he didn't know who he was.[12]

Director Val Guest contradicted Kneale: "It's absolute balls because he was not paralytic drunk. He wasn't stone-cold sober either. But he was a professional and knew his lines."[13] Donlevy's co-stars Bryan Forbes and William Franklyn recalled no problems when interviewed later.[14] Guest's more measured assessment of Donlevy was that he gave the films "absolute reality."[15] Guest added:

> (Donlevy) was a great guy to work with. He used to like his drink, however, so by after lunch he would come to me and say "Give me a breakdown of the story so far. Where have I been before this scene?" We used to feed him black coffee all morning but then we discovered he was lacing it. But he was a very professional actor and very easy to work with.[16]

None of the behind-the-scenes difficulties are in any way apparent in the finished movie, which sustains a slightly unsettling atmosphere for most of its running time. The scenario this time involves Quatermass and his assistant Marsh (Bryan Forbes) discovering a complex on the site of what *was* the village of Winnerden Flats. This complex of huge domes is

Quatermass 2 (1957), aka *Enemy from Space,* tapped into an undercurrent of unease in modern society which seemed to be losing its individuality. Donlevy's brusque approach was arguably more necessary than ever in an age that had almost stopped questioning. Sydney James is at right.

based almost entirely on Quatermass' own moon base project for which he tried but failed to get government backing. While Marsh is inspecting one of many small meteorites that have landed nearby, it bursts open and makes a black mark on his face. Suddenly armed security guards appear and take Marsh away. Quatermass tries to stop them, but is made to leave. He drives to the nearby town and attempts to find the police but is told they are 15 miles away. No one is willing to help. Eventually he makes contact with a crusading Parliament member, Broadhead (Tom Chatto), who organizes an official party to tour the complex and determine what is happening there.

The public is told the place manufactures synthetic food; actually, it houses an alien life form which has infected many people (including government officials) who become unthinking zombies. During the tour, several members of the visiting party are detained. Quatermass escapes and discovers Broadhead, who is covered in some kind of toxic ammonia substance and dies from the burns. After fleeing the plant, Quatermass finds an ally in Inspector Lomax (John Longdon), who believes his story. With the help of pressman Jimmy Hall (Sydney James), they manage to alert the outside world. Enraged workers march on the plant demanding to know what goes on inside the domes. They become trapped inside the control room and finally discover the conglomeration of alien matter which is being fed and threatens to take over; but the Quatermass rocket is launched and saves the day.

Quatermass 2 is a decent science fiction adventure. Only the ending was something of a letdown once the familiar blob-like amorphous creature made its appearance; for all his undoubted imagination, it is rather surprising that Kneale could not have come up with something more convincing. But the settings were admirable, particularly the plant with its domes and pipelines. These scenes were filmed at the Shell Haven Refinery in Essex.

Donlevy was entirely believable as Quatermass, brusque and persistent, a quick-thinking man of action when required. He had great support from an excellent cast of very familiar faces such as Percy Herbert and William Franklyn. The plot of an alien life form infecting mankind and creating a race of faceless non-entities has marked similarities to the contemporary Hollywood movie *Invasion of the Body Snatchers* (1956), but that was a product of the age as individuality seemed to be diminishing.

There is a very telling scene at a dance in the community hall which cleverly reflects shifting tensions. At first there is the happy atmosphere of the traditional dance; this turns to animosity at the presence of Quatermass and the inspector; and finally fear and anger at the intrusion of the armed security guards. Donlevy's portrayal of the professor is hardly likely to be universally admired any time soon, but was arguably more in tune with the thrusting spirit of the atomic age than the erudite gent that Kneale first imagined. Once a written creation is manifested on screen, he is out of his creator's hands and takes on a life of his own. The test of the strength or weakness of any invented character is if he or she can be reinterpreted time and again and retain his or her essential self. On any scale, Quatermass passes that test.

After making that movie in England from May to July 1956, Brian traveled on to France where he met up with his daughter and admitted to feeling weary. "I'm played out," he announced. "No more work until I've had a good rest."[17] The same team of Guest, Hammer and Donlevy were all set to assemble for the third time in a follow-up, *Quatermass and the Pit*. However the success of *The Curse of Frankenstein* encouraged Hammer to instead pursue the gothic tale at the expense of science fiction; it would be another decade before the third Quatermass film was made. But Donlevy twice returned to the science fiction/horror genre, in *Curse of the Fly* (1965) and *Gammera, the Invincible* (1966).

Frank Tuttle's excellent crime film *A Cry in the Night* teamed Donlevy with Edmond O'Brien, another noir stalwart. Teenager Liz Taggart (Natalie Wood), daughter of Police Capt. Taggart (O'Brien), is with her fiancé Owen Clark (Richard Anderson) at a lovers' lane with all the other couples. Peeping Tom Harold Loftus (Raymond Burr) knocks out Clark and drives off in his car, abducting Liz. He takes Liz to his hideout at the abandoned brickworks on the edge of town. During the course of the investigation, the identity of the attacker is discovered and police find the car. Finally they locate him and all ends satisfactorily.

Cry in the Night stands out from the run-of-the-mill police thriller: It has a good story with interesting characters and is well-acted by a great cast. This was Tuttle's penultimate film; his career had started in silent days. His credits included *This Gun for Hire* (1942) and *Lucky Jordan* (1942). He was accused of being a Communist during the McCarthy hearings and escaped censure by naming names. He famously named Jules Dassin, which prompted Dassin to go to Europe.

There is a depth of insight into the motivations of the protagonists that is not apparent in the original Whit Masterson novel *All Through the Night*. Burr made a convincingly menacing mother's boy who might be capable of anything, and Wood was perfect as the frightened girl. O'Brien was a marvelous actor and his performance was well-judged; he was suitably on the edge of exploding, but not quite. Donlevy was spot-on as the captain in charge of the case. He does his level best to do the difficult job of restraining O'Brien and marshalling all the strands of the case and had a good insight into human behavior. He understands his friend O'Brien's frustrations, but also sees that he is too involved and over-protective of his daughter. The two veterans worked seamlessly together, and the whole ensemble was successful. The intriguing story effectively centered on the damaging effects of too much love from a parent.

By appearing in the movie, Donlevy missed out on the chance to revive his lead role in the play *King of Hearts* at the Carthay Circle Theater in Los Angeles, which had been due to open on November 7, 1955.[18] Always a great lover of opera, Brian almost won a role as a barman in Mark Blitzstein's *Reuben, Reuben* (1955), an experimental urban folk opera based on the Faust legend.[19] The show was a total failure and the audience walked out during the Boston tryout.[20]

In December 1956, Donlevy was suggested as a replacement for Arthur Kennedy, who had suffered a brain hemorrhage while starring in Broadway's *The Loud Red Patrick*, but the show closed just before Christmas.[21] The following year he was announced as Stephen A. Douglas in *The Rivalry,* Norman Corwin's dramatization of the famous Lincoln-Douglas debates. Raymond Massey was Abraham Lincoln and Agnes Moorehead played Adele Douglas. Rehearsals began on August 25, 1957, but Donlevy had problems memorizing his lines, and with the show due to open a week later at Santa Barbara, he was replaced by Martin Gabel.[22]

Most of the films Donlevy made in this later period were unmemorable, and his contribution to them minimal. Increasingly he turned his attention to television. He also tried to mount another production of his own, *The Golden Spur.*[23]

Donlevy was next seen on screen in the B-Western *Escape from Red Rock* (1957) for director Edward Bernds. This modest film concerned a young rancher forced to take part in robberies in order to save his brother's life. He flees with his sweetheart and makes for the Mexican border, pursued by Donlevy's gang and Sheriff Jay C. Flippen's posse. Although Donlevy essayed yet another baddie, he nonetheless protects the young woman and her baby from harm when they are threatened by his men. In this rather jaded Western, only the two oldtimers stood out, especially Donlevy as "an uninhibited outlaw with a heart only slightly lined with gold."[24] Bernds is chiefly remembered for his many Three Stooges comedy shorts. In the late 1940s he graduated to B-movies, some of which have achieved latter-day cult status such as *Reform School Girl* (1957), *High School Hellcats* (1958) and *Queen of Outer Space* (1958).

Delmer Daves' unusual Western *Cowboy* (1958) teamed Glenn Ford and Jack Lemmon as reluctant partners on a hard cattle drive from Chicago to Mexico and back. Ford insisted on Lemmon for the role of Harris, the daydreaming hotel clerk who toughens up on the trail to the point where he is running the outfit. It was a major departure for Lemmon, who was initially skeptical. Ford managed to convince him over the course of several drinks.[25] Donlevy played one of the trail hands, the lonely Doc Blender, who is trying to escape from his former life as sheriff of Wichita and is tired of a life of killing.

The movie focused on the unfolding dramatic tensions between the two leads, particularly Harris, who loses himself *and* finally finds himself en route. Seldom has a cattle drive seemed so convincing and oddly engrossing. At the end, Doc decides to leave the trail and return to Wichita to seek out an old friend. However, the men hear that the friend pulled a gun on Doc, who shot him; Doc later hanged himself. Harris' lack of reaction upon hearing of the death of Doc points up how callous he has become. Donlevy looked tired and much older, which underlined the pathos of the character. This was something of a valedictory performance by the veteran. There is about him the ghost of former Western glories, the sense of outliving his time, and never finding a place to belong. He appears rather lost, and it comes as no real surprise to hear of Doc's eventual suicide.

Despite the relatively small size of the role, fourth-billed Donlevy still had a distinct presence. This interesting but often overlooked movie was well shot in color by the legendary Charles Lawton Jr. on location in Santa Fe. Writer-director Daves had an intriguing career including the co-writing of *The Petrified Forest* (1936) and directing thoughtful Westerns such as *3:10 to Yuma* (1957).

Donlevy next popped up in teenage cult favorite *Juke Box Rhythm* (1959), which was mostly notable for its music by the Earl Grant Trio, the Treniers and the Nitwits. There was a particularly rousing set by Johnny Otis playing "Willie and the Hand Jive." Donlevy's George Manton is a struggling music impresario whose son Riff (Jack Jones) is photographed with a visiting European princess choosing her wedding wardrobe. Riff persuades the princess to see the designs of a friend, Balenko (Hans Conreid). When she gives Balenko her patronage, he in turn gives Riff money to produce a show, Juke Box Jamboree, and help out his father in the process. The story and characters took a backseat to the music in this pleasantly diverting movie which featured several other familiar faces from Hollywood's heyday, also on the way down.

Donlevy next popped up in the big-name big-budget Frank Sinatra World War II movie *Never So Few* (1959), directed by John Sturges. Although allegedly based on fact, it was mostly a glossy star vehicle for Sinatra and Gina Lollobrigida. Set in Burma, the story centered on American army officer Tom Reynolds (Sinatra), who is ordered to lead an attack on Ubachi. Along with an eccentric, monocle-wearing British sidekick (Richard Johnson) and a group of assorted guerrillas, he is successful up to a point. However, he comes across an American convoy that has been attacked by renegade Chinese troops. Incensed, he disobeys orders and crosses the border into China, capturing 25 raiders. Later, all the prisoners are massacred. On his return, Reynolds is placed under military arrest, but is saved at the end by the intervention of a brigadier general (Donlevy) who upholds his actions.

"Sinatra meets Lollobrigida—and the screen catches fire!" declared MGM's trailer for this film, which was promoted as "first-rate mass-market entertainment."[26] There are lots of explosions and plenty of philosophizing but for all its gloss and its apparent profundity, *Never So Few* seems rather hollow. The screenplay condones any and every cruelty that takes place in the name of "justice." This was a showcase for the two leads, although their love affair becomes rather tiresome and further elongates an already lengthy movie. Noticeable in smaller roles were Steve McQueen and Paul Henreid.

Donlevy only had a few short scenes near the end, but again had problems remembering his lines. In his five minutes of screen time he was strong and thoroughly convincing. According to Sturges' biographer, "the shoot, scheduled for an afternoon, took two days, Sturges patiently standing by as the actor read his lines from a blackboard."[27] Despite everything, Donlevy was judged to be strong and thoroughly convincing in his five minutes of screen time. One reviewer commented that he gave "one of the finest performances of 1959."[28] His fee for two days' work was $6,000, but he was sued for $15,000 by Curtis Roberts, a man who claimed he had helped him to get the role. Donlevy successfully established that his usual agents had procured him the part, and won the case.[29]

In March 1959, Donlevy had an offer from director Richard E. Cunha to work in Brazil on a movie entitled *Leave Me Alone*. The title was later changed to *A Moco do Quarto Treze* or, in English, *The Girl in Room 13*. Cunha was renowned for his low-budget opuses *Frankenstein's*

Daughter (1958) and *Missile to the Moon* (1958) which earned him a cult following.

The story concerns detective Steve Marshall (Donlevy) who arrives at Congonhas airport in Sao Paulo at the same time as a smuggler is being chased by police. The smuggler slips some negatives into Steve's pocket; these negatives are for the production of counterfeit banknotes. Steve has been mysteriously summoned to Brazil by letter. He hopes to find Kitty Herman (Andrea Bayard), who is wanted for the murder of her husband, and discovers that she killed him in self-defense. Kitty is the lover of Victor (Victor Merinow), who is involved in the counterfeiting gang. When Steve and Kitty arrive backstage, Kitty is attacked by Victor, who is looking for the negatives. Steve discovers the negatives are in his possession and Johnny is in charge of taking the negatives to the police, but double-crosses Steve and tries to do business with the gang, demanding $25,000. The gang is eventually foiled by Steve, who returns to the U.S. while Kitty decides to stay in Brazil.

Shot in Eastman Color in the studios at Sao Paulo, this was a typically low-budget Cunha venture. The director aimed to make his films for less than $80,000; usually they cost around $65,000 and were shot in only six days. The studio facilities were not of the standard Donlevy had been used to in his heyday, although he never complained. Other Hollywood actors were working there at the same time. One was young William Wellman, Jr., son of the director with whom Donlevy had made *Beau Geste* and *The Great Man's Lady*. Wellman Jr. remarked that the studio—and the dressing rooms—had a dirt floor. He recalled:

> There were a couple of soundstages, and all the stuff that you'd find at a studio. There was a little commissary and there were dressing rooms and there was (for a small studio) a *big* backlot—they had plenty of land. Brian Donlevy was doing a picture on another soundstage ... while we were there. It was towards the end of his career, and he was not in very good shape. I used to go talk to him a little bit. No one else was there.[30]

Starlet June Wilkinson was also filming there at the same time and often went to talk with Donlevy. While with him, she was approached about a new film project, *Career Girl*.[31]

The Girl in Room 13 had the feeling of a decent television adventure, and some elements that others have termed post-noir. Donlevy performed admirably under the circumstances and there was sufficient intrigue to hold the interest. The movie is very obscure and only turned up occasionally on late night television, but has never been released on DVD. The production might have lacked prestige, but Donlevy lifted it immeasurably. Sao Paulo was then in its early days of moviemaking and keen to entice famous artists from Hollywood. This was one of Donlevy's better later films and one of the last proto-noir-crime movies that recalled in essence the ghost of the great days of that genre of which he had been a part.

12

Fade Out

"Everywhere we went—and we crossed the U.S. three times—the public response was terrific. When you stick your kisser into 99 cities—and the people seem to like what they see—man, that's really something."
—Donlevy discusses the success of *The Andersonville Trial* with Harold Heffernan, "Donlevy Returning to Comedy," *The Pittsburgh Press,* September 7, 1961, 13

As the 1960s dawned, Donlevy sought to return to his theatrical roots and embarked on a lengthy tour of the country with *The Andersonville Trail.* In movies he tried to branch out into more comedy roles and also became a regular with the A.C. Lyles stock company in a series of low-budget but well-made Westerns. In between he retired, but soon became bored and returned for a few more years.

Despite the problems he had encountered remembering his lines while rehearsing *The Rivalry* in 1957, Brian made a successful return to the stage in 1958 in *No Time for Sergeants* and in 1960 as the Defense Counsel in Saul Levitt's *The Andersonville Trial.* This courtroom drama was based on the real-life trial of Henry Wirz, commandant of a Confederate prison during the Civil War. In 1865, Wirz was tried and executed for his inhumane treatment of thousands of Union soldiers who died of malnutrition, exposure and disease.

The nationwide tour was long and grueling, but proved very popular. It began on the West Coast in mid–June 1960 and ended there in mid–September 1961 after playing in most major cities for several nights and many small towns for one-night stands. The company played all kinds of venues, from high schools to aircraft carriers. Donlevy was praised for his work in this enthralling drama. One critic commented: "His swashbuckling days are over, but his skill is still consummate. Even in a secondary role as Otis H. Baker, Donlevy dominates the stage when he must."[1]

In 1961, Brian returned to comedy in an attempt to send up his own "tough guy" image. One of the first was Jerry Lewis' *The Errand Boy*, in which Donlevy appeared as the head of Paramutual Films, a thinly veiled satire of Paramount. The movie was shot while he was taking a break from his *Andersonville Trial* tour. He told a reporter about his new lease on life: "I'm a light-hearted guy and I've always liked to have plenty of laughs out of life. Going sour and heavy never sat well with me. Comedy is a lot of fun to do—and I'm sure glad Jerry picked me out of the rut."[2]

The Errand Boy begins with the blustery Tom "T.P." Paramutual (Donlevy) condemning his money-wasting employees and deciding to hire an industrial spy to root out the problems. His sister persuades him to hire someone who is so stupid that no one will have any idea that he is a spy. Enter Morty S. Tashman (Lewis), who sets about spoiling scenes and disrupting every single department. Soon the whole studio is in an uproar.

The Errand Boy has some great set-piece scenes that have become part of comic folklore. The comedian was memorably inventive at times,

In the 1960s, Donlevy attempted to change tack by moving back into comedy and played the head of Paramutual Films in *The Errand Boy* (1961), one of Jerry Lewis' most popular and critically acclaimed films. Left to right: Donlevy, Lewis and Howard McNear.

particularly in the rightfully acclaimed lift sequence, and in a mimed boardroom accompaniment to Count Basie's "Blues in Hoss' Flat." But Lewis is an acquired taste, and has always divided opinion. Although acclaimed as a genius in Europe, especially in France, where his miming skills have seen him lauded as the rightful heir to Chaplin, he is also equally pilloried. One critic called *The Errand Boy* "a feeble comedy with the star at his self-satisfied worst."[3] Lewis was a dedicated comic seen to best advantage perhaps in his partnership with Dean Martin and his earlier successes such as *The Nutty Professor*. However, his comedy leaves little room for the other performers, who are reduced to expressing bemusement, boredom or anger at his antics.

Donlevy was a good choice as someone to represent the forces of order against which Lewis is working, and the veteran actor appeared to enjoy playing with his established on-screen image. One critic remarked that Donlevy's "polished, tongue-in-cheek artistry contrast and compliment [Lewis'] broad clowning…."[4]

Donlevy continued in the light-hearted vein in *The Pigeon That Took Rome* (1962), which had appealing performances by some of the Italian members of the cast, especially the endearing child actor Livio Massimo. The surprising star was Charlton Heston, in a role that had been planned for Bob Hope. Heston was ill-suited to comedy and later considered making this movie a mistake. The often moody black-and-white photography lent itself more towards drama and somewhat deadened the comedic elements.

The rather slight story, set towards the end of the war, concerned two Americans behind enemy lines in Italy who send messages back to base via carrier pigeon and become entangled in the lives of the local girls and their families. Donlevy played Heston's commanding officer, a colonel—another in his gallery of high-ranking officers. He appeared briefly at the beginning to give Heston his assignment. Rarely seen since its release, the movie was amiable but heavy going after a while, and not especially funny.

In 1962, Donlevy practically retired and said that he intended to spend his time writing. However, he began to feel restless and by 1964 was tempted back to work. "I sort of quit for a while," he said in an interview. "But I got tired of the grass and jack-rabbits and came back to town where it's civilized."[5] There was talk of a part in a Broadway musical, and he also hoped to return to the summer theater circuit. During his time away, he had written 41 stories and said he hoped to interest NBC-TV in some of his ideas. Retirement was not the rest cure he hoped, and after so many years working, he longed to be active again. "All of a sudden I woke up and found I was getting lazy," he observed. "To waste your time is the biggest sin in the world. Who wants to take pills and stay young? I haven't fallen apart yet."[6]

After a two-year screen absence, he accepted the offer of another British science fiction film. *Curse of the Fly* was the last in a series of

Donlevy accepted an offer to travel to England to make *Curse of the Fly* (1965). This effective but curiously overlooked period horror was one of the best of his later films. Donlevy is seen here as Henri Delambre with George Baker as his son.

movies which began with *The Fly* (1958) and continued with *Return of the Fly* the following year. The original, based on a short story by George Langelaan, had been a memorable thriller starring David Hedison as a scientist whose experiments lead to disaster. Especially poignant was the episode where the man who becomes a fly is trapped in a spider's web and a tiny voice appeals for help. In *Curse*, Henri Delambre (Donlevy) is the grandson of the original scientist and the story centered on his attempts to perfect his experiments in teleportation, in this case between Quebec and London.

The film begins in Canada with a very attractive brunette, Patricia Stanley (Carole Gray), clad only in her underwear, escaping from a large house in the middle of the night. The house turns out to be a mental hospital and as she sprints across the road, she is nearly run over by Martin Delambre (George Baker). He installs her at a nearby hotel. In time, he falls in love with her. His brother Albert and father Henri (Donlevy) in London are embroiled in their experiments to perfect their teleportation system and Henri uses it to transport himself to the house in Quebec. Martin arrives at the house with Patricia, who is now his wife. She begins to suspect that all is not right; her husband has a recurring attack of a mysterious illness and at night she sees a strangely disfigured woman playing the piano. Martin and his father try and convince her it that it is just her imagination. The woman is Judith, Martin's first wife, who was disfigured in a previous experiment. Two other unfortunates are kept in the grounds and tended by rather strange servants. When the Delambres attempt to teleport the two creatures, something goes disastrously wrong and everything begins to unravel for them all.

A surprisingly effective period horror film, *Curse of the Fly* does not deserve its obscurity. It is a great advantage that it was filmed in black and white and did not follow the sensationalist route; there are no monsters for instance. A most notable feature is the score composed by Bert Shefter, who had also provided the music for the first two *Fly* movies and is justly famous for many other science fiction soundtracks. The music sets the tone admirably from the beginning; it is plaintive *and* slightly chilling, subtly underlining the inevitability of the fate of the family—their curse.

Donlevy was fully in sync with the atmosphere of the movie: also curiously plaintive and looking older, his voice sometimes weak. Interesting philosophical questions are raised about the ethics of progress. The Delambres' mantra of advancement whatever the human cost is brought home starkly when the victims of previous experiments are so callously dealt with. Henri seems urbane and composed, but when the semi-human thing in the sack tries to escape, he beats it furiously, taking out all his fear on the unseen creature in a particularly unsettling scene. This brutality appears to scare him. He is later remorseful although oddly powerless to change. Donlevy ably reflects all these conflicting emotions.

It is unfair to compare the movie to the previous ones in the series because it stands well enough on its own and instead of slavishly following the original, it tries to develop the theme rather than the substance. It failed at the box office, but that could be partially explained by marketing it as a sequel and thus setting up unreasonable expectations, when in fact it was the story of what became of the descendants of the Delambres.[7] The franchise was resurrected successfully some 20 years later when Jeff Goldblum and much improved special effects brought it back to life; recently there was talk that it would be filmed yet again. *Curse of the Fly* was shot in England with a good British cast including stalwarts such as Burt Kwouk. Rachel Kempson, mother of the famous Redgrave acting dynasty, played the head of the hospital from which Patricia escapes. It was directed efficiently by Australian-born Don Sharp, also known for *The Kiss of the Vampire* (1962) and *The Face of Fu Manchu* (1965). The movie marked Donlevy's last association with Twentieth Century–Fox, the studio which had given him his start 30 years before.

Made in Japan, *Gammera, the Invincible* was the first kaiju (monster film) about a giant turtle-like creature unleashed by atom bombs; it was created to compete with a rival studio's hugely successful *Godzilla* series. All attempts to deal with the monster are thwarted as it eats fire and thrives on the weaponry used against it. Although destructive, it shows compassion when it saves a falling child. Only freezing temperatures will thwart the monster and in the end it is announced that Plan Z, "the hope of the world," will send the creature into space on a rocket bound for Mars.

This movie's mostly Japanese cast was augmented by Donlevy and fellow Hollywood veteran Albert Dekker to directly appeal to the American market.[8] A purely Japanese version would have made much more sense and subtitles would have been preferable to dubbing which is seldom successful. Donlevy had a few scenes sitting around a table discussing the situation with the other American actors and then later at the United Nations where he has more to say about the monster and how to deal with it. These scenes appeared not to relate to the rest of the film and were clearly inserted; in all likelihood it was probably the same table turned the other way around with a United Nations logo behind. The giant turtle is not so terrifying, but the underlying theme of the terrors unleashed by the atom bomb perhaps explains why so many of these films were made at that time. For Donlevy it was not such a leap from playing the head of the atom bomb project to a general deciding how to combat the dangers awakened in the world by that terrible device.

One can only imagine that money induced Donlevy to participate in AIP's *How to Stuff a Wild Bikini* (1964); that at least was the excuse offered by Mickey Rooney and Buster Keaton. Samuel Z. Arkoff helped put the Z in Z-grade movies and they surpassed themselves in willful banality here in what the *New York Times* called "the answer to a moron's prayer."[9] In their defense, Messrs. Rooney, Keaton and Donlevy provided the only moments of relief in the whole tedious ensemble of 30-year old "teenagers" dancing on beaches to the sounds of nondescript '60s groups that never made the grade.

As if to hammer home his decline, Donlevy next turned up in the execrable farce *The Fat Spy* (1966) with Jayne Mansfield as his daughter. If anything, this was even worse than the previous entry and, to paraphrase the *New York Times,* could be dubbed the answer to a sub-moron's prayer. No wonder that George Raft turned down the part. As Mansfield's biographer noted, the movie did not even warrant an American premiere and first saw the light of day in Mexico: "Jayne and Phyllis [Diller] attended the premiere in Venezuela. The movie was so bad that Diller said she sneaked out of the theater, and went straight to confession—and she wasn't even Catholic."[10]

From here, Donlevy could only go up, and he returned to the sanity of old-fashioned filmmaking with A. C. Lyles and his ever-growing stock company of old players seeking refuge from the breakdown of the studio system. Lyles commented:

> One of the best friends I ever had on the studio lot was Brian Donlevy. I came to the studio in '37, and for a number of years, Brian was the star of some of the biggest pictures made—I mean big pictures, starting out ... with Preston Sturges and Bill Wellman. So we always became friends when I started making these pictures. We were having lunch one day, and I said, "I'm going to start making these pictures." And he said, "Now you just call me, tell me where you want me, and I'll be there." And that's the way it was, he did it for me all the time.[11]

Donlevy had a brief role in *Waco* (1966) as an ex-penitentiary friend of the title character (Howard Keel), but doesn't stay around when he recognizes the trouble in store from the townspeople and a belligerent local family with a score to settle. Also featured were a serious Jane Russell in her last starring role and a gaunt-looking Wendell Corey. Donlevy was third-billed but he hardly appeared in it. He next turned up as a marshal in *Hostile Guns* (1967) starring Tab Hunter and Yvonne De Carlo. He was only seen at the beginning and soon bashed on the head. A highlight of the film was the fight between Tab and his Uncle Joe portrayed by Emile Meyer, who was unforgettable as Ryker in *Shane*. Donlevy got to play a mayor in Lyles' *Arizona Bushwhackers* (1968), enhancing the atmosphere of this rather routine adventure alongside all the other familiar faces from Hollywood's golden age.

As a change from so many horse operas, Lyles branched out to mystery drama with *Rogue's Gallery* (1968). The plot concerned a perennially hard-up private detective, John Rogue (Roger Smith), who sleeps in his office and has not paid his secretary (Mala Powers) for months. He agrees to take the case of a girl who is judged to be a potential suicide case. During the course of his investigation, he uncovers an insurance racket and encounters numerous familiar faces from the golden age of Hollywood including Jackie Coogan, Farley Granger and Donlevy as a detective. A period curio, *Rogue's Gallery* was directed by Leonard Horn, who made his reputation on television with such series as *Mission: Impossible, Voyage to the Bottom of the Sea* and *Wonder Woman*. He made very few features; the most infamous was *The Magic Garden of Stanley Sweetheart* (1970), described by Andy Warhol as "the quintessential, most truthful studio-made film about the '60s counter-culture."[12]

Rogue's Gallery comes across as a tongue-in-cheek take on the 1940s detective genre: not so much a parody of *The Maltese Falcon* as an affectionate, mischievous tribute to the era. The presence of so many over-the-hill B-movie favorites adds to the atmosphere, and provides a touch of pathos. Although it now seems very much of its time, it is entertaining and likable. Roger Smith retired through ill health after making the film, and director Horn died a few years later at the age of 48. For some reason, *Rogue's Gallery* was not released until 1973.

Donlevy had another guest spot in the crime caper *Five Golden Dragons* (1967), filmed on location in Hong Kong. This poorly conceived movie consisted mostly of hapless playboy Bob Mitchell (Bob Cummings) and two Swedish girls being chased through a variety of locations—across junks along the waterside, in speedboats while waterskiing and even on rickshaws. Donlevy was one of the dragons of the title, part of a mysterious syndicate with control of the gold market. This syndicate appears to be responsible for several deaths being investigated by Shakespeare-addicted Police Commander Sanders (Rupert Davies). The idea was that none of the dragons had ever met before, despite working together for the past few years. All are due to meet for the first time at a shady club. The other dragons are eventually revealed as Dan Duryea, George Raft and Christopher Lee. They do not appear until over two-thirds of the way into the film. They are first seen arriving in Hong Kong and later seated around a table wearing kimonos and gold dragon masks. Each in turn is required to open a small door in a miniature pagoda in front of them with a special key; if it is the wrong key, he is shot automatically. On opening the door, each one removes his mask. They are not required to say many lines and Duryea does most of the talking, but none of them seemed to have any idea what they were doing there. Donlevy appeared unsure of his cues and looked bemused, which is unsurprising considering the unintelligible plot. Over the years, Raft, Donlevy and Duryea had made major contributions to the art of noir, and Christopher Lee was a horror legend.

Five Golden Dragons was a typical film of its period with familiar ingredients: an international cast in an exotic location, saddled with a weak screenplay that did not hang together. This was the penultimate movie for both Donlevy and Duryea, and it was sad to see fine actors wasted in such a way. Lee observed in an interview, "I was in Hong Kong doing a Fu Manchu film when this opportunity presented itself. Did I want to appear with George Raft, Dan Duryea and Brian Donlevy, three Hollywood legends?" Lee gave an emphatic "Yes!"[13]

Jack Hill's *Pit Stop* (1969), previously known as *The Winner,* was an underrated gem of the era and now a cult favorite. It deserves to be seen more widely and appreciated fully. Latterly released on DVD and Blu-ray,

In Jack Hill's cult racing movie *Pit Stop* (1969), Donlevy had in a key role as a ruthless businessman with Richard Davalos as his protégé. Donlevy brought an unexpected pathos to his role in what turned out to be his final film.

it has recently begun to garner deserved attention. The story concerns a rebellious, thrill-seeking kid, Rick Bowman (Richard Davalos), hired by track owner Grant Willard (Donlevy) to drive his cars on the dangerous figure eight track. It is a crazy way to drive and only the craziest people such as Hawk Sidney (Sid Haig) seem to succeed. Rick spends all his spare time working on a car and eventually beats Sidney in a race, becoming the darling of the circuit. Willard gives him a chance at a big race at Indianapolis, but things go wrong because of Rick's gamesmanship inspired by his determination to win at all costs.

Writer-director Hill has often been cited by Quentin Tarantino as a major influence on him. It is also noteworthy that Tarantino often uses older character actors associated with other genres. *Pit Stop* looks strikingly modern; the moody black-and-white photography undoubtedly adds to the atmosphere. Hill was criticized for not shooting in color but this was a smart move on his part and adds to the movie's timeless quality. The surging music of the Daily Flash is perfect to the time and its subject and is used to great effect throughout. The characters are interesting and plausible and there is a strong although slightly elusive narrative. There is plenty of footage of cars colliding, and the scenes inside the cars and during races are convincingly shot.

The other characters are well-played by Haig and young Ellen Burstyn; the combination of old and new actors made for an interesting dynamic that Tarantino later utilized to good effect. Grant Willard seems friendly, but is a ruthless man who says more than once that he is a businessman. Even so, Rick looks to him as something like a benefactor as though there is a transient bond between them. The stark ending leaves the feeling that Rick has become merely a reflection of Willard. Donlevy plays a rather ruthless individual who has no real feeling for his protégé, but who gives the impression he cares although he really only cares about making money. Even so, the veteran actor imbued his character with a distinct pathos. Although a far cry from the quality of movies of earlier years, this was a decent movie. *Pit Stop* was Donlevy's final role and was far more substantial than any other of his later years. It was a fitting end to an intriguing if very uneven career.

13

Happiness with Lillian

"He was an absolute angel, an absolute doll...."
—Lillian Donlevy recalls her late husband Donlevy
in *The Immortal Count* by Arthur Lennig.

Although his name had been linked with a succession of actresses since his divorce from Marjorie, Donlevy never came close to marriage with any of them. He was then busy on television, and when his successful show *Dangerous Assignment* was up and running, he had much to occupy his time. As both actor and producer of the show, he assembled a small team around him and enjoyed being busy again. His bookkeeper was the sister of Lillian Lugosi (*nee* Arch). Lillian had been married to legendary horror movie actor Bela Lugosi for 20 years. In 1953 she was seeking work of her own, and a life of her own away from her husband. Her sister wanted to leave her job and arranged for Lillian to meet Donlevy and perhaps land a job:

> The star was finishing up the day's shoot, and made a dashing first impression on Lillian. "I thought he looked very handsome," she said. [He] took Lillian and her sister to his dressing room to discuss the job, and the first thing he did was to tear off his toupee. "I was shocked," remarked Lillian, "because I didn't know he wore one."[1]

Although they were already separated, Bela heard that she was working on the show and about her friendship with Donlevy. Unsurprisingly, he became suspicious:

> One day, Bela called the *Dangerous Assignment* office and Brian picked up the phone; Bela wasn't aware whom he was talking to. "I want to speak to Mr. Donlevy," demanded Bela. "That man is destroying my marriage."[2]

In truth, the marriage, which began in 1933, had often been difficult and in 1944 they very nearly divorced. They got back together on that occasion but later separated again. Lillian finally divorced him on the grounds of "cruel and inhumane treatment" in May 1953.[3] Lillian testified to Bela's jealous nature: "He kept me under his thumb 24 hours a day. He'd listen in on an extension phone when I talked to my mother; he checked up on me when I went to the dentist's office. He charged me with infidelity."[4]

Lillian was given custody of their son Bela Jr., then 15, and the impoverished Bela had to pay $50 a month for his son and "token $1 alimony" to his ex. Bela remarried two years later and died in 1956. Lillian paid for his funeral.[5]

Brian and Lillian were constant companions after first meeting in 1953 but did not marry until February 25, 1966. The ceremony was performed by Judge Merrill Brown at his chambers in Indio, California. The couple honeymooned near Lake Tahoe.[6] They had much in common, being both retiring in nature and essentially loners. Both had friends of their own; many of Donlevy's fellow actors were among his best friends, including William Holden, Lloyd Nolan and Fred McMurray. But he was not a gregarious Hollywood partygoer. If he joined any social clubs, they tended to be rather select and low-key. For instance, he was listed as a member of the West Coast Lambs, an offshoot of the Lambs Theater Club of New York.[7] He was also a Mason and a member of the Mount Olive Lodge No. 506 of Los Angeles, referred to as a "Scottish Rite Freemason and Shriner."[8]

One of Donlevy's greatest loves was flying, and he was a charter member of the Aircraft Owners and Pilots Association.[9] He first took flying lessons in 1940 from Herb White, a veteran stunt flyer who worked on many movies. Donlevy's original motivation was to travel to his mining claims without having to charter a plane every time.[10] He owned a four-seater which he flew all over the country. "I can't go too far at any one time without stopping to refuel," he said in a 1960 interview. "I've been in probably every big and little airport in the country in the last 10 or 15 years. Met a lot of friends that way."[11] Donlevy and co-pilot Ed Denault once crashed in a cow pasture at Solvang, California, after a propeller fell off. Neither was hurt.[12]

In addition to his mines, Donlevy often liked to contemplate business ideas, but most of them came to naught. He once considered going into partnership with cowboy star Roy Rogers in a joint investment in a hotel and health camp they hoped to construct near Las Vegas.[13]

During the summer of the year he married Lillian, Donlevy played in one last stage role: the retired sea captain father in Ruth Gordon's touching autobiographical drama *Years Ago*. The play had recently enjoyed a good Broadway run and was well received at the quaint-sounding Avondale Theater-in-the-Meadow at Indianapolis. The story concerned a stage-struck Boston-area girl whose parents want her to become a physical culture instructor, but who is determined to pursue a theatrical career. It was Donlevy's final appearance on stage after 42 years.

After Donlevy retired from movies in 1969, he and Lillian lived a quiet and rather contented life, alternating between their home in Desert Springs and an apartment at Culver City. Lillian was described by one of Lugosi's biographers as "kind, candid, a little shy."[14] She was always helpful to the author and seemed by all accounts to be a calm, down-to-earth and good-humored soul. Bela Jr. had only good memories of his stepfather Brian, whom he described as "a good person, very generous ... he would give you the shirt off his back."[15] It appears that at last Brian found some measure of happiness in his private life.

These later years were overshadowed by a rift between Donlevy and his daughter Judy, the causes of which are not entirely clear. All her life he had doted on her; after his bitter divorce, he once admitted, "I'm afraid I'd have come unglued but for her."[16] He had spent six months of every year with her as far as possible and met up with her in Europe for vacations between film engagements; she visited him often on film sets and accompanied him on summer theater tours. With no wife and only occasional girlfriends, Judy became his consort, his home and almost everything to him. The breach came about when she was older.[17]

By late 1969, Donlevy's voice had become little more than a hoarse whisper, and in April 1970 he was diagnosed with throat cancer. In June 1971, he underwent an operation. He spent over a year recovering in hospital, and was readmitted to the Motion Picture Hospital at Woodlands in the following March 1972. By the end, he could no longer swallow, and "Lillian had to feed him through a hole in his stomach."[18] Brian died on April 5, 1972. A wake was held at Strother's mortuary at 6240 Hollywood Boulevard, the venue for the wake of many other famous stars—including Lugosi.[19] As requested, Donlevy was cremated and his ashes scattered over Santa Monica Bay. According to his widow, "Judy refused to see him while he was in the hospital, didn't attend the funeral nor contact her after her father's death."[20]

Lillian once said of her late husband "We were well-suited for each other, same likes, same dislikes, and we were both loners; we did not need other distractions. I still miss him terribly; he was the love of my life."[21]

Brian left only $8000 when he died. Lillian, in failing health, eventually had to leave the apartment they shared and move to a smaller place where she died October 9, 1981, at age 71.

Epilogue

"There was a lot of good in George...."
—Logan Stuart (Dana Andrews) recalls his friend
George Camrose (Donlevy) in *Canyon Passage* (1946).

Donlevy was a paradox. For most of his life he was presenting an image of himself to the world as an assured personality who inspired confidence in others. On screen he often played sassy, smart-talking larger-than-life tough guys, and was usually the one left nursing his jaw, and his grievances having been socked by the righteous hero. But he always maintained that the man on screen was not him at all. Indeed those who knew him best present him as essentially a shy, generous and gentle person. It was only very occasionally that his real persona was allowed to emerge on screen. Perhaps he hid behind the villains who he played so often. Some only saw the outward appearances, and while working on *Beau Geste* he seemed to be a different person altogether according to director William Wellman. However, Wellman's account was at variance with all the other memories of Donlevy in about 100 films. But few in Hollywood really knew him. For instance a reporter once bewailed him for complaining about his star status:

> "One day I heard Brian Donlevy moaning that public curiosity makes him feel like a goldfish in a bowl—and the next time I saw him he was driving down the boulevard in a block-long [chromium-plated] sports job, wearing dark glasses, an Alpine hat, a green overcoat and a neck scarf that would make a tropical sunset look colorless."[1]

Others' recollections are tempered with humanity. "Pepper" Paire Davis became one of the most famous female baseball players. During the 1940s she worked at a service station near Brentwood and met several Hollywood stars of the era. She had fond memories of him:

> "Donlevy would come rolling in driving a bright, canary yellow Cadillac convertible. It had steer horns on the hood and one of those musical horns.... It played "Merrily We Roll Along," while I was servicing his car. He always gave

me a big smile! He wore a great, big white Stetson hat. When I was done and he was ready to "merrily roll along" he would say "Thanks, Honey," and flip me a brand new silver dollar! That was a lot of money in those days. So I smiled pretty in those purple overalls."[2]

Robert Wagner remembered as a fourteen-year-old he used to polish the private planes of movie stars, among them Donlevy who once tipped him $5 and told him to go and buy himself a book on acting. Wagner was rich, so hardly needed the money. He did buy a book on acting and also kept the $5 bill which he always considered lucky, and indubitably the advice was lucky.[3]

Sometimes it is impossible to get past what one perceptive commentator aptly called Donlevy's "fierce diffidence."[4] He seemed to inherit the reserve of his father and the romanticism of his mother. Although he never achieved his childhood ambition to be a writer he had some poems published in his teens and eventually published a volume of poetry, *Leaves in the Wind* under the pen name of Porter Down.[5]

The received wisdom is that Donlevy's career was largely a failure. But if failure includes an Academy Award nomination for *Beau Geste*, admiration from the New York critics and the Soviet government for *Wake Island,* acclamation for many of his films, a successful theater, television and radio career, and a hit tv series, then perhaps failure is not so bad after all. Few actors before or since quite had his ability to make villains likeable. He had besides a sure gift for satire and a surprising range.

Donlevy cared about his acting and always tried to give his best. From his earliest days he kept a scrapbook of all his notices, good and bad. He was never complacent and took all the many criticisms on board: "I know that it is impossible to please everyone," he once said, "but I think it is good mental discipline to be reminded of the fact."[6] While rehearsing at home he wore the carpet out pacing up and down until he felt he had mastered a role to his satisfaction. He recorded himself reciting his lines over and over until he was certain he was word-perfect.[7]

In retrospect the war years at Paramount were Donlevy's most successful. After *The Great McGinty* he was elevated to leading roles and enjoyed two or three years when everything seemed to be going his way and almost anything was possible. He was riding high around the time of the release of *Wake Island* and a magazine featured a short resume about him which in a few words attempted to encapsulate the elusive Donlevy: "He has gray-green eyes, straight brown hair, and a great, generous heart."[8] This seems a fitting epitaph for a much undervalued actor who contributed to the tapestry of his era in his own unique way.

Appendices

FILMOGRAPHY

Jamestown. Chronicles of America #2. Short. Chronicles of America Productions, 1923 Director: Edwin L. Hollywood. Donlevy, uncredited, played an minor role.

Damaged Hearts. Pilgrim Pictures, 1924. Director: T. Hayes Hunter. Donlevy played Jim Porter

Monsieur Beaucaire. Paramount, 1924. Director: Sidney Olcott. Donlevy, uncredited, played a bath guest at a ball. (DVD)

The Eve of Revolution. Chronicles of America #15. Short. Chronicles of America Productions, 1924. Director: Kenneth Wells. Donlevy played Paul Revere.

School for Wives. Victor Halperin Productions, 1925. Director: Victor Halperin. Donlevy played Ralph.

A Man of Quality. Excellent Pictures, 1926. Director: Wesley Ruggles. Donlevy played Richard Courtney.

Striving for Fortune. Excellent Pictures, 1926. Director: Nat Ross. Donlevy was uncredited.

His Rise to Fame. Excellent Pictures, 1927. Director: Bernard McEveety. Donlevy was uncredited.

Gentlemen of the Press. Pathe Exchange, 1929. Director: Millard Wells. Donlevy played Kelly, a reporter.

Mother's Boy. Pathe Exchange, 1929. Director: Bradley Parker. Donlevy played Harry O'Day.

Ireno. Short. Paramount, 1932. Director: Aubrey Scott. Donlevy played a drunk.

A Modern Cinderella. Short. Warner Brothers, 1933. Director: Roy Mack. Donlevy played Charlie. (DVD)

Barbary Coast. Samuel Goldwyn, 1935. Directors: Howard Hawks, William Wyler. Donlevy played Knuckles Jacoby. (DVD)

Mary Burns, Fugitive. Paramount, 1935. Director: William K. Howard. Donlevy played Spike.

Another Face. RKO, 1935. Director: Christy Cabanne. Donlevy played "Broken Nose" Dawson/Spencer Dutro III.

Strike Me Pink. Samuel Goldwyn, 1936. Director: Norman Taurog. Donlevy played Vance.

Thirteen Hours By Air. Paramount, 1936. Director: Mitchell Leisen. Donlevy played Dr. James L. Evarts.

Human Cargo. 20th Century-Fox, 1936. Director: Allan Dwan. Donlevy played "Packy" Campbell.

Half Angel. 20th Century-Fox, 1936. Director: Sidney Lanfield. Donlevy played Duffy Giles.

High Tension. 20th Century-Fox, 1936. Director: Allan Dwan. Donlevy played Steve Reardon.

36 Hours to Kill. 20th Century-Fox, 1936. Director: Eugene Forde. Donlevy played Frank Evers. (DVD)

Crack-Up. 20th Century-Fox, 1936. Director: Malcolm St. Clair. Donlevy played Ace Martin. (DVD)

Midnight Taxi. 20th Century-Fox, 1936. Director: Eugene Forde. Donlevy played Charles "Chick" Gardner.

This is My Affair. 20th Century-Fox, 1937. Director: William A. Seiter. Donlevy played Batiste Duryea. (DVD)

Born Reckless. 20th Century-Fox, 1937. Directors: Malcolm St. Clair, Gustav Machaty. Donlevy played Bo "Hurry" Kane.

In Old Chicago. 20th Century-Fox, 1937. Director: Henry King. Donlevy played Gil Warren. (DVD)

Battle of Broadway. 20th Century-Fox, 1938. Director: George Marshall. Donlevy played Chesty Webb. (DVD)

We're Going to be Rich. 20th Century-Fox, 1938. Director: Monty Banks. Donlevy played Yanky Gordon.

Sharpshooters. 20th Century-Fox, 1938. Director: James Tinling. Donlevy played Steve Mitchell.

Jesse James. 20th Century-Fox, 1939. Director: Henry King. Donlevy played Barshee. (DVD)

Union Pacific. Paramount, 1939. Director: Cecil B. DeMille. Donlevy played Sid Campeau. (DVD)

Beau Geste. Paramount, 1939. Director: William Wellman. Donlevy played Sgt. Markoff. (DVD)

Behind Prison Gates. Columbia, 1939. Director: Charles Barton. Donlevy played Agent Norman Craig/Red Murray.

Allegheny Uprising. RKO, 1939. Director: William A. Seiter. Donlevy played Callendar. (DVD)

Destry Rides Again. Universal, 1939. Director: George Marshall. Donlevy played Kent. (DVD)

When the Daltons Rode. Universal, 1940. Director: George Marshall. Donlevy played Grat Dalton. (DVD)

The Great McGinty. Paramount, 1940. Director: Preston Sturges. Donlevy played Dan McGinty. (DVD)

Brigham Young—Frontiersman. 20th Century-Fox, 1940. Director: Henry Hathaway. Donlevy played Angus Duncan. (DVD)

I Wanted Wings. Paramount, 1941. Director: Mitchell Leisen. Donlevy played Capt. Mercer.

Billy the Kid. MGM, 1941. Directors: David Miller, Frank Borzage. Donlevy played Jim Sherwood. (DVD)

Hold Back the Dawn. Paramount, 1941. Director: Mitchell Leisen. Donlevy, uncredited, played an actor performing in a scene from *I Wanted Wings.*

South of Tahiti. Universal, 1941. Director: George Waggner. Donlevy played Bob.

Birth of the Blues. Paramount, 1941. Director: Victor Shertzinger. Donlevy played Memphis. (DVD)

The Great Man's Lady. Paramount, 1942. Director: William A. Wellman. Donlevy played "Steely" Edwards. (DVD)

The Remarkable Andrew. Paramount, 1942. Director: Stuart Heisler. Donlevy played Gen. Andrew Jackson.

Two Yanks in Trinidad. Columbia, 1942. Director: Gregory Ratoff. Donlevy played Vince Barrows.

A Gentleman After Dark. Edward Small Productions/United Artists, 1942. Director: Edwin L. Maron. Donlevy played "Heliotrope" Harry Melton.

Wake Island. Paramount, 1942. Director: John Farrow. Donlevy played Major Geoffrey Caton. (DVD)

War Bond Appeal. 1942. Short. Patriotic Appeal for War Bond Drive. Donlevy was the spokesman.

The Glass Key. Paramount, 1942. Director: Stuart Heisler. Donlevy played Paul Madvig. (DVD)

Nightmare. Universal, 1942. Director: Tim Whelan. Donlevy played Daniel Shane.

Stand By for Action. MGM, 1942. Director: Robert Z. Leonard. Donlevy played Lt. Comdr. Martin J. Roberts. (DVD)

Stalingrad aka *The City That Stopped Hitler: Heroic Stalingrad.* Tsentralnaya Studio Dokumentalnikh Filmov (Central Studio for Documentary Film), 1943. Director: Leonid Vermalov. Donlevy narrated.

Hangmen Also Die! Arnold Pressburger Films/United Artists, 1943. Director: Fritz Lang. Donlevy played Dr. Franticek Svoboda/Karel Vanek. (DVD)

Our Enemies Speak. John C. Flinn/Tom Baily, 1944. Short. Director: Bill Russell. Donlevy was a spokesman.

The Miracle of Morgan's Creek. Paramount, 1944. Director: Preston Sturges. Donlevy played Governor McGinty. (DVD)

The Four Freedoms Show. 1944. Newsreel. Personal appearances by the stars at Portland, Oregon, celebrating the sale of 32,000,000 War Bonds. Donlevy played a guest.

An American Romance. MGM, 1944. Director: King Vidor. Donlevy played Stefan Dubechek aka Steve Dangos. (DVD)

Duffy's Tavern. Paramount, 1945. Director: Hal Walker. Donlevy played himself.

Two Years Before the Mast. Paramount, 1946. Director: John Farrow. Donlevy played Richard Henry Dana. (DVD)

The Virginian. Paramount, 1946. Director: Stuart Gilmore. Donlevy played Trampas. (DVD)

Our Hearts Were Growing Up. Paramount, 1946. Director: William D. Russell. Donlevy played Tony Minetti.

Canyon Passage. Universal, 1946. Director: Jacques Tourneur. Donlevy played George Camrose. (DVD)

The Beginning or the End. MGM, 1947. Director: Norman Taurog. Donlevy played Major Gen. Leslie R. Groves.

Song of Scheherazade. Universal, 1947. Director: Walter Reisch. Donlevy played Capt. Vladimir Gregorovitch. (DVD)

The Trouble with Women. Paramount, 1947. Director: Sidney Lanfield. Donlevy played Joe McBride.

Unusual Occupations. Paramount, 1947. Short. Director: Robert Carlisle. Donlevy played himself.

Kiss of Death. 20th Century-Fox, 1947. Director: Henry Hathaway. Donlevy played Assistant District Attorney Louis D'Angelo. (DVD)

Heaven Only Knows. Nero Films, 1947. Director: Albert S. Rogell. Donlevy played Adam "Duke" Byron. (DVD)

Killer McCoy. MGM,1947. Director: Roy Rowland. Donlevy played Jim Caighn. (DVD)

A Southern Yankee. MGM, 1948. Director: Edward Sedgwick. Donlevy played Kurt Devlynn.

Command Decision. MGM, 1948. Director: Sam Wood. Donlevy played Brigadier Gen. Clifton I. Garnet. (DVD)

The Lucky Stiff. Amusement Enterprises, 1949. Director: Lewis R. Foster. Donlevy played John J. Malone.

Impact. Cardinal Pictures, 1949. Director: Arthur Lubin. Donlevy played Walter Williams. (DVD)

Shakedown. Universal, 1950. Director: Joseph Pevney. Donlevy played Nick Palmer.

Kansas Raiders. Universal, 1950. Director: Ray Enright. Donlevy played Col. William Clark Quantrill. (DVD)

Fighting Coast Guard. Republic, 1951. Director: Joseph Kane. Donlevy played Comdr. McFarland.

Slaughter Trail. RKO, 1951. Director: Irving Allen. Donlevy played Capt. Dempster. (DVD).

Hoodlum Empire. Republic, 1952. Director: Joseph Kane. Donlevy played Senator Bill Stevens. (DVD)

Ride the Man Down. Republic, 1952. Director: Joseph Kane. Donlevy played Bide Marriner.

Woman They Almost Lynched. Republic, 1953. Director: Allan Dwan. Donlevy played Col. Charles Quantrill. (DVD)

The Big Combo. Security Pictures/Theodora Productions, 1955. Director: Joseph H. Lewis. Donlevy played Joe McClure. (DVD)

The Creeping Unknown aka The Quatermass Xperiment. Hammer Films, 1955. Director: Val Guest. Donlevy played Prof. Bernard Quatermass. (DVD)

A Cry in the Night. Ladd Enterprises/Jaguar Productions, 1956. Director: Frank Tuttle. Donlevy played Capt. Ed Bates.

Enemy from Space aka *Quatermass 2.* Hammer Films, 1957. Director: Val Guest. Donlevy played Prof. Bernard Quatermass. (DVD)

Escape from Red Rock. Regal Films, 1957. Director: Edward Bernds. Donlevy played Bronc Grierson.

Cowboy. Columbia, 1958. Director: Delmer Daves. Donlevy played Doc Bender. (DVD)

Juke Box Rhythm. Clover Productions, 1959. Director: Arthur Dreifuss. Donlevy played George Manton.

Never So Few. MGM/Canterbury Productions, 1959. Director: John Sturges. Donlevy played Gen. Sloan. (DVD)

Girl in Room 13. Cinidistri/Sino Filmes/Layton Film Productions, 1960. Director: Richard E. Cunha. Donlevy played Steve Marshall.

The Errand Boy. Jerry Lewis Productions, 1961. Director: Jerry Lewis. Donlevy played Tom "T.P." Paramutual. (DVD)

The Pigeon that Took Rome. Lenoc Productions/Paramount, 1962. Director: Melville Shavelson. Donlevy played Col. Sherman Harrington.

Curse of the Fly. 20th Century-Fox, 1965. Director: Don Sharp. Donlevy played Henri Delambre. (DVD)

How to Stuff a Wild Bikini. American International, 1965. Director: William Asher. Donlevy played B.D. "Big Deal" Macpherson. (DVD)

Waco. A.C. Lyles Productions, 1966. Director: R.G. Springsteen. Donlevy played "Ace" Ross. (DVD)

The Fat Spy. Phillip Productions, 1966. Director: Joseph Cates. Donlevy played George Wellington. (DVD)

Gammera the Invincible. Daiei Film Company, 1966. Director: Noriaki Yuasa. Donlevy played Gen. Terry Arnold. (DVD)

Hostile Guns. A.C. Lyles Productions, 1967. Director: R.G. Springsteen. Donlevy played Marshal Willett.

Five Golden Dragons. Blansfilm/Constantin Film Production/Sargon, 1967. Director: Jeremy Summers. Donlevy played Dragon #2. (DVD)

Arizona Bushwhackers. A.C. Lyles Productions, 1968. Director: Leslie Selander. Donlevy played Mayor Smith.

Pit Stop. Jack Hill Productions, 1969. Director: Jack Hill. Donlevy played Grant Willard. (DVD)

Rogue's Gallery. A.C. Lyles Productions, 1973. Director: Leonard Horn. Donlevy played Detective Lee.

THEATER

What Price Glory? War drama by Maxwell Anderson and Laurence Stallings. Plymouth Theater, New York (September 3, 1924, to September 12, 1925), and tour (September 30, 1925, to July 1926). Donlevy played Corporal Gowdy.

Hit the Deck. Musical comedy. Belasco Theater, New York (April 1927 to February 25, 1928). Donlevy played Donkey.

The High Hatters. Farce by Louis Sobol. Klaw Theater, New York (May 1928).

Ringside. Drama by Edward E. Paramore, Jr., Hyatt Daab and George Abbott. Broadhurst Theater, New York (August 29 to October 5, 1928). Donlevy played Huffy.

Rainbow. Musical drama. Gallo Opera House, New York (November 21 to December 15, 1928). Donlevy played Capt. Robert Singleton.

Queen Bee. Comedy by Louise Fox Connell and Ruth Hawthorne. Belmont Theater, New York (November 12 to 25, 1929). Donlevy played John Talbot.

Up Pops the Devil. Comedy by Albert Hacker and Frances Goodrich. Theater Masque, New York (September 1, 1930, to January 1931). Donlevy played George Kent.

Peter Flies High. Comedy by Myron C. Fagan. Gaiety Theater, New York (November 9 to 15, 1931). Donlevy played Bill Curdy.

Society Girl. Comedy by John Larkin, Jr. Booth Theater, New York (December 30, 1931, to January 1932). Donlevy played Briscoe.

The Inside Story. Drama by George Bryant and Francis Vedri. National Theater, New York (February 22 to March 5, 1932). Donlevy played Nick Lipman.

The Boy Friend. Comedy by John Montague. Morosco Theater, New York (June 7 to 14, 1932). Donlevy played the Eel.

Honeymoon. Comedy. Vanderbilt Theater, New York (January 17 to February 25, 1933). Donlevy played Bob Taylor.

Three-Cornered Moon. Comedy by Gertrude Tonkonogy. Cort Theater, New York (March 16 to May 1933). Donlevy played Dr. Alan Stevens.

Another Man's Son. Drama by Len D. Hollister. Peterborough Dramatic Festival, Providence, Rhode Island (July 27 to August 4, 1933). Donlevy played Jim Mason.

Talent. Comedy drama by Rachel Crothers. Cape Playhouse, Dennis, Massachusetts (September 4 to 12, 1933). Donlevy played the lead role.[1]

Three and One. Comedy by Denys Amiel, adapted from the French by Lewis Galantiere and John Houseman. Longacre Theater, New York (October 25 to December 30, 1933). Donlevy played Charles Valois.

No Questions Asked. Comedy by Anne Morrison Chapin. Theater Masque, New York (February 5 to 12, 1934). Donlevy played Ernie Dulaney.

The Perfumed Lady. Comedy by Harry Wagstaff Gribble. Ambassador Theater, New York (March 12 to April 14, 1934). Donlevy played Warren Pasquale.

The Milky Way. Comedy by Lynn Root and Harry Clork. Cort Theater, New York (May 8 to July 1, 1934). Donlevy played Speed McFarland.

Life Begins at 8:40. Musical comedy revue. Winter Garden Theater, New York (August 27, 1934, to March 16, 1935). Five sketches: "The Radio Announcer's Bride" (Donlevy played the Radio Announcer), "The Samaritan" (Donlevy played the Barker), "She Loves Me" (Donlevy played the Intruder), "Quartet Erotica" (Donlevy played De Maupassant) and "A Day at the Brokers" (Donlevy played the Broker).

The Man in the Bowler Hat. Drama by A.A. Milne. Malibu Little Theater, tennis court, Malibu Beach Colony, California (August 1946). Donlevy may have played the chief villain.

What Price Glory? War drama. Music Hall, Detroit (October 6 to 25, 1947). Donlevy played Capt. Flagg.

Joan of Lorraine. Drama by Maxwell Anderson. Music Hall, Detroit (October 26 to November 9, 1947). Donlevy played the Inquisitor.

Dear Brutus. Drama by J.M. Barrie. Tour (July to September 1950). Donlevy played Lob.

King of Hearts. Drama by Matthew Boulton. Myrtle Beach, South Carolina (circa 1953). Donlevy played Bill Saunders.

The Country Girl. Drama by Clifford Odets. Tour (July to September 1954), including Norwich Theater, Connecticut, with Genevieve Griffin (July 12 to 20, 1954); Olney, Maryland, with Jean Peters (July 28 to August 10, 1954); Somerset, Massachusetts (August 13 to 20, 1954); Salt Creek Theater, Chicago, with Maria Riva; Connecticut, with Armina Marshal (August 30 to September 5, 1954). Donlevy played Frank Elgin.

No Time for Sergeants. Comedy by Ira Levin. May 26 to June 8, 1958. Oakdale Musical Theater, Wallingford, Connecticut (June 23 to June 30, 1958), Shubert Theater, Cincinnati. Donlevy played Sgt. King.

The Andersonville Trial. Drama by Saul Levitt. National Tour, September 1960 to June 1961. Dates included: Appleton High School, Appleton, Wisconsin, National Theater, Washington (December 26, 1960, to January 1961), Auditorium Theater, Rochester, New York (January 19 to 21, 1961), Bushnell Stage, Hartford, Connecticut (January 27 to 28, 1961). Donlevy played Otis H. Baker, the Defense Counsel.

Years Ago. Drama by Ruth Gordon. Avondale Theater-in-the-Meadows, Indianapolis, Indiana (July 26 to 31, 1966).

RADIO

Eno's Crime Club. CBS/NBC crime series with Clyde North, Edward Reese, Walter Glass, Ray Collins and Helene Dumas. February 9, 1931, to June 30, 1936. Donlevy played Various roles.

Hillbilly Heart Throbs. NBC musical drama anthology series based on folk songs with Agnes Moorehead, Ray Collins, Carson Robison, Frank Luther and the Vass family. May 2, 1933, to October 27, 1938. Donlevy played various roles.[1]

The Court of Human Relations. NBC, CBS and Mutual dramatized human interest stories with Percy

Hemus, Lucille Wall, Florence Baker, Van Heflin, Janet Lee and Rita Vale. January 1, 1934, to January 1, 1938. Donlevy played various roles.[2]

The Perfumed Lady. Extract from a Broadway play with June Martel, a benefit for the Stage Relief Fund broadcast on WOR/NBC, on March 16, 1934. Donlevy played Warren Pasquale.

Our Neighbors. NBC Interviews broadcast from Hollywood. With Jerry Belcher (host), Jimmie Fidler, Andy Devine and Jane Withers. July 25, 1937. Donlevy was a guest.

Hollywood Hotel. CBS drama series. "In Old Chicago," scenes with Alice Faye, Tyrone Power, Alice Brady. January 21, 1938. Donlevy played Gil Warren.

Lux Radio Theater. CBS drama series. "Jezebel" with Loretta Young, Jeffrey Lynn, Cecil B. DeMille. November 25, 1940. Donlevy played Preston Dillard. "They Drive by Night" with George Raft, Rita Hayworth. June 2, 1941. Donlevy played Paul Fabrini. "Wake Island" with Henry Fonda, Robert Preston, Broderick Crawford. October 26, 1942. Donlevy played Major Caton.

The Gulf Theater. CBS drama. "Torrid Zone" with James Cagney, Joan Bennett. December 8, 1940. Donlevy played Steve Case.

These Are Your Brothers. CBS Christmas drama by Arch Oboler, with Benny Rubin, December 26, 1940. Donlevy played a man dressed as Santa.

Bundles for Britain. NBC celebrity charity appeal, with Judy Garland, Mickey Rooney, Claudette Colbert, Charles Boyer, the Merry Macs, Jack Benny, James Cagney *et al.* January 1, 1941. Donlevy was a guest.

Bing Crosby's Music Hall. NBC music and variety show. February and

November 4 1941. Donlevy was a repeat guest.

Lincoln Highway Radio Show. NBC drama series. "Gambler's Wife," June 28, 1941. Donlevy played a lead role.[3]

Thousand and One Nights. CBS variety show, with Marlene Dietrich *et al.* "Two Gobs and a Gal" farce with Andy Devine, Lucille Ball, July 14, 1941. Donlevy was a guest.

Thanksgiving Day—1941 by Steven Vincent Benet. NBC Broadcast essay, November 19, 1941. Donlevy was a reader.[4]

Navy Relief Program. Mutual war charity broadcast, "Navy skit," with Walter Huston, January 7, 1942. Donlevy was a guest.

Philip Morris Playhouse. CBS drama. "The Great McGinty." January 23, 1942. Donlevy played Daniel McGinty.

Keep 'Em Rolling. Mutual patriotic broadcast with songs and dramatic interludes. "Joe Smith, American" by Paul Gallico. January 25, 1942. Donlevy played Joe Smith.

Vox Pop. CBS variety show. "Hollywood at War" Discussion of the theme of Hollywood at war, with Joan Bennett, Franchot Tone, Gregory Ratoff, Joe E. Brown and Claire Trevor. January 26, 1942. Donlevy was a guest. Live from Camp Elliott Marine Base, San Diego, for the premiere of *Wake Island*, August 25, 1942. Donlevy was an interviewer and co-host.

The Kate Smith Hour. NBC variety show. January 30, 1942. Donlevy was a guest.

Flyers Don't Die by Robert Presnell. ABC drama. January 31, 1942. Donlevy played a pilot.

Three Sheets to the Wind by Ken England. NBC adventure serial in 26

episodes, with John Wayne, Mary Anderson, Knox Manning, Helga Moray, Frank Worlock. February 15 to July 5, 1942. Donlevy played a leading role.[5]

Crime Doctor. CBS crime drama series, with Walter Greaza, Jeannette Nolan and Edith Arnold. November 8, 1942, to January 1943. Donlevy played Dr. Benjamin Ordway.[6]

Lady Esther Screen Guild. CBS drama series. "Stand By for Action" with Charles Laughton, Chester Morris, March 8, 1943. Donlevy played Lt. Comdr. Martin J. Roberts. "A Night to Remember" with Herbert Marshall (host), Lucille Ball, May 1, 1944. Donlevy played Jeff Troy. "Love Before Breakfast" with Virginia Bruce, David Bruce, January 22, 1945. "The Great McGinty" with Akim Tamiroff, Ruth Hussey, August 27, 1945. Donlevy played Daniel McGinty. "A Night to Remember" with Claire Trevor, April 8, 1946. Donlevy played Jeff Troy.

Philip Morris Audition Show. NBC variety show with Alvino Rey and the King Sisters. March 24, 1943. Donlevy was an emcee.[7]

Memorial Day Broadcast. NBC patriotic broadcast. May 29, 1943. Donlevy was a reader. "Letter from His Commanding Officer" by John Farrow.

The Cavalcade of America. NBC drama. "Double Play" by Jacland Marmar. Two brothers in love with the same girl use a double play scheme to sink a Japanese ship. With Kent Smith, Hal Gerard, Gayne Whitman. Steve Yancey. September 6, 1943. "Navy Doctor," war saga of the U.S.S. *Astoria*, with Will Geer, Paul Stewart. December 6, 1943. Donlevy played Dr. Charles Flower. "Odyssey to Freedom" by Isabel Leighton, story of a Navy hero who had previously escaped from Nazi camps. March 6, 1944. Donlevy played Edward Kowalski. "My Fighting Congregation," the story of a courageous army chaplain with Wally Maher. June 12, 1944. Don-

levy played William Taggart. "The Conquest of Pain" by Morton Wishengrad, the history of surgical anesthetic. December 11, 1944. Donlevy narrated. "Doctor in Crinoline," the story of a pioneering woman doctor, Elizabeth Blackwell, with Walter Huston, Loretta Young, Gayne Whitman, Robert Armbruster. December 18, 1944. Donlevy played a doctor. "The Case of the Tremendous Trifle" by Bernard Feins, the story of the American petroleum industry. March 4, 1946. Donlevy played Edwin L. Drake. "The Old Fall River Line," the story of a steamship company. September 23, 1946. Donlevy played Capt. Dan Hamilton. "Big Boy" by Brice Disque Jr., the biography of baseball star Babe Ruth, with Alan Reed, Howard McNear. September 29, 1947. Donlevy played Herman "Babe" Ruth. "Joe Palmer's Beard," the story of a man of principle in Massachusetts. September 13, 1949. Donlevy played Joe Palmer. "Greeley of the Tribune," the story of Daniel Webster and the free press, with Chester Stratton. February 6, 1951. Donlevy played Horace Greeley.

The Burns & Allen Show. CBS comedy variety show. January 19, 1943. Donlevy was a guest. Skit "The Sin of Madeline Fudnick," September 14, 1943. Donlevy was a guest.

The Philco Radio Hall of Fame. Blue Network variety show with Bob Burns, Walter O'Keefe, the Xavier Cugat Orchestra, Lina Romay. December 19, 1943. Donlevy was a guest.

Front Line Theater. AFRS Request plays and music show, "The Good Old Days." Circa 1943. Donlevy played Steve Brody. "Suez Road," with Ann Sothern. May 8, 1944. Donlevy was a guest star.

The Silver Theatre. CBS drama. "Steve Brodie." March 19, 1944. Donlevy played Steve Brodie. "Suez Road" with Ann Sothern. June 25, 1944. Donlevy was a guest star. "Backfire." July 14, 1946. Donlevy played Bob Corey.

Yarns for Yanks. AFRS human interest stories and plays. Broadcast circa 1944. "The Lemon Drop Kid." Donlevy played Sidney Milburn. "Broadway Financier." Donlevy played the lead role. "A Very Honorable Guy." Donlevy played "Feet" Samuels.

The Hottest Guy in the World by Damon Runyon. AFRS syndicated drama broadcast to American troops. Circa 1944. Donlevy narrated.

Suspense. CBS mystery drama series. "The Black Path of Fear" by Cornell Woolrich, with Hans Conreid, John McIntire. August 31, 1944. Donlevy played Bill Scott. "Lazarus Walks" by J.M. Speed, with Hans Conreid, Cathy Lewis. October 31, 1946. Donlevy played Dr. Graham. "Out of Control" by Baynard Kendrick, with Wally Maher, Cathy Lewis. March 28, 1946. Donlevy played Duncan Maclaine.

University of the Air: We Came This Way. NBC series about the Greek War Relief Association. "The Story of Andreas" by Morton Wishengrad, with Katina Paxinou, Dana Andrews, Skip Homeier. October 27, 1944. Donlevy played a partisan.

The American Romance Caravan. WLW-MGM syndicated promotional broadcast for the *An American Romance* tour. Hosted by Bill McClusky, with Walter Abel, Nancy Walker, Jean Porter. October 21, 1944. Donlevy was a guest.

Screen Guild Theater. "Love Before Breakfast" with Virginia Bruce, David Bruce. January 22, 1945. Donlevy played Scott Miller.

The Adventures of Jungle Jim. Syndicated serial. December 15, 1945.

Academy Award Theater. CBS drama. "The Great McGinty." April 20, 1946. Donlevy played Daniel McGinty.

Theater of Romance. CBS mystery drama. "Shadow of a Doubt." April 30, 1946. Donlevy played Uncle Charlie.

Hollywood Star Time. CBS mystery drama. "Hot Spot" with Vincent Price, Lurene Tuttle. July 27, 1946. Donlevy played Frankie Christopher.

The Radio Reader's Digest. CBS Drama. "The Story of Hans Pieterson." September 26, 1946. Donlevy played Hans Pieterson.

The Eddy Duchin Show. NBC variety show. April 24, 1947. Donlevy was a guest.

Claudia. "The Great Dane Debate," syndicated advertisement, with Kathryn Bard, Paul Crabtree. November 30, 1948. Donlevy was a guest.

The New National Guard Show. Syndicated recruiting series. "Turnabout," circa 1948. Donlevy played Ernest Haynes.

Sealtest Variety Theater. NBC variety show, with Dorothy Lamour. February 24, 1949. Donlevy was a guest.

The Camel Screen Guild Theater. NBC drama. "Command Decision" with Clark Gable, John Hodiak, Van Johnson, Edward Arnold. March 3, 1949. Donlevy played Brigadier Gen. Clifton I. Garnett.

Dangerous Assignment. NBC crime drama series. With William Conrad, Herb Butterfield, Alice Backes, Leon Belasco, Raymond Burr. July 9, 1949, to July 1, 1953. Donlevy played Steve Mitchell. The following is a partial list of episodes: "Relief Supplies," July 9, 1949. "Sunken Ships," July 16, 1949. "Nigerian Safari," July 23, 1949. "The Millionaire Murders," August 6, 1949. "Alien Smuggling," August 13, 1949. "File 307," August 20, 1949. "Captain Rock," February 13, 1950. "The Greek Connection," February 20, 1950. "International Blackmail," March 20, 1950. "The Sheik's Secret," March 27, 1950. "Pirate Loot," April 10, 1950. "Flying Saucers Over Santa Rosa," April 17, 1950. "The Nazi and the Physicist,"

April 24, 1950. "Sabotage in Paris," May 3, 1950. "The Professor Is a Spy," May 10, 1950. "The Lost City," May 17, 1950. "Burmese Witness," May 24, 1950. "Little White Pill," May 31, 1950. "Deadly Bacteria," June 7, 1950. "Lefty and Sam," June 21, 1950. "Five Gardenias," July 26, 1950. "Vienna Mystery," August 2, 1950. "Death Drums," August 9, 1950. "Hired Killer," August 16, 1950. "Bombay Gun Runners," August 23, 1950. "Guided Missile Plans," August 30, 1950. "Assignment Mine Disaster," September 6, 1950. "Trained Seal," September 20, 1950. "Latin America," September 27, 1950. "Smash Forged Identification Papers Ring," September 29, 1950. "Tokyo," October 10, 1950. "Dangling from the Wrong End of a Rope," November 18, 1950. "The Football Play," November 25, 1950. "The Empty Matchbook," December 2, 1950. "Berlin Kidnapping," December 9, 1950. "Assignment Richmond," December 16, 1950. "Assignment Eastern Europe." December 30, 1950. "Anti-Sub Plans," January 6, 1951. "Missing Scientist," January 13, 1951. "Mighty Power Puff," January 20, 1951. "A Box of Busted Bells," January 27, 1951. "Nazi Fugitive," February 3, 1951. "The Kroner Cutlass," February 10, 1951. "Malaya," February 17, 1951. "The Bronx and the Buzz Bomb," February 23, 1951. "London and the Secret Code," March 3, 1951. "Assignment South America," March 10, 1951. "The Canal Zone and a Piece of String," March 24, 1951. "The Balkans File," April 7, 1951. "The Middle East," April 14, 1951. "Pen Mightier Than the Sword," April 21, 1951. "Assignment: The Balkans," April 28, 1951. "Find Rudolph Karpel," May 4, 1951. "Needle in a Haystack," May 11, 1951. "Operation Hot Foot Microbes," May 18, 1951. "Assignment Japan," June 16, 1951. "South American Democracy," July 3, 1951. "Assignment Ghost Hunters," March 10, 1952. "Assignment Turkey," November 12, 1952. "Assignment Mexico," January 28, 1953.

Brian Donlevy. KPMC (Bakersfield, CA), variety show, January 2, 1950. Donlevy was the host.

Night Beat. NBC mystery series. April 9, 1950. Guest Donlevy talked about *Dangerous Assignment.*

Skippy Hollywood Theater. CBS drama. "Seven Seas to Danger," April 13, 1950.

Boomer Jones. Mutual Labor Day broadcast for the International Association of Machinists. "Unfinished Business," by Morton Wishengrad, with William Holden, Marie McDonald. September 4, 1950. Director: Mel Ferrer.

MGM Theater of the Air. WMGM syndicated drama. "Thunder Afloat," October 27, 1950. Donlevy played Pop Thorson.

Bob Considine. NBC News & Interviews. April 21, 1951. Donlevy was a guest.

Hollywood Calling. Syndicated interviews with the stars, hosted by George Fisher, with Vincent Price, Helen Walker, circa 1951. Donlevy was a guest.

Franz Lehar Festival: American Cancer Society. Syndicated public service broadcast sponsored by the American Cancer Society. One-minute charity appeals by Donlevy, Vivien Leigh, Laurence Olivier, Sophie Tucker, Herman Wouk, Dana Andrews, Mimi Benzell, Shirley Booth, Dick Powell, Jersey Joe Walcott, Brian Aherne, Fred MacMurray, Jane Wyman. September 1953.

Guest Star. Syndicated Treasury Department program. "Pick Up" with Barbara Luddy, Lawrence Dobkin. April 25, 1954. Donlevy was a guest.

TELEVISION

The Texaco Star Theater. NBC music variety show. "The Milton Berle

Show" with Max "Slapsie" Rosenbloom, the Lange Troupe Acrobats, Ken Shapiro. June 7, 1949. Donlevy was a guest.

The Chevrolet Tele-Theater. NBC drama. "Weather Ahead" by Ernest Kinoy. June 13, 1949. Donlevy played a captain.

Pulitzer Prize Playhouse. ABC drama. "The Pharmacist's Mate" by Budd Schulberg, based on a George Weller story, with Gene Raymond, John Baer, Richard Bartlett, George Conrad, Darryl Hickman and Alan Hale, Jr. December 22, 1950. Donlevy played Lt. Comdr. Miller.

Dangerous Assignment. NBC mystery crime series. Circa January 6 to October 1952, with Herbert Butterfield as the Commissioner. Donlevy played Steve Mitchell. "The Alien Smuggler Story" with Jane Adams, Paul Marion, Ralph Moody, 1952. "The Submarine Story" with Robert Easton, Paul Dubov, Dayton Lummis, 1952. "Displaced Persons Story" with Henry Rowland, Pamela Duncan, 1952. "The Memory Chain" with Jeanne Bates, 1952. "The Manger Story" with Maria Palmer, Hugh Beaumont, Gavin Muir, 1952. "The Key Story" with Suzanne Dalbert, Stanley Waxman, Hans Herbert, 1952, "The Bhandra Story" with Neyle Morrow, Leonard Strong, Shep Menken, 1952. "The Salami Story" with Elena Verdugo, Laura Mason, Dan Seymour, 1952. "The Mine Story" with Fritz Feld, Joseph Mell, 1952. "The Italian Movie Story" with Jorja Cartwright, Fritz Feld, 1952. "The Blood-Stained Feather Story" with Bruce Lester, Wyott Ordung, Martha Wentworth, 1952. "The Burma Temple Story" with Arthur Space, Elizabeth Frazer, Robert Moody, 1952. "The Sunflower Seed Story" with Steve Pendleton, Frank Lackteen, Edgar Barrier, 1952. "The Caboose Story" with Lyle Talbot, Frank Gerstle, Maria Palmer, 1952. "The Missing Diplomat Story" with Edgar Barrier, Lyle Talbot, 1952. "The Briefcase Story" with Laura Mason, Richard Gaines, 1952. "The Civil War Map Story" with Waldron Boyle, Betty Lou Gerson, 1952. "The Piece of String Story" with Ralph Smiley, Hugh Beaumont, 1952. "The Iron Banner Story" with Ivan Triesault, Roland Varno, 1952. "The Dead General Story" with John Dehner, Nestor Paiva, 1952. "The Parachute Story" with Kristine Miller, Peter Coe, 1952. "The Stolen Letter" with Nestor Paiva, Laura Mason, 1952. "The Venetian Story" with Shannon O'Neal, Larry Dobkin, Strother Martin, 1952. "The Bodyguard Story" with James Flavin, Laura Mason, March 10, 1952. "The Art Treasure Story" with Adele Jergens, Joseph Mell, John Parish, March 17, 1952. "The Death in the Morgue Story" with Harry Guardino, Franchesca de Scaffia, David Ormont, March 24, 1952. "The Atomic Mine Story" with Lisa Clark, Herbert Deans, March 31, 1952. "The Red Queen Story" with Alfred Santos, Percy Helton, Mabel Paige, April 7, 1952. "The One Blue Chip Story" with Michael Ansara, Douglass Dumbrille, Ted Stanhope, April 14, 1952. "The Assassin Ring Story" with Beverly Tyler, Larry Blake, April 21, 1952. "The Lagoon Story" with Patrick O'Moore, Christine Larson, April 28, 1952. "The Black Hood Story" with Gloria Eaton, Joseph Turkel, May 5, 1952. "The Pat and Mike Story" with Nelson Leigh, John Warburton, May 12, 1952. "The Havana Microfilm Story" with Jeanne Tatum, Howard Joslin, May 19, 1952. "The Perfect Alibi" with Byron Kane, Jan Arvan, Dolores Moran, May 26, 1952. "The Knitting Needle Story" with Clancy Cooper, Frances Rafferty, June 2, 1952. "The Paris Sewer Story" with Carol Thurston, Leonard Penn, June 9, 1952. "The Decoy Story" with Laura Mason, Jim Davis, June 16, 1952. "The Archeological Story" with Lyle Talbot, Henry Corden, June 23, 1952. (DVD)

The Name's the Same. ABC panel game show, with Robert Q. Lewis, Carl

Reiner, Joan Alexander, "I'd Like to Be … Tom Corbett, Space Cadet." May 19, 1953. Donlevy was a guest.

Lux Video Theater. CBS drama. "Tunnel Job" by Carey Wilbur, with Ruth Warrick, George Matthews, Olin Howlin, Joseph Foley. May 21, 1953. Donlevy played Dan Carmody. "The Great McGinty" by Preston Sturges, with Nancy Gates, William Schallert, Lillian Molieri, Paul Harvey. April 28, 1955. Daniel McGinty. "Betrayed." April 19, 1956. Donlevy was the intermission guest.

Your Show of Shows. NBC music variety show. May 30, 1953. Donlevy was a guest star.

I've Got a Secret. CBS panel game show. Garry Moore, Laraine Day. August 26, 1953, and March 14, 1956. Guest. (DVD)

Robert Montgomery Presents Your Lucky Strike Theater. NBC drama. "First Vice-President," based on the novel by Joan Transue, with Olive Blakeney, June Dayton, Dean Harris. August 31, 1953. Donlevy played the president.

The Colgate Comedy Hour. NBC variety show, with Eddie Cantor (host), Eddie Fisher, Frank Sinatra, Connie Russell. November 29, 1953. Donlevy was a guest. (DVD)

The Motorola Television Hour. ABC drama anthology series. "At Ease" by Rod Serling, with Madge Evans, Horace MacMahon, Pat Harrington. December 15, 1953. Donlevy played a sergeant.

Place the Face. CBS panel game show, with Joan Bennett, Gilda Gray. February 18, 1954. Donlevy was a guest.

Chrysler Medallion Theater. CBS drama series. "Safari" by Ben Zavin. April 3, 1954.

The Judy Maxwell Story. A syndicated broadcast explaining the work of AMVETS, the National Service Foundation. September 13, 1954. Donlevy was a presenter.

The Valiant Men by Nicholas Montserrat, CBS Drama Trilogy. February 10, 1955. Donlevy played Lt. Comdr. Knowles.

The Ford Television Theater. NBC comedy-drama. "The Policy of Joe Aladdin." May 12, 1955. Donlevy played Joe Aladdin. (DVD) "Double Trouble," adapted from a story by Selden M. Loring, with Richard Denning, Yvette Dugay, Frank De Kova, Richard Erdman, Damian O'Flynn. March 22, 1956. Donlevy played Charlie Brock. (DVD)[1]

Star Stage. NBC drama anthology series. "Honest John and the Thirteen Uncle Sams" by Joel Carpenter. October 7, 1955. Donlevy played Honest John Gaminski.

Climax! CBS anthology drama series. "The Pink Cloud" by Ben Starr, with Doris Dowling, Jay C. Flippen, Sally Forrest. October 27, 1955. Donlevy played Sam Marvin.

Crossroads. ABC drama anthology. "Mr. Liberty Bell." November 18, 1955. Donlevy played Dr. Roy Bell. "The Judge" by George Bruce, with Donald Curtis, Willis Bouchey, Hal Baylor. May 18, 1956. Donlevy played the Rev. Robert McClure. "God of Kandikur" with Eve Miller, Robert Cornthwaite. January 25, 1957. Donlevy played the Rev. Jacob Chambers.

Damon Runyon Theater. CBS mystery drama. "Barbecue" by Robert Blees and Jack Harvey, with Donald Woods (host), Jean Parker, Ben Welden, Vince Barnett. December 3, 1955. Donlevy was a guest star.

Charity Telethon. KPTV (Portland, Oregon). A 16-hour fund-raising telethon for cerebral palsy, with Victor Jory, Jeff Donnell, Tommy Bartlett, Martha Tilton and Magda Gabor.

December 10–11, 1955. Donlevy was a guest.[2]

Kraft Television Theater. NBC drama. "Home Is the Hero" by Walter Macken, with Anthony Perkins, Pat O'Malley, Glenda Farrell, Ann Thomas, Loretta Leversee. January 25, 1956. Donlevy played Paddo.

Westinghouse Studio One. CBS drama. "The Laughter of Giants" by Paul Crabtree, with Rita Gam, Patrick McVey, Biff McGuire. March 19, 1956. Donlevy played Jim.

The DuPont Show of the Week. CBS/NBC drama. "Beyond This Place" by A.J. Cronin, with Peggy Ann Garner, Max Adrian, Russell Collins, Shelley Winters, Farley Granger, Torin Thatcher, Hurd Hatfield, Fritz Weaver. November 27, 1957. Donlevy played Constable Dale. "Jeremy Rabbitt—The Secret Avenger" by Robert Thom, with Frank Gorshin, Franchot Tone, Jennifer West, Jim Backus, Carolyn Jones, Walter Matthau. April 5, 1964. Donlevy played Cheese Karapolis.

The Texan. CBS Western series. "The Man Behind the Star" with Rory Calhoun, Richard Jaeckel, Russell Simpson, February 9, 1959. Donlevy played Sherriff Bob Gleason. (DVD) "Traildust." October 19, 1959. Donlevy was a guest star. (DVD)

Rawhide. CBS Western series. "Incident of the Power and the Plough" with Clint Eastwood, Sheb Wooley. February 13, 1959. Donlevy played Jed Reston. (DVD)

Wagon Train. CBS Western series. "The Jasper Cato Story" with Ward Bond, Robert Horton. March 4, 1959. Donlevy played Jasper Cato. (DVD)

Hotel de Paree. CBS Western series. "Juggernaut" with Earl Holliman, Strother Martin, Jeanette Nolan, Judi Meredith. October 9, 1959.

The June Allyson Show. CBS drama series. "Escape" by Gene Roddenberry, with Frank Lovejoy, Silvia Sidney, Margaret O'Brien, Norman Leavitt. February 22, 1960. Donlevy played John Ridges.

Zane Grey Theater. CBS Western series. "The Sunday Man" with Dick Powell (host), Leif Erickson, Dean Jones, Trudi Ziskind. February 26, 1960. Donlevy played Fred Childress.

The Red Skelton Show. CBS comedy series. "Deadeye the Blacksmith." March 9, 1960. Donlevy played Big Dan.

Spotlight. ABC/KUTL (Tulsa, Oklahoma). Interview-variety show with Louise Bland (hostess). Crca 1961. Donlevy was a guest.[3]

Here's Hollywood. NBC daytime talk show. Jack Linkletter (interviewer) with Brian Donlevy and Jill St. John, October 19, 1961.

Target: The Corrupters. ABC drama series. "A Man Is Waiting to Be Murdered" by Louis Lantz, with Stephen McNally, Jack Flood, George Lane, Mike Jessan. January 5, 1962. Donlevy played Pete.

Saints and Sinners. NBC drama series. "Dear George, the Siamese Cat Is Missing" by Adrian Spies, with Nick Adams, Lola Albright, Barbara Rush, Gary Lockwood. September 17, 1962. Donlevy played Preller.

Perry Mason. CBS crime-courtroom drama series. "The Case of the Positive Negative" with Raymond Burr, Dabbs Greer, Ted de Corsia. May 1, 1966. Donlevy played Gen. Roger Brandon. (DVD)

Family Affair. CBS comedy series. "Hard Hat Jody," with Brian Keith, Sebastian Cabot, Anissa Jones, Kathy Garver. January 2, 1967. Donlevy played Owen Pennington. (DVD)

The Name of the Game. NBC mystery series. "The Perfect Image" with

Ida Lupino, Stephen McNally, Gene Barry, Hal Holbrook, Clu Gulager, Charles Drake, Jill Townsend. November 7, 1969.[4]

RECORDINGS

Life Begins at 8:40. Original cast show recording (1934), with Ray Bolger, Bert Lahr, Lusela Gear. Capitol Records 20096 BD-43 LP, 1950. Donlevy was a cast member.[1]

"Columbus" by Joaquin Miller and *"The American Flag"* by Joseph Redman Drake. Reciter/Singer accompanied by the Victor Young Orchestra, Decca 40030 78. 1947.

Franz Lehar Festival: American Cancer Society. This 16" radio transcription disc promotional record features one-minute appeals by Donlevy, Vivien Leigh, Laurence Olivier, Sophie Tucker, Shirley Booth *et al.* American Cancer Society 1953 Campaign. LAT 64309. 1953.

Worlds of Literature. A series of six records of songs, poems and recitals by Donlevy, Richard Dyer-Bennett, Burl Ives, Ames Brothers, Fredric March, Woody Guthrie *et al.* Audio Education, New York. 1955.[2]

Our Common Heritage. Patriotic readings featuring Donlevy, Agnes Moorehead, Walter Huston, Pat O'Brien, Bing Crosby and Fredric March. Reciter-singer of "Columbus" and "The American Flag," with Victor Young Orchestra: Decca DL-9072 LP. 1959.

How to Stuff a Wild Bikini. Soundtrack featuring the Kingsmen *et al.* Singer with Mickey Rooney of "Madison Avenue," Wand WDM/S 671 LP. 1966. Reissued on Real Gone Music RGM-0280 CD. 2014.

Chapter Notes

Preface

1. Barry Farrer: "Pin-Up Man," *Screenland,* March 1944, 70.

Chapter 1

1. "Here's the Real Brian Donlevy Minus All the Press Agent Malarkie," *The Milwaukee Journal,* March 5, 1940, 1–2. Navy Records list Donlevy as being born in 1902, but his death certificate and immigration records cite 1901.

2. "Rites Saturday for Thomas Donlevy of Sheboygan Falls," *The Sheboygan Press,* January 29, 1931, 12.

3. United States Census, 1920: *Family Search,* https://familysearch.org/ark:/619 03/1:1:MFV6-DXS. Thomas Donlevy, Sheboygan Falls, Sheboygan, Wisconsin, 1920.

4. "Tough Guy movie actor Brian Dunlevy was born in Castle Street," *Portadown Times,* February 10, 2015, 1.

5. Richard K. Bellamy, "Riding the Airwaves; Wuxtry! Donlevy Birthplace Believed Found," *The Milwaukee Journal,* August 7, 1944, 2.

6. Massachusetts State Census, 1855, Worcester, Southbridge, Massachusetts: Family Search https://familysearch.org/ark:61903/:1:MQ4X-LNL.

7. G. H. Hack, *The Genealogical History of the Donlevy Family* (Columbus, Ohio: Printed for private distribution by Chaucer Press, Evans Publishing Company, 1901), 8, 23.

8. Massachusetts Death Indexes 1841–1915, Christopher Dunleavy, Uxbridge, Massachusetts, 1892: Ellen Dunleavy,

Uxbridge, Massachusetts, January 11, 1909: Family Search https://familysearch.org/ark:610903/1:1:N4SQ-751.

9. "Rites Saturday for Thomas Donlevy of Sheboygan Falls," *The Sheboygan Press,* January 29, 1931, 12.

10. Massachusetts Town Clerk, Vital and Town Records, 1626–2001, *Family Search,* https://familysearch.org/ark/1:1:FH M1-YYW. Thomas H. Dunlavey and Elizabeth C. Murray, 1885.

11. United States Census, 1910: *Family Search,* https://familysearch.org/ark:/61903/ 1:1:M2KQ-XJY. Thomas H. Donlevy, Medway, Norfolk, Massachusetts.

12. "Not Brian, But Waldo," Letter from C. F. Leavens, *The Milwaukee Journal,* August 10, 1944, 2: "Waldo, But Not Ripon," Letter from Mrs. La Verne Van Erden, *The Milwaukee Journal,* August 10, 1944, 2.

13. Theater Program for *The Andersonville Trial,* Auditorium Theater, Rochester, January 19–21, 1961.

14. www.americanwoolen.com/brand/

15. "Here's the Real Brian Donlevy Minus All the Press Agent Malarkie," *The Milwaukee Journal,* March 5, 1940, 1–2.

16. "Waldo, But Not Ripon," Letter from Mr. La Verne Van Erden, *The Milwaukee Journal,* August 10, 1944, 2.

17. "Here's the Real Brian Donlevy Minus All the Press Agent Malarkie," *The Milwaukee Journal,* March 5, 1940, 1 2.

18. Buck Herzog, "On Amusement Row; Dick Jurgens Can't Pass Up Pins; Auto Accident Made Him Band Leader; Off the Cuff," *The Milwaukee Sentinel,* April 11, 1939, 14.

19. "Waldo Donlevy is the Youngest

Soldier in Entire Guard," *The Sheboygan Press,* October 16, 1916, 1.

20. Liza, "Mr. America," *Screenland,* October 1944, 46.

21. Buck Herzog, "On Amusement Row," *The Milwaukee Sentinel,* November 17, 1940, 24.

22. "Here's the Real Brian Donlevy Minus All the Press Agent Malarkie," *The Milwaukee Journal,* March 5, 1940, 1–2.

23. "Waldo Donlevy is the Youngest Soldier in Entire Guard," *The Sheboygan Press,* October 16, 1916, 1.

24. Gregory Mank, "Brian Donlevy," *Films in Review,* April 1975, 209.

25. "Waldo Donlevy is the Youngest Soldier in Entire Guard," *The Sheboygan Press,* Ocotber 16, 1916, 1.

26. "Waldo Donlevy Writes Home," *The Sheboygan Press,* November 8, 1917, 2.

27. "News," *The Sheboygan Press,* December 22, 1917, 3.

28. www.32nd-division.org/history/32hist.htm.

29. wiki/32nd_Infantry_Division_(United_States)

30. www.32nd-division.org/history/32hist.htm.

31. Philip M. Flammer, *The Vivid Air: The Lafayette Escadrille* (Athens: The University of Georgia Press, 1981), 32: New England Air Museum Exhibition www.neam.org/lafayette-escadrille/index.html.

32. "News," *The Sheboygan Press,* September 18, 1918, 2.

33. www.digitaldeliftp.com/Digital DeliToo/dd2jb-Dangerous-Assignment.html.

34. Harrison Carroll, "Brian Donlevy Meets Former Soldier Pal from War," *The Deseret News,* June 9, 1943, 28.

35. Stephen Curley & Frank Joseph Wetta, *Celluloid Wars: A Guide to Film & the American Experience of War* (Westport, CT: Greenwood Press, 1992); Michael Paris, *From the Wright Brothers to Top Gun: Aviation, Nationalism & Popular Culture* (Manchester University Press, 1995), 35.

36. "Here's the Real Brian Donlevy Minus All the Press Agent Malarkie," *The Milwaukee Journal,* March 5, 1940, 1–2.

37. Ibid.

38. Ibid.

39. John R. Franchey, "Don't Hitch Your Wagon," *Photoplay,* January 1942, 35.

40. Ibid., 72.

41. Naval Records, Tammie Kahnhauser, Education Technician, Nimitz Library, Email February 26, 2016; tkahnhau@usna.edu.

42. Ibid.

43. Gregory Mank, "Brian Donlevy," *Films in Review,* April 1975, 211.

44. Hedda Hopper, "Looking at Hollywood," *Toledo Blade,* June 17, 1942, 17.

45. Naval Records, Tammie Kahnhauser, Education Technician, Nimitz Library, Email February 26, 2016; tkahnhau@usna.edu.

46. "Hollywood Filled with Failures of Other Vocations," *The Milwaukee Sentinel,* June 28, 1944, 2.

47. Buck Herzog, "On Amusement Row," *The Milwaukee Sentinel,* November 17, 1940, 24.

Chapter 2

1. John R. Franchey, "Don't Hitch Your Wagon," *Photoplay,* January 1942, 36.

2. "Hollywood Filled With Failures of Other Vocations," *The Milwaukee Sentinel,* June 28, 1944, 2: "If These Stars Ever Go Broke," *The World's News,* March 3, 1945, 9: "Brian Donlevy's Beef," *Variety,* December 9, 1942, 22.

3. "Hoyts Ritz," *Goulburn Evening Post,* February 3, 1939, 2.

4. Lawrence S. Cutler, and Judy Goff Cutler, *J. C. Leyendecker: American Imagist* (Abrams, Ann Arbor: University of Michigan, 2008), 38.

5. *The Masonic Philatelist Quarterly: Volume 7 No. 4* (New York: The Masonic Stamp Club of New York, December 2014), 15: Musenews www.americanillustration.org/pressRelease/NMAI_Press_1_4_07.html

6. "Dale Evans," *The North Western Courier,* Narrabi, NSW, June 19, 1952, 7.

7. "Don Gets the Last Laugh," *Pittsburg Post-Gazette,* December 25, 1935, 14.

8. Gregory Mank, "Brian Donlevy, 1901–72," *Films in Review,* April 1975, 211–212.

9. Paul Grainge, *Memory & Popular*

Film (Manchester: Manchester University Press, 2003), 25–26.

10. www.imdb.com/title/tt0135479/trivia?ref_=tt_trv_trv

11. L. C. Moen, "F. B. O.—Damaged Hearts," *Motion Picture World,* March 8, 1924, 1105.

12. "School for Wives," *The Moving Picture World,* April 11, 1925, 583.

13. Mank, "Brian Donlevy, 1901–72," 211.

14. Ibid.

15. John R. Franchey, "Don't Hitch Your Wagon," *Photoplay,* January 1942, 72.

16. Ken Bloom, *Broadway: An Encyclopedia* (London: Routledge, 2004), 411.

17. Ibid.

18. "Waldo Donlevy in Chicago," *Sheboygan Journal,* October 16, 1926, 2.

19. Leon Surmelian, "Sitting Pretty: Many Broadway Actors Prefer Hollywood," *Screenland,* March 1937, 78.

20. "A Man of Quality; George Walsh Mixes Up with Smugglers," *Motion Picture News,* November 6, 1926, 78.

21. "After "Rising to Fame" was Completed," (Caption Under Picture), *Motion Picture World,* August 7, 1926, 348.

22. "Excellent's "Striving for Fortune" set for December," *Motion Picture News,* December 26, 1926, 2419.

23. "Hit the Deck," *Variety,* April 13, 1927, 52.

24. Louella O. Parsons, "Musical Film Waits Berlin's Pen," *The Deseret News,* December 2, 1940, 5; Norton Mockridge, "How to Drive to Maine Without Really Trying," *Toledo Blade,* February 12, 1969, 39.

25. Edward Cushing, "The Theaters; Mr. Sobol's High-Hatters Arrive at the Klaw Theater Unaccompanied by Cheers," *The Brooklyn Daily Eagle,* May 11, 1928, 44.

26. "Plays Out of Town; Ringside, Detroit," *Variety,* July 10, 1928, 52.

27. Ibid., 59.

28. "New York, New York City Marriage Records, 1829–1940," *Family Search:* (https://familysearch.org/ark:/61903/1:1:24C B-FVY) Waldo Brian Donlevy and Yvonne Grey Bailey, 05 Oct 1928; Marriages, Manhattan, New York.

29. www.ibdb.com/: "Mr. White and His Girls," *The Brooklyn Daily Eagle,* April 12, 1925, 67.

30. Edwin Hessler: "Yvonne Grey," *Hessler's Garden of Girls,* November 1925, 43.

31. www.streetswing.com/

32. Yvonne Grey: "Hand Me a Lemon, Yvonne Says: By Yvonne Grey of the Ziegfeld Follies," *The Evening Independent,* June 15, 1925, 19.

33. Thomas S. Hischak, *The Rodgers and Hammerstein Encyclopedia* (Westport, CT: Greenwood Press, 2007), 127.

34. Thomas S. Hischak, *Boy Loses Girl: Broadway's Librettist* (Lanham, MD: Scarecrow Press, 2003), 35.

35. Leon Surmelian, "Sitting Pretty: Many Broadway Actors Prefer Hollywood," *Silver Screen,* March 1937, 78.

36. "Queen Bee," *Variety,* November 20, 1929, 63.

37. "Lady Alone: 'Queen Bee' Unconvincing Comedy at the Belmont," *The Brooklyn Daily Eagle,* November 13, 1929, 23.

38. Lynn Kear and John Rossman, *Kay Francis: A Passionate Life & Career* (Jefferson, N.C.: McFarland, 2006), 44.

39. Benjamin de Casseres: "The Stage in Review: Up Pops the Devil," *Screenland,* December 1930, 95.

40. "Up Pops the Devil," *Variety,* September 10, 1930, 60.

41. "Thomas Donlevy Taken," *The Sheboygan Press,* January 29, 1931, 8.

42. Ed Sullivan, "Little Old New York: The Passing Show," *Toledo Blade,* June 13, 1941, 22.

43. Ed Sullivan, "Little Old New York: Strictly Personal," *Toledo Blade,* March 10, 1942, 24.

44. Ed Sullivan, "Looking at Hollywood: Donlevy Does Impossible; Steals Cooper's Picture," *Chicago Sunday Tribune,* August 13, 1939, 2.

45. Charles K. Moore, "Hollywood Film Shop," *Lodi News-Sentinel,* January 30, 1942, 4.

46. "'Peter' in the Shop," *Variety,* October 13, 1931, 56.

47. Ethan Mordden, *The Golden Age of Broadway:1919–59* (New York: St. Martin's Press, 2015), 183.

48. Arthur Pollack, "The Theaters," *The Brooklyn Daily Eagle,* January 20, 1931, 21.

49. Arthur Pollack, "The Theaters; 'So-

ciety Girl' A Play About Blueblood Who Leads Prize Fighter Astray, Opens at the Broadway Majestic," *The Brooklyn Daily Eagle,* December 22, 1931, 22.

50. "'Society Girl' Sold," *The Brooklyn Daily Eagle,* January 16, 1932, B9.

51. Buck Herzog, "On Amusement Row," *The Milwaukee Sentinel,* December 29, 1939, 13.

52. Jimmie Fidler, "Hollywood Shots," *Reading Eagle,* January 4, 1940, 12.

53. "Plays on Broadway: The Inside Story," *Variety,* March 1, 1932, 54.

54. "Pictures Possibilities," *Variety,* March 1, 1932, 23.

55. Gerald Broman, *American Theater: A Chronicle of Comedy and Drama: 1930–69* (New York: Oxford University Press, 1996), 57.

56. "Plays on Broadway: The Boy Friend," *Variety,* June 14, 1932, 53.

57. Arthur Pollack, "'The Boy Friend' at the Morosco Theater is Crowded with Happenings of a Great Variety of Sorts," *The Brooklyn Daily Eagle,* June 8, 1932, 20.

58. Ibid.

59. "Picture Possibilities," *Variety,* July 12, 1932, 25.

60. "Bride and Groom," *Columbia Daily Spectator,* January 18, 1933, 2.

61. Arthur Pollack: "The Theaters," *The Brooklyn Daily Eagle,* March 17, 1933, 22: "Whispering Galleries: Puss in the Corner," *Columbia Daily Spectator,* March 20, 1933, 2.

62. Gerald Broman, *American Theater: A Chronicle of Comedy & Drama: 1930–69* (New York: Oxford University Press, 1996), 78.

63. "Another Man's Son," *Variety,* August 8, 1933, 47.

64. Bernard F. Dick, *Forever Mame: The Life of Rosalind Russell* (Jackson: University Press of Mississippi, 2006), 28.

65. "Mild Comedy," *Variety,* December 12, 1933, 57.

66. Arthur Pollack, "The Theaters," *The Brooklyn Daily Eagle,* October 26, 1933, 8.

67. "Stage and Screen," *Pittsburgh Post-Gazette,* February 5, 1934, 6.

68. "Plays on Broadway; No Questions Asked," *Variety,* February 13, 1934, 96.

69. "Bunker Bean," *Modern Screen,* August 1936, 90.

70. https://en.wikipedia.org/wiki/Owen_Davis,_Jr.

71. Gregory Mank, *Women in Horror* (Jefferson, N.C.: McFarland, 2005), 12.

72. "Plays on Broadway; 'The Perfumed Lady,'" *Variety,* March 20, 1934, 55; "The Perfumed Lady," *Motion Picture Herald,* April 7, 1934, 28.

73. L. Stevenson, "Lights of New York," *Lafayette Ledger,* May 10, 1935, 11. 60; "Plays Out of Town: Ringside, Detroit," *Variety,* July 10, 1928, 52 & 59.

74. Benjamin de Cassares, "Should Climb on Screen Like Taxi," *Motion Picture Herald,* May 19, 1934, 37.

75. "The Theaters," *The Brooklyn Daily Eagle,* May 9, 1934, 10; "The Milky Way; Critical Moments," *Jewish Telegraph Agency,* May 11, 1934, 12.

76. L. Stevenson, "Lights of New York," *Lafayette Ledger,* May 10, 1935, 11.

77. Hedda Hopper, "Whispering Galleries; Who Held the Horse?" *Columbia Spectator,* May 18, 1934, 18.

78. "The Milky Way," *Variety,* May 15, 1934, 66.

79. "Plays on Broadway; Life Begins at 8:40," *Variety,* September 4, 1934, 54.

80. "Plays on Broadway; Life Begins at 8:40," *Variety,* September 4, 1934, 54.

81. Paul Harrison, "Stage Folk Cook Up Things on Sideline," *The Tuscaloosa News,* January 18, 1935, 4.

82. Yvonne Grey-Donlevy, Champlain, May 8, 1934, from Plymouth, England to New York, New York Passenger and Crew Lists 1909, 1925–57, *Family Search,* https://familysearch.org/ark:/61903/1:1:24NB-7WZ.

83. Yvonne Donlevy or Grey, Britannic, September, 1935; New York, New York Passenger and Crew Lists, 1909, 1925–57, *Family Search,* https://familysearch.org/ark:/61903/1:1:24VL-FHR

84. J. P. Wearing, *The London Stage: 1930–39: A Calendar of Producers, Performers & Personnel* (Lanham, MD: Rowman & Littlefield, 2014), 551. "Wife of Actor Donlevy Gets Reno Divorce" *Los Angeles Times,* February 2, 1936, 53.

85. "Casamento de Uma Artista Cinematographica," (Marriage of a Cinema Artiste), *Correo Paulistano,* December 11, 1937, 15.

86. "Wedding of American Actress," *The Glasgow Herald,* December 11, 1937, 13.

87. "Yvonne Nothman, born 20-08-1907, 1 January, 1939-December 31, 1946, Collection Records of Special Operations Executive, The National Archives, Kew Gardens, London," www.academia.edu/2315071/THE_MOST_SECRET_LIST_OF_SOE_AGENTS_N.

88. "Senhor G. Rothman," *The Times,* April 7, 1958, 9.

89. "Yvonne Grey Nothman, November, 1999, Torbay, Devon, England," England & Wales Death Registration Index 1937–2007, *Family Search,* https://familysearch.org/ark:/61903/1:1:QVZX-RLSB.

90. John R. Franchey, "Don't Hitch Your Wagon," *Photoplay,* 72.

Chapter 3

1. Thomas Nord Riley, "The Art of Mr. Donlevy," *Hollywood,* April 1940, 54.

2. "Bits That Blossomed into Careers," *Silver Screen,* January 1936, 34.

3. Gregory Black, *Hollywood Censored* (Cambridge: Cambridge University Press, 1994), 218–20.

4. "Real Brian Donlevy Minus All the Press Agent Malarkie," *The Milwaukee Sentinel,* March 5, 1940, 2.

5. Leon Surmelian, "Sitting Pretty: Many Broadway Actors Prefer Hollywood," *Silver Screen,* March 1937, 78.

6. Harold Heffernan, "It Happens in Hollywood; Fashion Plate Menjou Is a Male Film Rarity," *The Sunday Morning Star,* October 4, 1942, 34.

7. "She's Mary Burns, Fugitive," *San Jose News,* December 28, 1935, 13.

8. Leslie Halliwell, "Mary Burns, Fugitive," *Halliwell's Film Guide* (London: Guild, 1983), 532.

9. "Mary Burns, Fugitive," *Variety,* November 20, 1935, 16.

10. "Mary Burns, Fugitive," *Modern Screen,* January 1936, 34.

11. "Mary Burns, Fugitive," www.tcm.com/tcmb/title/83015/Mary-Burns-Fugitive/notes.html.

12. "Tenement on Stilts Seen in 'Mary Burns,'" *Catskill Mountain News,* January 3, 1936, 10.

13. Richard B. Jewell, *The RKO Story* (New York: Octopus, 1982), 91.

14. "Theater Reviews: Shea's County," *Buffalo Courier-Express,* March 20, 1936, 22.

15. David Shipman "Eddie Cantor," *The Great Movie Stars: The Golden Years* (New York: Hamlyn, 1971), 94.

16. "Paramount Readies Aviation Film," *Prescott Evening Courier,* December 13, 1935, 9.

17. "Human Cargo," *St. Petersburg Times,* June 17, 1936, 9.

18. "Romance Rises and Falls in Hollywood," *Daily News,* March 10, 1938, 10.

19. Harold V. Cohen, "The Drama Desk: East and West," *Pittsburgh Post-Gazette,* April 23, 1936, 8.

20. "Real Brian Donlevy Minus All Press Agent Malarkie,"

21. "Theater Gossip," *The Evening Independent,* March 21, 1936, 11.

22. "Entertainments: New Films in London; 'Thirty Six Hours to Kill,'" *The Times,* November 9, 1936, 10.

23. Martin Dickstein, "Picture Parade," *The Brooklyn Daily Eagle,* August 10, 1936, 12.

24. Leon Surmelian, "Sitting Pretty," *Silver Screen,* March 1937, 78.

25. "Reviews: 'Crack-Up,'" *Independent Exhibitors' Film Bulletin,* December 16, 1936, 8.

26. "Midnight Taxi," *The Sydney Morning Herald,* May 17, 1937, 6.

27. "Midnight Taxi," (www.tcm.com/tcmdb/title/83450/Midnight-Taxi/notes.html.)

28. Graham Greene, "This Is My Affair," in *Halliwell's Film Guide* (London: Guild, 1983), 822.

29. "Real Brian Donlevy Minus All Press Agent Malarkie,"

30. Gregory Mank, "Brian Donlevy, 1901–72," *Films in Review,* April 1975, 211.

31. Thomas Nord Riley, "The Art of Mr. Donlevy," *Hollywood,* April 1940, 55.

32. Harold Heffernan, "Bad Public Relations? Job or Not, Don Keeps Lip-Whiskers," *Toledo Blade,* February 18, 1960, 23.

33. David Shipman "Gracie Fields," *The Great Movie Stars: The Golden Years* (New York, Hamlyn, 1971), 192.

34. Patricia Higgins, "Eleanor Dances but Marjorie Sings," *The Sydney Morning Herald,* June 2, 1938, 20.

35. www.tvhistory.tv/1937%20QF.htm.

36. "Sharpshooters," *The Sydney Morning Herald,* January 23, 1939, 4.

37. Mank, "Brian Donlevy: 1901–72," 215.

38. Kenneth W. Munden, executive ed., *The American Film Institute Catalogue of Motion Pictures: Feature Films: 1931–40* (Los Angeles: University of California Press, 1993), 205.

39. Kenneth W. Munden, *The American Film Institute Catalogue of Motion Pictures: Feature Films: 1931–40* (Los Angeles: University of California Press, 1993), 205.

40. "News of the Screen," *New York Times,* June 18, 1937.

41. "News from Hollywood, " *New York Times,* December 11, 1936, 21.

Chapter 4

1. "Hollywood," *Variety,* January 25, 1939, 62: "Stars Excited Over Mothers Day," *Truth,* May 8, 1938, 33.

2. E. J. Smithson, "Beau Geste Comes Back," *Hollywood,* June 1939, 65.

3. "Charles Bickford Won't Be Flogged," *The Straits Times,* January 15, 1939, 15.

4. Mark A. Vierra, *Majestic Hollywood: The Greatest Films of 1939* (Philadelphia, PA: Running Press, 2013), 107.

5. "Donlevy's Brit Veto," *Variety,* January 12, 1939, 4.

6. William Wellman, Jr., *Wild Bill Wellman: Hollywood Rebel* (New York: Pantheon Books), 345–351.

7. Ibid.

8. Ibid.

9. Gregory Mank, "Brian Donlevy, 1901–72," *Films in Review,* April 1975, 216.

10. Barry Farrer, "Pin-Up Man," *Screenland,* March, 1944, 71.

11. William Wellman, Jr., *Wild Bill Wellman: Hollywood Rebel* (New York: Pantheon Books), pp345–51.

12. Malcom H. Oetlinger, "I Hate Your Face," *Screenland,* March 1941, 34.

13. Buck Herzog, "Up and Down Amusement Row," *The Milwaukee Sentinel,* June 27, 1941, 6-A.

14. "Theater Gossip," *The Evening Independent,* November 30, 1939, 8.

15. Ed Sullivan, "Looking at Hollywood: Donlevy Does Impossible; Steals Cooper's Picture," *Chicago Sunday Tribune,* August 13, 1939, 2.

16. Jimmy Fidler, "Hollywood Shots," *Reading Eagle,* August 16 1939, 8.

17. "Pittsburgh to Play Host to Hollywood 'Great' at World Premiere," *The Pittsburgh Press,* October 29, 1939, 1.

18. "Walsh to Direct Republic's 'Command,'" *Motion Picture Herald,* October 28, 1939, 65.

Chapter 5

1. William Lynch Vallee, "The Truth About Mrs. McGinty," *Silver Screen,* September, 1940, 36; 88–9.

2. Gregory Mank, "Brian Donlevy: 1901–72," *Film in Review,* April 1975, 216.

3. Diane Jacobs, *Christmas in July: The Life and Art of Preston Sturges* (Berkeley: University of California Press, 1992), 205.

4. "Critics Quotes," *Motion Picture Daily,* August 26, 1940, 9.

5. Bosley Crowther, "The Screen; The Great McGinty, Rowdy Satire on Crooked Politics at Paramount," August 15, 1940, 21.

6. "Brian Donlevy on Tour," *Motion Picture Daily,* July 9, 1940, 8.

7. "'Great McGinty' Star Feted in Philadelphia," *Showmen's Trade Review,* August 10, 1940, 11.

8. "Fans Vote During "McGinty" Review, *Showmen's Trade Review,* July 27, 1940, 13.

9. Si Stenhauser, "Axis Radio Lies Aimed at States," *The Pittsburgh Press,* February 2, 1942, 14.

10. John P. Reilly, "Mayors, From Joe to Phil to Rudy," *The Hour,* March 23, 2003, A9.

11. Raymond Durgnant, quoted by Leslie Halliwell, *Halliwell's Film Guide* (London: Guild Publishing, 1983), 342.

12. "Theater Gossip," *The Evening Independent,* December 27, 1941, 18.

13. Juanita Brooks, *The Mountain Meadows Massacre* (Palo Alto, CA: Stanford University Press, 1950), 101–105.

14. Edwin Schallert, "Daltons Cast

Named for Follow-Up," *Los Angeles Times,* August 1, 1940, A10.

15. Harold V.Cohen, "From Hollywood," *Pittsburgh Post-Gazette,* October 21, 1940, 23.

16. Louella O. Parsons, "Hot Off the Hollywood Wires," *The Milwaukee Sentinel,* November 2, 1940, 16.

17. "Round the Studios," *New Zealand Herald,* February 17, 1940, 10.

18. Louella O. Parsons, "Musical Film Waits Berlin's Pen," *The Deseret News,* December 2, 1940, 5.

19. "Screen News Here and in Hollywood," *The New York Times,* December 30, 1940, 20.

20. Louella O. Parsons, "Best Seller Brings Top Movie Price," *The Deseret News,* October 11, 1940, 19.

21. Harold V. Cohen, "The Drama Desk," *The Pittsburgh Press,* October 15, 1940, 23.

22. Harold V. Cohen, "The Drama Desk," *Pittsburgh Post-Gazette,* January 15, 1940, 11.

23. "Actor's Knife," *The Milwaukee Sentinel,* February 16, 1941, 14.

24. "Taylor Gift," *The Pittsburgh Press,* April 22, 1941, 14.

25. "Star Just 'Trucks Along' to Location," *The Pittsburgh Press,* December 28, 1940, 12.

26. Buck Herzog, "Up and Down Amusement Row: Don Refused to Stay a Villain," *The Milwaukee Sentinel,* June 27, 1941, 6A.

27. "Stars Plan Hunting Trip with Cameras," *The Pittsburgh Press,* July 19, 1941, 10.

28. Leslie Halliwell, *Halliwell's Film Guide* (London: Guild Publishing, 1983), 762–763.

29. "Studio Size-Ups," *The Film Daily,* November 1, 1941, 11.

30. Harold Conrad, "Gotham Grapevine," *The Brooklyn Daily Eagle,* October 3, 1941, 13.

31. "'Stars of Tomorrow' cast," *Motion Picture Herald,* November 22, 1941, 38.

32. Hedda Hopper, "But Can He Cook?" *The Washington Post,* February 27, 1942, 11.

33. Hedda Hopper, "Lucky! Donlevy Getting Breaks Thanks to Sturges," September 10, 1941, 23.

34. "Product Digest The Release Chart Showmen's Review: Reviews; Two Yanks in Trinidad," *Motion Picture Herald,* March 28, 1942, 573.

35. "Paramount Story Cost $10,000—is Shelved," *The Deseret News,* January 18, 1941, 6.

36. Larry Ceplair and Christopher Trumbo, *Dalton Trumbo: Blacklisted Hollywood Radical* (Lexington: University of Kentucky Press, 2014), 108.

37. "The New Pictures," *Time,* March 30, 1942, 21.

38. "The Remarkable Andrew," *The Film Daily,* January 19, 1942, 6.

39. Jim Henaghan, "Don't Call Me Mister," *Modern Screen,* October 1950, 90.

40. Bob Thomas, *Golden Boy: The Untold Story of William Holden* (London: Weidenfeld & Nicholson, 1983), 42.

41. Edwin Schallert, "Newlyweds Ball, Arnaz Will Co-Star for RKO," *Los Angeles Times,* March 12, 1941, 12.

42. "Studio Size-Ups," *Film Bulletin,* November 1, 1941, 11.

43. "Wings for Democracy for Morros," *The Film Daily,* January 24, 1941, 4.

44. Charles H. Moore, "Hollywood Film Shop," *Lodi News-Sentinel,* April 21, 1941, 14.

45. Victoria Wilson, *Steel-True: A Life of Barbara Stanwyck 1907–41* (New York: Simon & Schuster, 2013), 746.

46. Patricia King Hanson, and Amy Dunkleberger, *The American Film Institute Catalogue of Motion Pictures* (Los Angeles: University of California Press, 1999), 935.

47. Thomas L. Pryor, "The Great Talent Hunt," *New York Times,* September 14, 1941, 14.

48. "Screen News Here and There," *New York Times,* September 4, 1942, 12.

49. Douglas W. Churchill, "Frederic March Gets Lead in 'One Foot in Heaven," *New York Times,* April 1, 1941, 20.

50. "Screen News Here and There," *New York Times,* February 12, 1943, 21.

Chapter 6

1. "Regional Newsreel: Portland," *Showmen's Trade Review,* April 22, 1944, 34.

2. Bosley Crowther, "The Screen; 'Wake

Island' A Stirring Tribute to the U.S. Marines with Brian Donlevy in the cast, at the Rivoli," *New York Times,* September 2, 1942, 23.

3. John Douglas Eames, *The Paramount Story* (New York: Octopus, 1982), 162.

4. www.imdb.com/title/tt0035530/awards?ref_=ttawd.

5. Hedda Hopper, "Donlevy Dons Laurels," *The Washington Post,* September 12, 1942, B6.

6. Edwin Schallert, "Khyber Rifles May Become Film," *Los Angeles Times,* July 18, 1941, A12.

7. Kenneth W. Munden, *The American Film Institute Catalog of Motion Pictures: Feature Films 1931–40* (Oakland, CA: University of California Press, 1993), 343, 696.

8. Ibid.

9. "Four Films Open This Week," *New York Times,* November 4, 1942, 28; "Brian Donlevy," *Motion Picture Herald,* Jul 18, 1942, 18.

10. Louella O. Parsons, "Jerome Kern Musical Planned," *The Deseret News,* April 17, 1941,

11. Louella O. Parsons, "Close-Ups and Long Shots of the Motion Picture Scene," *The Washington Post,* May 2, 1941, 8.

12. "Kayoing the Caterpillars," *Variety,* February 16, 1941, 4.

13. "Talking of Talkies," April 25, 1943, *Truth* (Brisbane, Queensland), 17.

14. Niven Busch, "I, Veronica Lake…: How I Punched Brian Donlevy," *Life,* May 17, 1943, 83.

15. Ibid.

16. Sheilah Graham, "Today's Film News," *The News,* May 8, 1941, 14; "13 Stage Productions Bought," *Motion Picture Herald,* April 12, 1942, 44.

17. Ron Base, *Starring Roles: How Hollywood Stardom is Won and Lost* (New York: Little, Brown & Co., 1994), 62.

18. "B.G. De Sylva, Hollywood Program Notes from the Studios," *Showmen's Trade Review,* December 20, 1941, 26.

19. "Hollywood Program Notes from the Studios," *Showmen's Trade Review,* January 11, 1941, 18.

20. "'Nightmare' at the Princess," *Montreal Gazette,* May 8, 1943, 7.

21. Gregory Mank, "Brian Donlevy, 1901–72," *Films in Review,* April 1975, 226.

22. Diana Barrymore and Frank Gerold, *Too Much Too Soon* (New York: Henry Holt & Co., 1957), 63.

23. Charles Tranberg, *Robert Taylor: A Biography* (Albany, GA: Bear Manor Media, 2011), 154.

24. Leslie Halliwell, *Halliwell's Film Guide* (London: Guild, 1983), 770.

25. "Cargo of Innocents; New Films in London," *The Times,* March 22, 1943, 8.

26. "Sequel Planned for Casablanca," *The Montreal Gazette,* January 1, 1943, 3; "Rita Hayworth Given Suspension," *The Deseret News,* January 21, 1943, 17

27. "Program Notes From the Studios: Donlevy gets 'Sahara,'" *Showmen's Trade Review,* January 23, 1943, 28.

28. Hedda Hopper, "Hollywood," *The Pittsburgh Press,* December 19, 1942, A7.

29. Edwin Schallert, "Drama and Film," *Los Angeles Times,* May 14, 1943, A15.

30. Hedda Hopper, "Looking at Hollywood," *Los Angeles Times,* March 8, 1942, A3.

31. *Storm,* "Coast Flashes," *Motion Picture Daily,* August 11, 1942, 3.

32. "Coast Flashes," *Motion Picture Daily,* September 17, 1942, 2.

33. William R. Weaver, "Stars Set for Caribbean Patrol," *Motion Picture Herald,* September 12, 1942, 41.

34. Louella O. Parsons, "Looking at Hollywood," *The Milwaukee Sentinel,* November 1, 1943, Part 2, p5.

35. "Paramount Suspends Donlevy," *Variety,* September 15, 1943, 2.

36. "Donlevy Wows Girls at Baxter," *The Spokesman-Review,* April 5, 1944, 15.

37. "Brian Donlevy in Hospital," *Variety,* October 6, 1943, 3.

38. "Now They're All Joining Up," *The Australian Women's Weekly,* August 2, 1941, 16.

39. William R. Weaver, "Hollywood," *Motion Picture Daily,* May 11, 1943, 4.

40. "Notes from Hollywood," *Motion Picture Daily,* November 21, 1941, 7.

41. Hedda Hopper, "Bright Dawns the Day," *The Washington Post,* December 26, 1942, 4.

42. Hedda Hopper, "Hollywood," *The Pittsburgh Press,* October 28, 1942,

43. Barbara Roisman Cooper, *Anna Lee: Memoir of a Career on General Hospital and in Film* (Jefferson, N.C.: McFarland, 2007), 147.

44. www.imdb.com/title/tt0035966/awards?ref=tt_awd.

45. Hedda Hopper, "Hollywood," *Berkeley Daily Gazette,* June 19, 1943, 14.

46. Stephan Jaeger, Elena V. Barabon and Adam Muller, *Fighting Words and Images: Representing War Across the Disciplines* (Ontario: University of Toronto Press, 2012), 152.

47. Buck Herzog, "Theater Showing Stalingrad Epic," *The Milwaukee Sentinel,* February 26, 1944, 11.

48. Jaeger, Barabon, and Muller, *Fighting Words and Images,* 152.

49. "Film's Narration Made After Hours," *The Pittsburgh Press,* October 25, 1943, 12.

50. "Associated British Will Get Wilcox Next Picture," *The Film Daily,* December 20, 1943, 11.

51. "Hollywood Stars Surround President on Birthday," *St. Petersburg Times,* January 31, 1944, 1.

52. Hedda Hopper, "Looking at Hollywood," *Toledo Blade,* February 7, 1944, 25.

53. "Pictures in the City of Stars," *The Coaticook Observer,* April 13, 1945, 9.

54. Buck Herzog, "Along Amusement Row," *The Milwaukee Sentinel,* August 8, 1944, section 2, 8.

55. James Curtis, *Spencer Tracy* (London: Hutchinson, 2011), 501.

56. "Caniff is Flooded With Movie Titles," *The Wilmington News,* April 8, 1949, 2.

57. "'Romance' Premieres; Exhibition of Drawings," *Showmen's Trade Review,* October 7, 1944, 20.

58. "Movie of the Week; Illustrators Depict Scenes from King Vidor's 'American Romance,'" *Life,* October 2, 1944, 75–79.

59. "WLW-MGM Tie-Up Promotes 'Romance' in 130 city Hook-Up; Premieres Planned for Film," *The Pittsburgh Press,* September 29, 1944, 28.

60. Ibid.

61. "War Bond Show Set Tonight at the Palmetto House," *Herald-Journal,* December 11, 1944, 2.

62. Charles Higham and Joel Greenberg, *The Celluloid Muse: Hollywood Directors Speak* (London: Angus & Robinson, 1969), 28.

63. "Burlington Theater; 'An American Romance,'" *National Advocate,* November 22, 1946, 4.

64. Kenneth W. Munden, *The American Film Institute Catalog of Motion Pictures: Feature Films 1931–40* (Oakland, CA: University of California Press, 1993),70.

65. Buck Herzog, "Along Amusement Row; 'An American Romance,'" *The Milwaukee Sentinel,* December 7, 1944, 6.

66. "Brian Donlevy May Make Mexican Film," *Atlanta Constitution,* August 1, 1944, 10.

67. Alan Gevinson, *Within Our Gates: Ethnicity in American Feature Films, 1911–60* (Oakland, CA: University of California Press, 1997), 721.

68. "Theater Gossip," *The Evening Independent,* January 7, 1944, 14.

69. Hugh Dixon, "This and Data," *Pittsburgh Post-Gazette,* June 29, 1944, 24.

70. Edwin Schallert, "'Boys' Ranch' Needs Donlevy, Metro Insists," *Los Angeles Times,* October 2, 1944, 12.

71. Richard B. Jewell and Vernon Harbin, *The Paramount Story* (London: Octopus Books, 1983), 175.

72. Louella Parsons, "Hollywood," April 27, 1947, Section 2, 8.

73. Harmony Hayes, "Fans & Fan Clubs," *Silver Screen,* January 1937, 76.

74. Barry Farrer, "Pin-Up Man," *Screenland,* January 1937, 35, 70.

75. Virginia Vale, "Star Dust; Odds & Ends," *Madison Lake Times,* February 13, 1941, 8.

76. "Theater Gossip," *The Evening Independent,* January 8, 1944, 14.

77. Barry Farrer, "Pin-Up Man," 70.

Chapter 7

1. "Brian Donlevy Gets Lonesome and Proposes," *The Milwaukee Sentinel,* July 15, 1936, 19.

2. Louella O. Parsons, "Warners Get a Lawd for Connelly Hit," *Pittsburgh Post-Gazette,* December 9, 1935, 10.

3. Hugh Dixon, "Hollywood: Sarong-Song," *Pittsburgh Post-Gazette,* December 30, 1940, 21.

4. Louis Sobol, "The Voice of Broadway," *The Miami News,* April 16 1940, 41.

5. Eileen Percy, "MacMurray Drops Six-Shooter for Gladys Swarthout Musical," *The Milwaukee Sentinel,* June 5 1936, 19.

6. E. J. Smithson, "Tamed By a Redhead," *Hollywood* August 1941, 50–51.

7. "Brian Donlevy Gets Lonesome and Proposes," *The Milwaukee Sentinel.*

8. U.S. Marriage Records, Family search Marriage certificate Waldo B. Donlevy and Marjorie Lane, December 31, 1936: https://www.familysearch.org/ark:/61903/1:1:K8JT-611.

9. Harold V. Cohen, "The Movie Lots Beg to Report," *Pittsburgh Post-Gazette,* June 4, 1936, 8.

10. "Versatile Lady," *Evening Post,* January 5, 1939, 16.

11. "Jane: Hollywood Gossip from the studios and around the Boulevard," *Lodi News-Sentinel,* March 12, 1936, 2.

12. "Versatile Lady," 16.

13. Liza, "Mr. America," *Screenland,* October 1944, 46–7.

14. Ibid.

15. John R. Franchey, "Don't Hitch Your Wagon," *Photoplay,* January 1942, 73.

16. "Film Star at Home," *The Grenfell Record & Lachlan Advertiser,* September 11, 1944, 3.

17. "Hollywood Budgets for National Clothing Effort Sensational Fight," *Sunday Times,* August 9, 1942, 8.

18. Jimmie Fidler, "Warner Brothers Plan to Give Priscilla Lane Big Build-Up," *St. Petersburg Times,* February 3, 1942, 3.

19. John R. Franchey, "Don't Hitch Your Wagon," 73.

20. Vern Haugland, "No Gold in Them Thar Hills," *St. Petersburg Times,* December 21, 1941, 37.

21. "Donlevy Donates Mine to Nation," *The Pittsburgh Press,* October 7, 1939, 10.

22. Jimmie Fidler, "Warner Brothers Plan to Give Priscilla Lane Big Build-Up."

23. "Donlevy to Hunt for Pirate Treasure," *The Sunday Morning Star,* June 29, 1941, 34.

24. Ed Sullivan, "Little Old New York," *Toledo Blade,* October 10, 1941, 19.

25. John R. Franchey, "Don't Hitch Your Wagon."

26. Gregory Mank, "Brian Donlevy, 1901–1971," *Films in Review,* April, 1971, 212.

27. "Actor's Rare Pipe Collection," *The Shepparton Advertiser,* September 15, 1936, 7.

28. John R. Franchey, "Don't Hitch Your Wagon."

29. Liza, "Mr. America."

30. Jack Hiatt, "Tough Mr. Donlevy Who Couldn't Date His Wife," *The American Weekly, The Milwaukee Sentinel,* July 9, 1947, 9.

31. "Are Movie Bachelors Wedding Ring Shy?" *The Australian Women's Weekly,* June 27, 1936, 32.

32. "Ex-Wife Claims Donlevy Tricked Her into Affair," *St. Petersburg Times,* September 27, 1947, 2.

33. "Donlevy Denies Urging Infidelity," *The Pittsburgh Press,* September 28, 1947, 2.

34. Ibid.

35. "Ex-Wife Claims Donlevy Tricked Her into Affair."

36. Ibid.

37. "Brian Donlevy Pays Detectives $15,000 to Have Wife Shadowed," *St. Petersburg Times,* November 15, 1947, 18.

38. "Wife of Brian Donlevy Charged With Adultery," *San Jose News,* September 13, 1947, 6.

39. "Actor Charges Wife Philandered," *The Milwaukee Sentinel,* September 23, 1947.

40. "Rival Attorney Insists Donlevy Pays $50,000," *The Brooklyn Daily Eagle,* September 13, 1947, 3.

41. "Brian Donlevy Pays Detectives $15,000 To Have Wife Shadowed."

42. "Wife Charges Cruelty in Suit Against Actor," *The Spokesman-Review,* October 1, 1947, 2.

43. "Brian Donlevy to Seek New Divorce," *Ottawa Citizen,* December 27, 1947, 2.

Chapter 8

1. "Carlton Cinema," *The Times,* January 31, 1946, 6.

2. *Wild Harvest,* "Screen Stars are Where You Find Them," *The Sydney Morning Herald,* September 3, 1946, 13; "Filming

Index Remains at 53 on Coast," *Showmen's Trade Review,* July 3, 1946, 8.

3. *Scruffy,* "Schaeffer in New Film to Finance Indie Films," *Showmen's Trade Review,* April 13, 1946, 5.

4. "Stand-Ins of Hollywood Unsung Heroes," *The World's News,* January 17, 1942, 16; Peter Kingson, "Stand-Ins on Films," *The Daily News,* April 13, 1946, 25.

5. Bob Thomas, *Golden Boy: The Untold Story of William Holden* (Weidenfeld & Nicholson, 1983), 89–90.

6. *Hollywood Reporter,* January 1945, Quoted by www.tcm.com/tcmdb/title/05926/Our-Hearts-Are-Growing-Up/notes.html.

7. BJP, "The Screen," *The Milwaukee Sentinel,* March 21, 1947, 22.

8. Ibid.

9. "Hollywood Sights and Sounds," *Prescott Evening Courier,* October 13, 1947, 4.

10. Sheilah Graham, "What's What in Hollywood," *The Milwaukee Journal,* May 12, 1946, A9.

11. Paula Walling, "Film Flash Cable; Orson Welles Not Worried by Student Scorn," *The Sunday Times,* April 20, 1947, 8.

12. "MGM Will Reissue 'Boys' Town,'" *Dunkirk Evening Observer,* July 11, 1948, 13.

13. Sheilah Graham, "What's What in Hollywood."

14. "Chicago," *Variety,* November 20, 1946, 71.

15. "Atom Bomb Film Causes Disputes," *The Straits Times,* March 6, 1947, 1.

16. Michael J. Yavenditti, "Atomic Scientists & Hollywood: The Beginning or the End?" *Film & History: An Inter-Disciplinary Journal of Film and Television,* December 1978, 5–6.

17. "Atom Bomb Film Causes Disputes."

18. Bosley Crowther, "Atomic Bomb Film Starts at Capitol; Beginning or End, Metro Study of Historic Weapon," *New York Times,* February 12, 1947, 21.

19. *The Night Watch,* Hedda Hopper, "Hollywood," *The Pittsburgh Press,* November 10, 1947, 22.

20. Kevin Thomas, "Victor Mature Hits Stride," *Los Angeles Times,* December 7, 1966, D15.

21. "Donlevy Starred in 'Kiss of Death' Discovers That Crime Doesn't Pay," *The Montreal Gazette,* January 22, 1947, 48.

22. Louella O. Parsons, "Hollywood," *The Milwaukee Sentinel,* March 23, 1947, Section 2, 8.

23. Hedda Hopper, "Screen Vehicle is Lined Up for New French Star," *Toledo Blade,* January 3, 1947, 37.

24. Hedda Hopper, "Peggy Ann Garner Set for Role Opposite Cary Grant," *Toledo Blade,* August 26, 1947, 29.

25. Hugh Dixon, "Movie Memories," *Pittsburgh Post-Gazette,* July 1, 1947, 16.

26. Marion Meade, *Buster Keaton: Cut to the Chase: A Biography* (London: Bloomsbury, 1996), 239.

27. Erskine Johnson, "False Reports Upset Judy Garland," *The Pittsburgh Press,* September 7, 1947, 53.

28. Hedda Hopper, "Looking at Hollywood," *The Evening Independent,* November 19, 1947, 14.

29. Hedda Hopper, "Twentieth Century Flirting with James Mason," *Toledo Blade,* May 8, 1947, 35.

30. *Pride of the Yankees,* www.tcm.com/tcmdb/title/87109/The-Pride-of-the-Yankees/notes.html.

31. Buck Herzog, "The Babe Ruth Story," *The Milwaukee Sentinel,* April 1, 1948, 29.

32. Kirtley Briskette, "Joe Lucky," *Modern Screen,* December 1945, 122.

33. Ron Backer, *Mystery Movie Series of 1940s Hollywood* (Jefferson, N.C.: McFarland, 2010), 307.

34. *Frontier Town,* "In Hollywood," *Variety,* November 20, 1946, 46.

35. Hedda Hopper, "Looking at Hollywood," *Chicago Tribune,* October 1, 1947, 17.

36. Edwin Schallert, "Industrialist Seeking Donlevy for Mr. Webster," *Los Angeles Times,* August 9, 1948, 13.

37. Hedda Hopper, "Engel Trying to Line Up Andrews, Darnell, Donlevy for 'Fire,'" *Toledo Blade,* November 5, 1948, 40.

38. "Hollywood Actors Plan Little Theater Project," *The Australian Women's Weekly,* October 26, 1946, 31.

39. "Donlevy to Open Detroit Music Hall Season," *Billboard,* October 3, 1947, 32.

40. "Glory Pulls in 13, 200 in Detroit Wind-Up," *Billboard,* November 1, 1947, 46.

41. "Hollywood Sights and Sounds," *Prescott Evening Courier,* October 13, 1947, 4.

Chapter 9

1. Hedda Hopper, "Doris Day Cast as Helen Morgan," *The Evening Independent,* September 1, 1948, 16.

2. "Names in the News," *The Milwaukee Sentinel,* November 1, 1948, 6.

3. *John Winton,* "New Films Launched, New Players Discovered," *The Film Daily,* December 27, 1943, 8.

4. Jack Lait, Jr., "Hollywood," *The Brooklyn Daily Eagle,* February 3, 1949, 5.

5. Louella O. Parsons, "In Hollywood," *The Milwaukee Sentinel,* January 18, 1949, 6

6. Edith Gwynn, "In Hollywood: Elliott Roosevelt to Pay Alimony to Faye Emerson," *St. Petersburg Times,* October 10, 1949, 20.

7. "Looking at Hollywood," *The Chicago Tribune,* November 5, 1949, 14-f.

8. Louella O. Parsons, "In Hollywood," *The Milwaukee Sentinel,* September 19, 1949, 6.

9. Edwin Schallert, "Tierney, Boyer Figure in Feldman Films," *Los Angeles Times,* April 16, 1949, 11.

10. Harrison Carroll, "Behind the Scenes in Hollywood," *The Dispatch,* May 18, 1949, 28.

11. Hedda Hopper, "Filmdom Chatterbox," *Toledo Blade,* June 4, 1949, 38.

12. Harrison Carroll, "Behind the Scenes in Hollywood," *The Dispatch,* June 4, 1949, 12.

13. Bob Thomas, "Hepburn to Tour in Shakespeare Play; Long Vacation from Films," *The Evening Independent,* June 9, 1949, 15.

14. Hedda Hopper, "Filmdom Chatterbox."

15. Harrison Carroll, "Behind the Scenes in Hollywood."

16. Louella O. Parsons, "Hollywood," *The Milwaukee Sentinel,* July 11, 1949, 8.

17. Louella O. Parsons, "Hollywood," *The Milwaukee Sentinel,* July 13, 1949, 7.

18. Cobina Wright, "Party Gossip," *Screenland,* January 1950, 35.

19. Sheilah Graham, "Directing at End for Lupino," *The Spokesman-Review,* April 7, 1950, 12.

20. Dorothy Kilgallen, "Joan Crawford and Brian Donlevy Have Discovered Each Other," *Schenectady Gazette,* October 26, 1949, 41.

21. Harrison Carroll, "Behind the Scenes in Hollywood," *The Dispatch,* December 13, 1949, 5.

22. Dorothy Kilgallen, "Voice of Broadway," *Schenectady Gazette,* February 18, 1950, 18.

23. Louella O. Parsons, "Hollywood," *The Milwaukee Sentinel,* January 31, 1950, 8.

24. Walter Winchell, "Ingrid Bergman's Ex-Husband Wants Celeste Holm For His Next Bride," *St. Petersburg Times,* November 14, 1951, 23.

25. Walter Winchell, "In Hollywood," *St. Petersburg Times,* October 10, 1951, 7: Louella O. Parsons, "Hollywood," *The Milwaukee Sentinel,* February 6, 1950, 6; www.glamourgirlsofthesilverscreen.com/show/448/Pamela+Duncan/index.html;

26. Lynn Bowes, "What Hollywood is Talking About!" *Screenland,* December 1950, 8.

27. Louella O. Parsons, "Hollywood," *The Milwaukee Sentinel,* March 13, 1950, 7.

28. Scott Dale, "Hollywood Calendar," *Los Angeles Times,* January 1, 1949, C9.

29. Bernard F. Dick, *The Merchant Prince of Poverty Row: Harry Cohn of Columbia Pictures* (Lexington, Kentucky: University of Kentucky Press, 2015), 177.

30. Harrison Carroll, "Behind the Scenes in Hollywood," *The Dispatch,* January 12, 1950, 10.

31. Leroy March, "Hollywood Jottings," *Northern Star,* Lismore, NSW, May 20, 1950, 6.

32. Leroy March, "Hollywood Jottings," *Northern Star,* September 1, 1950, 2.

33. Erskine Johnson, "Korea Places Curbs on Foreign Movie Locations," *Ottawa Citizen,* August 11, 1950, 12.

34. "Central Theater," *Raymond Terrace Examiner & Lower Hunter & Port Stephens Advertiser* (NSW), December 20, 1951, 6.

35. Hedda Hopper, "Looking at Hollywood," *Chicago Tribune,* June 21, 1948, 7.

36. Dorothy Kilgallen, "Nicky Now Dating Starlet of Liz Taylor's Type," *Toledo Blade*, March 2, 1955, 51.

37. "President and Wife Honor Guests at Premiere," *The Deseret News*, April 26, 1951, 2.

38. "Film Weekly," *Western Star* (Roma Toowoomba, Queensland), May 15, 1951, 4.

39. Virginia Grey interview by Mike Fitzgerald: www.westernclippings,com/interview/virginiagrey_interview.htmshl.

40. Ibid.

41. Margaret Bean, "Hoodlum movie is worth seeing; Donlevy Gives Kefauver Boost with his impersonation," *The Spokesman-Review*, April 30, 1952, 5.

42. "Hoodlum Empire," with Brian Donlevy, Claire Trevor, John Russell, Vera Ralston and Forrest Tucker," *Harrison's Reports*, February 23, 1952, 32.

43. "Ride the Man Down A Fine Western," *Film Bulletin*, November 3, 1952, 6.

44. Louella O. Parsons, "Scoops to Get Wally Cox on Screen," *Ottawa Citizen*, August 22, 1953, 18.

45. Hedda Hopper, "Susan Hayward Will Star with 1,000 Zulus," *Chicago Daily Tribune*, February 12, 1954, 12.

46. Anita Fagan "The Rosy Glow," Letter to *The Easthampton Star*, April 11, 2015: www.easthamptonstar.com/Letter-Editor/2015514/Letters-Editor-151415.

47. Gregory Mank, "Brian Donlevy, 1901–72," *Films in Review*, April 1975, 221.

48. Ibid.

Chapter 10

1. "Retrospect Reveals Achievements of the Past Year," *Pittsburgh Post-Gazette*, December 30, 1940, 24.

2. Erskine Johnson, "Hollywood Talk of Movies, Stars," *The Southeast Missourian*, April 6, 1950, 12.

3. "Reviews of TV Shows; Dangerous Assignment (30 mins-29 in series)" *Billboard*, October 3, 1953, 12.

4. Ibid.

5. Jack O'Brian, "Film's Follies," *Herald-Journal*, February 15, 1978, A6.

6. "Actress Files Suit in Nazi Spy Case," *Toledo Blade*, February 18, 1954, 4.

7. www.henryswesternroundup.blog

spot.co.uk/2010/10/republic-3-big-valley-2.html.

8. *Daily Independent Journal*, October 2, 1954, 16.

9. "Four California Studios to Shoot Pilot," *Billboard*, November 15,1 1955, 4.

10. Ultan Macken, *Walter Macken: Dreams on Paper* (Blackrock, Cork, Ireland: Mercier Press, 2009), 328.

11. Jack O' Brian, *St. Petersburgh Times*, May 20, 1956, 69.

12. "The National Spotlight: Portland," *Motion Picture Herald*, December 24, 1955, 32.

13. Rick du Brow, "'Saints and Sinners,' Debuts," *Eugene Register-Guard*, September 18, 1962, 8A.

14. "Complete Television Programs for Monday," *Pittsburgh Post-Gazette*, January 2, 1967, M-3.

Chapter 11

1. "Actor Convicted," *St. Petersburg Times*, April 7 1955, 3.

2. "Brian Donlevy Fined," *The Tuscaloosa News*, April 7 1955, 26.

3. Alain Silver, and Elizabeth Ward, *Film Noir* (London: Secker & Warburg, 1980), 29.

4. Ibid.

5. Francis M. Nevins, *Joseph H. Lewis: Overview, Interview & Filmography* (Lanham, MD: Scarecrow Press, 1998), 62.

6. Sheilah Graham, *The Spokesman-Review*, June 19 1951, 5.

7. "Back to the Moulin Rouge: Jean Renoir's New Film" *The London Times*, August 29 1955, 10.

8. "Film Stars Glow, But Queen Steals the Show," *Toledo Blade*, November 16, 1954, 6.

9. "Philip Tips Royal Taboos in Humanizing First Family," *Rome News-Tribune*, November 26 1954, 13.

10. Marcus Hearn, and Jonathan Rigby, Liner notes to DVD release of *The Quatermass Xperiment* (London, 2003) DD06157.

11. Ibid.

12. Andy Murray, *Into the Unknown: The Fantastic Life of Nigel Kneale* (London: Headpress, 2003) 56.

13. Tom Weaver, *Val Guest: Double Fea-*

ture Creature Attack (Jefferson, N.C.: Mc-Farland, 2003), 110.

14. Paul Welsh, "Blow By Blow Account," The Borehamwood & Elstree Times, February 8, 2007, 8.

15. Wayne Kinsey, Hammer Films: The Bray Studio Years (London: Reynolds & Hearn, 2002), 35.

16. John Brosnan, The Primal Screen: A History of Science Fiction Films (London: Orbit, 1991), 77.

17. Sheilah Graham, "Gadabout's Diary: Rita's Film Company Dockers Stage Hit," The Deseret News, July 1956, B9.

18. Edwin Schallert, "Drama; Gail Russell to Star as Pioneer Nurse," Los Angeles Times, October 26, 1955, B7.

19. Leonard Lyons, "The Lyons Den," Reading News, January 3, 1955, 8.

20. https:/en.wikipedia.org/wiki/Reuben_Reuben_(opera)

21. Mike Connolly, "Ingrid, Roberto, To Be Separated," The Desert Sun, December 13, 1956, B6.

22. Charles Tranberg, I Love the Illusion: The Life and Career of Agnes Moorehead (Jefferson, N.C.: McFarland, 2007), 178–9.

23. "Edwin Schallert, Brian Donlevy Will Do 'Golden Spur' On Own," Los Angeles Times, June 14, 1957, A9.

24. William R. Wilson, "Escape from Red Rock," Motion Picture Daily, January 3, 1958, 4.

25. Peter Ford, Glenn Ford: A Life (Madison, Wisconsin: University of Wisconsin Press, 2011), 178.

26. "Never So Few, with Frank Sinatra and Gina Lollobrigida, " Harrison's Reports, December 12, 1959, 198.

27. Lovell, Glenn, Escape Artist: The Life and Films of John Sturges (Madison: The University of Wisconsin Press, 2008), 169–170.

28. Harold Heffernan, "Bad Public Relations Job Or Not, Donlevy Keeps Lip-Whiskers," Toledo Blade, 23.

29. "Actor Brian Donlevy Wins $15,000 Lawsuit," The Southeast Missourian, January 25, 1960, 3.

30. William Wellman, Jr., Wild Bill Wellman, Hollywood Rebel (New York: Pantheon Books, 2015), 353.

31. Paul Parla, and Charles P. Mitchell, Scream, Sirens, Scream! Interviews with 20

Actresses from Science Fiction, Horror, Film Noir and Mystery Movies, 1930s to 1960s (Jefferson, N.C.: McFarland, 1999), 232.

Chapter 12

1. "'Andersonville Trial' Magnificent Production," The Post-Crescent, November 28, 1960, 8.

2. Harold Heffernan, "Donlevy Returns to Comedy," The Pittsburgh Press, September 7, 1961, 13.

3. Leslie Halliwell, Halliwell's Film Guide (London: Guild, 1983), 253.

4. Heffernan, "Donlevy Returns to Comedy."

5. "Donlevy Returns to Life in Hollywood After Exile," Schenectady Gazette, March 31, 1964, 10.

6. Ibid.

7. John Hamilton, The British Independent Horror Film 1951–70 (Hemlock Books, 2013), 132–6.

8. https://en.wikipedia.org/wiki/Gammera_(film)

9. "The Screen: "Wild Bikini" Arrives in Neighborhoods," New York Times, January 12, 1967, 48.

10. Frank Ferrucio, and Damien Santroni, Did Success Spoil Jayne Mansfield? Her Life in Pictures & Text (Parker, Colorado: Outskirts Press, 2010), 80.

11. C. Courtney Joyner, The Westerners: Interviews with Actors, Directors, Writers & Producers (Jefferson, N.C.: McFarland, 2009), 119.

12. www.imdb.com/title/tt0066036/trivia.

13. Tom Johnson, and Mark Miller, The Christopher Lee Filmography 1948–2003 (Jefferson, N.C.: McFarland, 2004), 161.

Chapter 13

1. Gregory Mank, Bela Lugosi and Boris Karloff: The Expanded Story of a Haunting Collaboration (Jefferson, N.C.: McFarland, 2009), 51–53.

2. Gary Don Rhodes, Lugosi: His Life in Films, on Stage, and in the Hearts of Horror Lovers (Jefferson, N.C.: McFarland, 1997), 52.

3. Ibid.

4. Arthur Lennig, *The Immortal Count: The Life and Films of Bela Lugosi* (Lexington: University Press of Kentucky, 2003), 430.

5. Rhodes, *Lugosi,* 52.

6. "Lillian Lugosi to Wed Brian Donlevy," *Park City Daily,* February 22, 1966, 22.

7. Lewis Hardee, *The Lambs Theater Club* (Jefferson, N.C.: McFarland, 2006), 193.

8. *The Masonic Philatelist Quarterly,* December 2014, Vol. 70, No. 4 (The Masonic Stamp Club of New York), 15.

9. www.aopa.org/

10. "Don Becoming Aerial Commuter," *The Pittsburgh Press,* April 29, 1940, 11.

11. Harold Heffernan, "Bad Public Relations; Job or Not, Don Keeps Lip-Whiskers," *Toledo Blade,* February 18, 1960, 23.

12. "Actor Crash Lands," *The Pittsburgh Press,* January 12, 1950, 2.

13. "Hollywood Film News," *South Western Advertiser,* February 6, 1948, 11.

14. Gregory Mank, "Brian Donlevy, 1901–72," *Films in Review,* April 1975, 222.

15. Bela G. Lugosi, telephone conversation with the author, November 23, 2015.

16. "Hollywood Sights and Sounds," *Prescott Evening Courier,* October 13, 1947, 4.

17. Bela G. Lugosi, telephone conversation with the author, November 23, 2015.

18. Arthur Lennig, *The Immortal Count: The Life and Films of Bela Lugosi* (Lexington: University Press of Kentucky, 2003), 433.

19. Gregory Mank, *Women in Horror Films* (Jefferson, N.C.: McFarland, 2005), 12.

20. www.metacritic.com/person/brian-donlevy: Confirmed by Bela G. Lugosi in telephone conversation with the author, November 23, 2015.

21. Gregory Mank, "Brian Donlevy, 1901–72," 222.

Epilogue

1. Jimmie Fidler, "Hollywood Shots," *Reading Eagle,* November 1, 1938, 6.

2. Praire Pepper Davis, *Dirt in the Skirt* (Bloomington, Indiana: Author House, 2009), 80.

3. Harold Heffernan, "Actors Harbor Many Silly Superstitions," *Toledo Blade,* May 13, 1960, 26.

4. Moira Finnie, "Brian Donlevy: A Tough Guy Not a Wrong Guy," September 24, 2008: moviemorlocks.com/2008/09124/brian-donlevy-a-tough-guy-not-a-wrong-guy/

5. Gregory Mank, "Brian Donlevy, 1901–72," *Films in Review,* April 1975, 219.

6. "Film News and Players Gossip," *Frankston and Somerville Standard,* June 5, 36, 3.

7. "Let's Look in on Hollywood," *The World's News,* April 22, 1944, 9.

8. "Here Comes the Marine!" (Page from an unknown magazine), circa 1942.

Theater

1. Wilella Waldorf: "Forecasts and Postscripts," *New York Evening Post,* August 19, 1933, 12.

Radio

1. Vincent Terrace, *Radio Programs 1924–84: A Catalog of More Than 1800 Shows* (Jefferson, N.C.: McFarland, 2010), 151.

2. John Dunning, *On the Air: The Encyclopedia of Old-Time Radio* (New York: Oxford University Press, 1998), 182.

3. *Lincoln Highway Radio Show,* The Lincoln Highway National Museum & Archives www.lincoln-highway-museum.org/Radio/Radio-index.html.

4. Vincent Terrace, *Radio Programs 1924–84: A Catalog of More Than 1800 Shows* (Jefferson, N.C.: McFarland, 2010), 334.

5. John Dunning, *On the Air: The Encyclopedia of Old-Time Radio* (New York: Oxford University Press, 1998), 185.

6. "Vick Knight Spurns Film Offer, Auditions Show for Morris," *Variety,* March 24, 1943, 29.

7. Harry Mackenzie, *The Directory of the Armed Forces Radio Service Series* (Westport, Connecticut: Greenwood Press, 1999), 19.

Television

1. "The Policy of Joe Aladdin," available on DVD Ford Theater Disc 3, and "Double Trouble" on Ford Theater Disc 22. From: www.rockandrollondvd.com/

2. "The National Spotlight: Portland," *Motion Picture Herald,* December 24, 1955, 32.

3. Louise Bland KUTL www.tulsatv memories.com/bland.html/

4. "Your TV Scout," *Times Daily,* November 7, 1969, 13.

Recordings

1. "Harold Arlen's Best Known Songs and Recordings Available," *Billboard* July 22, 1950 p440. Although this record was listed by *Billboard,* a modern-day recording of the show was made by the Library of Congress and released in June 2010 on the PS Classics label PS-1090 (See www. psclassics.com/cd_lifebeginsat840.html.)

2. Max U. Bildersee "Records on Review," *Educational Screen,* January, 1955, 37.

Bibliography

Affron, Charles, and Mirella Jona. *Best Years: Going to the Movies 1945–46.* New Brunswick, New Jersey: Rutgers University Press, 2009.

Ardmore, Jane. *The Self Enchanted: Mae Murray: Image of the Era.* New York: McGraw-Hill Book Company Inc., 1959.

Astor, Mary. *A Life on Film.* London: W. H. Allen, 1973.

Backer, Ron. *Mystery Movie Series of 1940s Hollywood.* Jefferson, NC: McFarland, 2010.

Barnouw, Erik. *Documentary: A History of the Non-Fiction Film.* New York: Oxford University Press, 2012.

Barris, Alex. *Hollywood's Other Men.* Brunswick, NJ: A. S. Barnes & Co., 1975.

Barrymore, Diana, and Frank Gerold. *Too Much, Too Soon.* New York: Henry Holt and Company, 1957.

Base, Ron. *Starring Roles: How Hollywood Stardom Is Won and Lost.* New York: Little, Brown & Co., 1994.

Basinger, Jeanine. *The Star Machine.* New York: Vintage, 2009.

Behlmer, Rudy. *Memo for Darryl F. Zanuck: The Golden Years at Twentieth Century-Fox.* New York: Grove Press, 1993.

Belafonte, Dennis. *The Films of Tyrone Power.* New York: Citadel Press, 1979.

Bergan, Ronald. *The United Artists Story.* London: Octopus Books, 1986.

Black, Gregory. *Hollywood Censored.* Cambridge: Cambridge University Press, 1994.

Bloom, Ken. *Broadway: An Encyclopedia.* London: Routledge, 2004.

Blum, Daniel. *A Pictorial History of Talkies.* London: Spring Books, 1964.

Bookbinder, Robert. *The Films of Bing Crosby.* New York: Citadel Press, 1977.

Boyer, Paul. *By the Bomb's Early Light: American Thought and Culture at the Dawn of the Atomic Age.* Chapel Hill: Orange County, University of North Carolina Press, 1985.

Brigham, Albert Perry. *The United States of America: Studies in Physical, Regional, Industrial and Human Geography.* London: University of London Press, Ltd., 1926.

Broman, Gerald. *American Theater: A Chronicle of Comedy and Drama 1930–69.* New York: Oxford University Press, 1996.

Brooks, Juanita. *The Mountain Meadows Massacre.* Palo Alto, CA: Stanford University Press, 1950.

Brosnan, John. *The Primal Screen: A History of Science Fiction Films.* London: Orbit, 1991.

Buscombe, Edward. *The BFI Companion to the Western.* New York: Atheneum Press, 1988.

Butler, Ivan. *The War Film.* Cranbury, NJ: A. S. Barnes & Co., 1974.

Ceplair, Larry, and Christopher Trumbo. *Dalton Trumbo: Blacklisted Hollywood Radical.* Lexington: University of Kentucky Press, 2014.

Chandler, Charlotte. *Marlene: A Personal Biography.* London: JR Books, 2011.

Chierichetti, David. *Mitchell Leisen: Hollywood Director.* Los Angeles, CA: Photoventures Company, 1995.

Curley, Stephen J., and Frank Joseph Wetta. *Celluloid Wars: A Guide to Film and the American Experience of War.* Westport, Connecticut: Greenwood Press, 1992.

195

Curtis, James. *Spencer Tracy A Biography.* London: Hutchinson, 2011.

Cutler, Lawrence S., and Judy Goff Cutler. *J. C. Leyendecker: American Imagist.* Ann Arbor: University of Michigan, 2008.

Davis, Pepper Paire. *Dirt in the Skirt.* Bloomington, IN: Author House, 2009.

Davis, Ronald L. *Hollywood Beauty: Linda Darnell and the American Dream.* Norman: University of Oklahoma, 1991.

Devine, Dennis. *Your Friend and Mine, Andy Devine.* Albany, GA: Bear Manor Media, 2013.

Dick, Bernard F. *Forever Mame: The Life of Rosalind Russell.* Mississippi: University Press of Mississippi, 2011.

_____. *The Merchant Prince of Poverty Row: Harry Cohn of Columbia Pictures.* Lexington: University of Kentucky Press, 2015.

Donati, William. *Ida Lupino: A Biography.* Lexington: University of Kentucky Press, 1996.

Dunning, John. *On the Air: The Encyclopedia of Old-Time Radio.* New York: Oxford University Press, 1998.

Durgnant, Raymond, and Scott Simmon. *King Vidor, American.* Oakland: University of California Press, 1988.

Eames, John Douglas. *The MGM Story.* London: Octopus Books, 1979.

_____. *The Paramount Story.* London: Octopus Books, 1985.

Elder, Jane Lenz. *Alice Faye: A Life Beyond the Silver Screen.* Jackson: University of Mississippi Press, 2002.

Everson, William C. *The Bad Guys: A Pictorial History of the Movie Villain.* New York: Citadel Press, 1964.

Fane-Saunders, Kilmeny. *Radio Times Guide to Films.* London: BBC Worldwide, 2003.

Ferruccio, Frank. *Did Success Spoil Jayne Mansfield? Her Life in Pictures and Text.* Parker, Colorado: Outskirts Press, 2010.

Flammer, Philip M. *The Vivid Air: The Lafayette Escadrille.* Athens: University of Georgia Press, 1981.

Fleming, E. J. *The Movieland Directory: Nearly 30,000 Addresses of Celebrity Homes, Film Locations and Historical Sites in the Los Angeles Area 1900-Present.* Jefferson, NC: McFarland, 2010.

Ford, Peter. *Glenn Ford: A Life.* Madison: University of Wisconsin Press, 2011.

Freedland, Michael. *Some Like It Cool: The Charmed Life of Jack Lemmon.* London: Robson Books, 2002.

Fyne, Robert. *The Hollywood Propaganda of WWII.* Lanham, MD: Scarecrow Press, 1997.

Gevinson, Alan. *Within Our Gates: Ethnicity in American Feature Films, 1911–60.* Oakland: University of California Press, 1997.

Grabbard, Krin. *Jammin' at the Margins: Jazz and the American Cinema.* Chicago: University of Chicago Press, 1996.

Grainge, Paul. *Memory and Popular Film.* Manchester: Manchester University Press, 2003.

Gussow, Mel. *Don't Say Yes Until I Finish Talking: A Biography of Darryl F. Zanuck.* New York: Doubleday, 1971.

Hack, G. H. *Genealogical History of the Donlevy Family.* Columbus, OH: Printed for private distribution by Chaucer Press, Evans Printing Company, 1901.

Halliwell, Leslie. *Halliwell's Film Guide.* London: Guild Publishing, Fourth Edition, 1983.

Hamilton, John. *The British Independent Horror Film 1951–70.* Hailsham, East Sussex: Hemlock Books, 2013.

Hanson, Patricia King, and Anny Dunkleberger. *AFI: American Film Institute Catalog of Motion Pictures: Feature Films 1941–50.* Oakland: University of California Press, 1999.

Hardee, Lewis. *The Lambs Theater Club.* Jefferson, NC: McFarland, 2006.

Harvey, James. *Romantic Comedy in Hollywood: From Lubitsch to Sturges.* New York: Da Capo Press, 1998.

Higham, Charles. *Olivia & Joan: A Biography of Olivia de Havilland and Joan Fontaine.* London: New English Library, 1984.

_____, and Joel Greenberg. *The Celluloid Muse: Hollywood Directors Speak.* London: Angus & Robinson, 1969.

Hirschhorn, Clive. *The Universal Story.* London: Octopus Books, 1983.

Hischak, Thomas S. *Boy Loses Girl: Broadway's Librettists.* Lanham, MD: Scarecrow Press, 2003.

_____. *The Rodgers and Hammerstein Encyclopedia.* Westport, Connecticut: Greenwood Press, 2007.

Hotson, Kim R. *Susan Hayward: Her Films and Life.* Jefferson, NC: McFarland, 2002.

Hughes, Howard. *Crime Wave: The Filmgoer's Guide to Great Crime Movies.* London: I. B. Taurus, 2006.

Hunter, Tab, and Eddie Muller. *Tab Hunter Confidential: The Making of a Movie Star.* Chapel Hill, NC: Algonquin Books.

Izzo, David Garrett, and Lincoln Konkle. *Stephen Vincent Benét: Essays on His Life and Work.* Jefferson, NC: McFarland, 2003.

Jacobs, Diane. *Christmas in July: The Life and Art Preston Sturges.* Berkeley: University of California Press, 1992.

Jaeger, Stephan, Elena V. Barabon, and Adam Muller. *Fighting Words and Images: Representing War Across the Disciplines.* Ontario: University of Toronto Press, 2012.

Jewell, Richard B., and Vernon Harbin. *The RKO Story.* London: Octopus Books, 1983.

Johnson, Tom, and Mark A. Miller. *The Christopher Lee Filmography: All Theatrical Releases 1948–2003.* Jefferson, NC: McFarland, 2004.

Joyner, C. Courtney. *The Westerners: Interviews with Actors, Directors, Writers and Producers.* Jefferson, NC: McFarland, 2009.

Kear, Lynn, and John Rossman. *Kay Francis: A Passionate Life and Career.* Jefferson, NC: McFarland, 2006.

Keylin, Arleen, and Suri Fleischer. *Hollywood Album: Lives and Deaths of the Hollywood Stars from the Pages of the New York Times.* NY: Arno Press, 1977.

Kinsey, Wayne. *Hammer Films: The Bray Studio Years.* London: Reynolds & Hearn, 2002.

Kolin, Philip C., and Colby H. Kullman. *Studies in American Drama 1945-Present* Volumes 4–6. University Park: Pennsylvania State University Press, 1990.

Larkins, Bob, and Boyd Magers. *The Films of Audie Murphy.* Jefferson, NC: McFarland, 2004.

Lee, Anna, and Barbara Roisman. *Anna Lee: Memoir of a Career on General Hospital and in Film.* Jefferson, NC: McFarland, 2007.

Lennig, Arthur. *The Immortal Count: The Life and Films of Bela Lugosi.* Lexington: University Press of Kentucky, 2003.

Liebmann, Roy. *Vitaphone Films: A Catalogue of Features & Shorts.* Jefferson, NC: McFarland, 2003.

Linet, Beverly. *Ladd: A Hollywood Tragedy.* New York: Berkley, 1980.

Lombardi, Frederic. *Allan Dwan and the Rise and Decline of the Hollywood Studios.* Jefferson, NC: McFarland, 2013.

Lovell, Glenn. *Escape Artist: The Life and Films of John Sturges.* Madison: The University of Wisconsin Press, 2008.

McInnes, Dick. *Dorothy Lamour: My Side of the Road.* Upper Saddle River, NJ: Prentice-Hall, 1980.

McKay, James. *Dana Andrews: The Face of Noir.* Jefferson, NC: McFarland, 2010.

Macken, Ultan. *Walter Macken: Dreams on Paper.* Blackrock, Cork, Ireland: Mercier Press, 2009.

Mackenzie, Harry. *The Directory of the Armed Forces Radio Service Series.* Westport, CT: Greenwood Press, 1999.

McLean, Adrienne. *Being Rita Hayworth: Labor, Identity, and Hollywood Stardom.* Brunswick, NJ: Rutgers University Press, 2004.

Mank, Gregory. *Bela Lugosi and Boris Karloff: The Expanded Story of a Haunting Collaboration* Jefferson, NC: McFarland, 2009.

_____. *The Very Witching Hour of Night: Dark Alleys of Classic Horror Cinema.* Jefferson, NC: McFarland, 2014.

_____. *Women in Horror Films.* Jefferson, NC: McFarland, 2005.

Marrill, Alvin H. *The Films of Anthony Quinn.* New York: Citadel Press, 1975.

Martin, Len D. *The Republic Pictures Checklist: Features, Serials, Cartoons, Short Subjects and Training Films of Republic Pictures Corporation 1935–59.* Jefferson, NC: McFarland, 2006.

Meade, Marion. *Buster Keaton: Cut to the*

Chase: A Biography. London: Bloomsbury, 1996.

Merck, Mandy. *America First: Naming the
Nation in U. S. Film*. London: Routledge,
2007.

Mitchell, Greg. *Hollywood Bomb: The Un-
making of 'The Most Important Movie
Ever Made.'* New York: Sinclair Books,
2013.

Monaco, James. *The Movie Guide*. New
York: Perigee, 1996.

Mordden, Ethan. *All That Glitters: The
Golden Age of Broadway 1919–1959*. New
York: St Martin's Press, 2015.

Munden, Kenneth W. *The American Film
Institute Catalog of Motion Pictures: Feature Films 1931–40*. Oakland: University
of California Press, 1993.

Murray, Andy. *Into the Unknown: The Fantastic Life of Nigel Kneale*. London: Headpress, 2006.

Nevins, Francis M. *Joseph H. Lewis:
Overview, Interview and Filmography*.
Lanham, Maryland: Scarecrow Press,
1998.

Noll, Roger, and The Dodge County Historical Society Inc. *Beaver Dam 1841–
1941*. Charleston, SC: Arcadia Publishing,
2003.

Nott, Robert. *The Films of Randolph Scott*.
Jefferson, NC: McFarland, 2004.

Paris, Michael. *From the Wright Brothers to
Top Gun: Aviation, Nationalism and Pop-
ular Culture*. Manchester: Manchester
University Press, 1995.

Parish, James Robert, and Bowers, Ronald
L. *The MGM Stock Company: The Golden
Era*. London: Ian Allan Ltd, 1973.

Parla, Paul, and Charles P. Mitchell. *Scream
Sirens Scream! Interviews with 20 Ac-
tresses from Science Fiction, Horror, Film
Noir and Mystery Movies, 1930s to 1960s*.
Jefferson, NC: McFarland,1999.

Quinlan, David. *The Illustrated Directory
of Film Stars*. London: B. T. Batsford Ltd,
1981.

Quirk, Lawrence J. *The Films of William
Holden*. New York: Citadel Press, 1973.

Reed, Alan, and Ben Ohmart. *Yabba Dabba
Doo! The Alan Reed Story*. Albany, GA:
Bear Manor Media, 2009.

Rhodes, Gary Don. *Lugosi: His Life in
Films, on Stage, and in the Hearts of Horror Lovers*. Jefferson, NC: McFarland,
1997.

Rollyson, Carl. *Dana Andrews: Hollywood
Enigma*. Jackson: University Press of
Mississippi, 2012.

_____. *A Real American Character: The Life
of Walter Brennan*. Jackson: University
Press of Mississippi, 2015.

Rooney, Mickey. *Life is Too Short: An Au-
tobiography*. London: Hutchinson & Co,
1992.

Santo Pietro, Mary Ann, and Gilbert V.
Hartke. *Father Hartke: His Life and
Legacy to the American Theater*. Wash-
ington, D.C.: The Catholic University of
America Press, 2002.

Schlossheimer, Michael. *Gangsters and Gun-
men*. Jefferson, NC: McFarland, 2001.

Sennett, Ted. *Masters of Menace: Greenstreet
and Lorre*. New York: E. P. Dutton, 1979.

Shepherd, David, and Frank Thompson.
*Henry King, Director: From Silents to
'Scope*. Los Angeles, CA: Directors Guild
of America, 1996.

Shipman, David. *The Great Movie Stars:
The Golden Years*. London: Hamlyn,
1970.

Shull, Michael J., and David Edward Wilt.
*Hollywood War Films 1937–45: An Ex-
haustive Filmography of American
Feature-Length Motion Pictures Relating
to World War II*. Jefferson, NC: McFarland,1996.

Silver, Alain, and Elizabeth Ward. *Film
Noir*. London: Secker & Warburg, 1979.

Smith, Don G. *Lon Chaney, Jr.: Horror Film
Star, 1906–73*. Jefferson, NC: McFarland,
2004.

Smith, J. D., and Len Gutteridge. *Jack Teagarden: The Story of a Jazz Maverick*.
London: The Jazz Book Club, 1960.

Sobol, Louis. *The Longest Street: A Memoir*.
New York: Crown Publishers, 1968.

Stuart, Gloria and, Sylvia Thompson. *I Just
Kept Hoping*. New York: Little, Brown &
Company, 1999.

Taylor, John Russell. *The Pleasure Dome:
Graham Greene: The Collected Film Criticism 1935–40*. London: Secker & Warburg, 1972.

Terrace, Vincent. *Radio Programs 1924–84:
A Catalog of More Than 1800 Shows*. Jefferson, NC: McFarland, 2010.

Thomas, Bob. *Golden Boy: The Untold Story of William Holden*. London: Weidenfeld & Nicholson, 1983.

Thomas, Tony. *Joel McCrea: Riding the High Country*. Burbank, CA: Riverwood Press, 1991.

_____, and Aubrey Solomon. *The Films of 20th Century Fox*. New York: Citadel Press, 1979.

Tierney, Tom. *Ziegfeld Follies Paper Dollies*. North Chelmsford, MA: Courier Corporation, 1985.

Tranberg, Charles. *I Love the Illusion: The Life and Career of Agnes Moorehead*. Albany, GA: Bear Manor Media, 2007.

_____. *Robert Taylor: A Biography*. Albany, GA: Bear Manor Media, 2011.

Van der Merwe, Ann Ommen. *The Ziegfeld Follies: A History in Song*. Lanham, MD: Scarecrow Press, 2009.

Viera, Mark A. *Majestic Hollywood: The Greatest Films of 1939*. Philadelphia: Running Press, 2013.

Wearing, J. P. *The London Stage: 1930–1939: A Calendar of Productions, Performers & Personnel*. Lanham, MD: Rowman & Littlefield, 2014.

Weaver, David E. *Black Diva of the Thirties: The Life of Ruby Elzy*. Jackson: University Press of Mississippi, 2015.

Weaver, Tom. *Return of the B Science Fiction and Horror: The Mutant Melding of Two Volumes of Classic Interviews*. Jefferson, NC: McFarland, 2000.

_____. *Science Fiction: 20 Interviews with Classic Science Fiction and Horror Filmmakers*. Jefferson, NC: McFarland, 2003.

_____. *Val Guest: Double Feature Creature Attack*. Jefferson, NC: McFarland, 2003.

Wellman, William, Jr. *Wild Bill Wellman: Hollywood Rebel*. New York: Pantheon Books, 2015.

Wilson, Victoria. *Steel True: A Life of Barbara Stanwyck 1907–1940, Volume 1*. London: Simon & Schuster, 2004.

Yavenditti, Michael J. 1978. "Atomic Scientists and Hollywood: The Beginning or the End?" *Film & History: An Interdisciplinary Journal of Film and Television Studies*. 8, no. 4: 51–66.

Index

Page numbers in **_bold italics_** indicate pages with illustrations

Abbey Theater 135
Abbott & Costello 52, 120
Abel, Walter 56, 88
Academy Awards 46, 51, 163
Across the Aisle aka *36 Hours to Kill* 37–8
Across the Pacific 72
Adams, Nick 136
The Addams Family 120
Adler, Luther 127, 128
Advance Agents to Africa 76
The Advertiser 46
Aircraft Owners and Pilots Association (AOPA) 161
Alexander, Ross 25
All Quiet on the Western Front 25
Allegheny Uprising 52–54
Alton, John 138
Ameche, Don 1, 43, 43, 81
American Cancer Society 132
"The American Flag" 88
An American Romance **85**, 85–6, 99
The American Vagabond 62
American Woolen Company 4
Amiel, Denys 24
Anderson, Eddie "Rochester" 65
Anderson, Maxwell 17, 76, 115
Anderson, Richard 144
The Andersonville Trial 150, 151
Andrews, Dana 1, 100, 115
Angelus, Muriel **56**
Annapolis Navy Academy 9–10, 30
Another Face 31–2
Another Man's Son 24
An Arctic Voyage 84
Arden, Eve 104, 122
Arizona Bushwhackers 157
Arlen, Harold 26
Asbury, Herbert 30
The Asphalt Jungle 118
Astor, Mary 60
"At Ease" 135
Aumont, Jean-Pierre 102, **103**, 104

The Babe Ruth Story 112
Bad Boy 124
Baker, George 153, 154
Baker, George Pierce 15
Balcon, Michael 76
Baldwin, Louise A. 89
Ball, Lucille 90
Barbary Coast 28–30, **29**, 69
The Barbary Coast, (Novel) 30
Barrie, J.M. 124
Barrymore, Diana **79**, 80
Barrymore, Lionel 105
Barton, Charles 52
Barton, Jim 22
Baruch, Bernard 105
Basie, Count 152
Bates, Sumner 96
Battle of Broadway 43
Bautzter, Greg 122
Baxter, Alan 30, 33
Baxter, Warner 115
Bayard, Andrea 148
Beach, Charles 13
Beau Geste 2, 46, 49–52, 54, 129, 148
Beau Hunks 50
Beck, Thomas 38, **39**
Beery, Wallace 49
Beginning or the End 104–6, 121
Behind Prison Gates 52
Bendix, William 76, 78, 81, 98, 99, 112
Benet, Steven Vincent 132
Bennett, Charles 104
Bennett, Joan 33
Benny, Jack 114
Bergman, Ingrid 87
Berkeley, Busby 19
Berlin, Irving 18
Bernds, Edward 145
The Best Years of Our Life 86
Beveridge, Colonel Byron 2
"Beyond This Place" 153
Bezzerides, A.I. 62
Bickford, Charles 48
"Big Boy" 112, 131

The Big Combo 2, 137–39, **138**
Big Town Girl 45
Billy the Kid 64, 72
The Bing Crosby Show 132
Birth of the Blues 64–5, 99
The Black Cat 110
"The Black Path of Fear" 131
Blackmer, Sidney 44
Blair, Janet 66
Blitzstein, Mark 145
Blyth, Ann 111
Boccaccio, Giovanni 26
Bogart, Humphrey 55, 78, 80, 123
Bohr, Dr. Niels 105
Bolger, Ray 26, 27
Bonanza 120
Bond, Ward 36, 101
"Boomer Jones" 132
Born Reckless 41–2
Born Yesterday (Film) 123
Born Yesterday (Play) 115
The Boy Friend 23–4
Boyer, Charles 63
"The Boys in the Backroom" 54
Boys' Own 50
Boys' Ranch 88
Breen, Joseph 30, 40
Brennan, Walter **29**, 61, 82
Brent, George 66
The Brian Donlevy Fan Club 89
Bridges, Lloyd 101
Brigham Young—Frontiersman 59–60
Broadway 124
The Broadway Drifter 17
"Broadway Review" 23
Broken Doll 24
Bronson, Charles 134
Brooklyn Daily Eagle 28
Brown, Judge Merrill 161
Brown, Kathryn 95
Buddies 9
Burke, James 38
Burnett, W.R. 38
The Burns & Allen Show 132
Burr, Raymond 144
Burstyn, Ellen 159
Butch Minds the Baby 66
Butterworth, Charles 35
Buy Me That Town 76
Byington, Spring 24

Cabanne, Christy 15, 32
Cagney, James 27, 53, 123, 124
The Caine Mutiny Court Martial 123
Calhern, Louis 23
Call Northside 777 120
Call of the Wild 30
Calleia, Joseph 77
Cameron, Rod 112, 128
Cantor, Eddie 2, 32–3

Canyon Passage 1, 2, 100–110
Cape Playhouse, Massachusetts 24
Capra, Frank 58
"Capricio Espagnol" 103–4
Captain Blood 25
Career Girl 148
Carey, Macdonald 82
Caribbean Patrol 81
Carlisle, Elsie 7
Carmichael, Hoagy 101
Carradine, John 47
Carriere, "Pokey" 65
Cartwright, Jorja **109**
The Cat and the Canary 30
Cat People 101
Cavalcade of America 131
Cavalcade of the Air 130
Celluloid War 8
Chadwick, Sir James 105
Chandler, Major "Speed" 130
Chaney, Lon, Jr. **47**
Chapman, Marguerite 123
Charlie Chan 38
Charlie Chan on Broadway 45
Chasing Danger 44
Chatto, Tom 143
Chevrolet Tele-Theater 132
Child, Barbara 21
Child, Richard Washburn 69
Christmas in July 55
Chronicles of America 15
Churchill, Sir Winston 121
The Cinderella Racket 21
Clark, Dane 123
Climax! 135
Coburn, Charles 118
Collins, Eddie 43
Colman, Ronald 49
Columbia University 9, 13
Coming Up For Air 121
Command Decision 112–3
Conreid, Hans 146
Conroy, Frank 40
Considine, Bob 105
Conte, Richard 137, **138**
Coogan, Jackie 157
Cook, Elisha, Jr. 24, 25
Coolidge, Calvin 12
Cooper, Gary 1, 46, 49, 112
Corey, Wendell 130, 157
Corrigan, Douglas "Wrong Way" 130
Cortina, Dr. Jose Manuel 94
Corwin, Norman 145
Cosmopolitan 71
Cotton, Joseph 87
The Count of Monte Cristo 123
The Country Girl 130
The Court of Human Relations 131
Cowboy 146
Cox, Wally 130

Crack Up 38–40, **39**
Craig, James 88
Craven, Frank 22
Crawford, Broderick 60, 65, 66
Crawford, Joan 122
Crime Doctor 132
Criterion Theater 22
Cronin, A.J. 136
Crosby, Bing 64, 65
Crossroads 133
Crothers, Rachel 24
The Crowd Roars 111
Crowther, Bosley 56, 57
A Cry in the Night 144
Cummings, Robert 109, 110, 157
Cunha, Richard E. 147–8
The Curse of Frankenstein 144–5
The Curse of the Fly 144, **153**, 153–5
Curtis, Tony 123

Dahl, Arlene 111
The Daily Flash 159
Dale, Esther 30
The Daltons Ride Again 61
Damaged Hearts 16
Dana, Richard Henry 97, 98
Dance Hall 72
Dangerous Assignment 70, 79, 130, 132, 133–4, 160
The Dark Corner 120
Dark of the Moon 82
Dark Passage 32
Darley, Brian 8
Darwell, Jane 1, 47, 48
Da Silva, Howard 98, 126
Dassin, Jules 144
Davalos, Richard **158**, 159
Davis, Owen, Jr. 25
Davis, "Pepper" Paire 163–4
Davis, Rupert 157
Day, Laraine 82
"A Day at the Brokers" 26
"Dear George, the Siamese Cat Is Missing" 136
De Balzac, Honore 26
De Carlo, Yvonne 102, **103**, 104, 157
Decca Records 88
De Cordova, Arturo 81
Dee, Frances 34, **35**
De Havilland, Olivia 63
Dekker, Albert 50, 74, 76, 155
Delmar, Vena 71
Demarest, William 55, 102
De Maupassant, Guy 26
De Mille, Cecil B. 2, 47–48
Denault, Ed 161
Desert Padre 88
Destry Rides Again 46, **53**, 54
Devine, Andy 65
Dietrich, Marlene 54

Dietz, Howard 86
Diller, Phyllis 156
Dinehart, Alan 40
Donat, Robert 80
Donlevy, Bridy (great-grandmother) 4
Donlevy, Christopher (grandfather) 4
Donlevy, Christopher, Jr. 4
Donlevy, Ellen (née Gilliman) 4
Donlevy, Frank 4
Donlevy, Frank Henry "Spink" (half-brother) 4, 6–7
Donlevy, James 4
Donlevy, Judith Ann (daughter) 88, 94–6, 104, 109, 139, 144, 162
Donlevy, Martha 4
Donlevy, Peter (great-grandfather) 4
Donlevy, Rebecca (née Parks, mother) 3, 4–5, 17, 46, 164
Donlevy, Thomas Henry (father) 3–5, 10, 17, 22, 164
Double Indemnity 81
"Double Trouble" 110
Douglas, Adele 145
Douglas, Melvyn 30
Douglas, Paul 115, 122, 139
Douglas, Stephen A. 145
Dowling, Doris 135
Downey, Morton 21
Drake, Frances 40
Drake, Joseph Redman 88
Dratler, Jay 120
Drew, Ellen 67, **68**
Duff, Howard 122, 123
Duffy's Tavern 88
Duna, Steffi 55
Duncan, Pamela 122
Dunn, James 110, 111
Dupont Show of the Week 135
Duryea, Dan 157–8
Dutch Treat 76
Dvorak, Ann 91
Dwan, Allan 35

Eagle-Lion 115
Ealing Studios 76
Earl Carroll Vanities 16
Earl Grant Trio 146
Early, Walter 87
Earth and Climactic Belts 84
Easton, Robert 134
"Ee By Gum" 44
Einstein, Albert 105
Elizabeth II, Queen 141
Elzy, Ruby 65
Enemy from Space 141–4, **142**
Engel, Sam 115
Eno's Crime Club 131
Enter Mr. Webster 115
The Errand Boy **151**, 151–2
"Escape" 135

Escape from Alcatraz aka *Escape from Red Rock* 145
Etting, Ruth 21
Eve of Revolution 15
Eve of Saint Mark 76
Evening Independent (Florida) 19
"Everybody's Crazy Ceptin' Me" 126
Everything Happens to Him 81
Excellent Pictures 17

Face of Fu Manchu 155
Fadden, Tom 69
Fairbanks, Douglas, Jr. 62
Fallon, William J. 135
Family Affair 52, 136
Farrand, Colonel Roy F. 3
Farrell, Glenda 36
Farrow, John 74, 98, 99, 132
The Fat Spy 156
Faye, Alice 42
Fernandez, Esther 98
Ferrer, Mel 132
Fetchit, Stepin 38
Fick, Dr. Bob 96
Fields, Gracie 2, 43–4
Fighting Coast Guard 124–6, **125**
Film Bulletin 128
The Film Daily 67
Fire 115
The First Rebel aka *Allegheny Uprising* 58
Fitzpatrick, Byron "Sugar" 99
Five Golden Dragons 157–8
Flagg, James Montgomery 15, 91
"Flight of the Bumblebee" 103
Flippen, Jay C. 135, 145
The Fly 154
Flying Fortress 66
Fonda, Henry 25
For Whom the Bell Tolls 72, 123
Forbes, Bryan 142
Ford, Glenn 146
Ford, John 60, 64
Ford, Wallace 31–2
Ford Television Theater 110
Forde, Eugene 38, 166
Forgotten Faces 69
Foster, Norman **20**
Foster, Preston 44, 69
The Four Freedoms Show 76
Fowler, Gene 35, 135
Fowley, Douglas 36
Francis, Kay 20, 60
Frankenstein's Daughter 148
Franklin, Benjamin 67
Franklyn, William 142, 143
Franz Lehar Festival 132
The Front Page 52, 104
Frontier Town 115
Fulton Theater 24

Gabel, Martin 145
Gable, Clark 30, 57, 105, **112**, 113–4
Gabor, Magda 135
Gaiety Theater 22
Gam, Rita 135
The Gamma People 139
Gammera the Invincible 144, 155–6
Gargan, William 28
Garner, Peggy Ann 136
Garnett, Tay 76
Garrett, Pat 64
Garrick Theater, Detroit 18
Gaynor, Janet 38
Gehrig, Lou 112
The General 111
A Gentleman After Dark 69–70
Gentlemen of the Press **20**, 20–1
George, Gladys 26
George White's Scandals of 1925 19
Gershwin, George 26
Gilkyson, Terry 126
Gilliman, Ann (née Riley) 4
Gilliman, Brian (great-grandfather) 4
The Girl in Room 13 134, 147–9
The Glass Key 76–8
Globe Theater 19
"God of Kandahar" 133
Godzilla 155
The Golden Spur 145
Goldwyn, Sam 28
Gomez, Thomas 135
Gone with the Wind 46, 113
Gordon, Mary 61
Gordon, Ruth 24, 161
Gould, Jay 115
Granach, Alexander 82
Granger, Farley 136, 157
Grant, Cary 81
Gray, Carole 154
Gray, Colleen 108
The Great John L. 88
The Great Man's Lady 51, 71–2, 148
The Great McGinty 2, 23, 47, 55–9, 61, 73, 74, 78, 163
The Great McGinty (radio) 131
The Great McGinty (television) 135
The Great Mouthpiece 135
Green Room Club 16
Greene, Graham 41
Greene, Richard 66
Gregory, Paul 130
Grey, Virginia 126–7
Grey, Yvonne 18–19, 20, 22–3, 27, 90
Groves, General 105–6
Guest, Val 141
A Guy Named Joe 81

Hague, Frank 57
Hahn, S.S. 96
Haig, Sid 158

The Hairy Ape 16
The Hairy Ape (Film) 81
Half Angel 34–5, **35**
Hall, Bert 8
Hall, Thurston 134
Halperin, Victor 16
Hamilton, Neil 15
Hammer Films 139, 144
Hammerstein, Oscar, II 19
Hammett, Dashiell 76
Hangmen Also Die! 1, 82–4, **83**
Hannan, James 95
"Hard-Hat Jody" 136
Harding, Warren G. 12
Harlow, Jean 91
Harrison, Rex 69
Hart, William S. 123
Hathaway, Henry 2, 46, 49, 59, 107
Hawks, Howard 28, 64
Hayward, Susan 1, 57, 100
Hayworth, Rita 33–4, **34**
Heaven Only Knows **109**, 109–11
Hedison, David 154
Heflin, Van 106
Heisler, Stuart 67
Hellmann, Lillian 26
Helton, Percy 134
Hemingway, Ernest 72
Henreid, Paul 147
Henry, O. 62
Herbert, Hans **119**
Herbert, Percy 142
Hessler's Garden of Girls 19
Heston, Charlton 152
Heydrich, Reinhard 82, 83
Heydt, Jean Louis 55
Hickman, Darryl 98
The High Hatters 18
High School Hellcats 146
High Tension 35–6
Hill, Jack 158
Hillbilly Heart Throbs 131
Hitchcock, Alfred 104
Hold Back the Dawn 63
Holden, William 62, **63**, 67, **68**, 99, 132, 161
Holmes, Taylor 108
"Home Is the Hero" 135
Homeier, Skip 88
"Honest John and the Thirteen Uncle Sams" 135
Honeymoon 24
Hoodlum Empire **127**, 127–8
Hope, Bob 152
Hopkins, Arthur 16, 17
Hopkins, Miriam 28, 69
Horn, Leonard 157
Horvick, Louise 43
Hostile Guns 157
Houston, Margaret Bell 82
Houston, Sam 82

How to Stuff a Wild Bikini 155
Howard, Mary 64
Huber, Harold 70
Hudson, Rochelle 41
Hull, Henry 47
Human Cargo 33–34, 35
The Human Side 71
Hunter, Ian 64
Hunter, Tab 156–7
Hunter's College, New York 89
Hussey, Ruth 119
Huston, Walter **20**, 88
Hutton, Betty 59, 81

I Live in Grosvenor Square 81
"I Remember You" 65
I Walked with a Zombie 101
I Wanted Wings 51, 62–3, **63**, 65, 78, 133
"I Wish I Wuz" 126
Impact 2, 117–21, **119**, **120**
In Old Chicago 42–3
In Old Oklahoma 110
Incendiary Blonde 81
Independent Exhibitors Film Bulletin 39–40
The Inside Story 23
International Settlement 45
Invasion of the Body Snatchers 143
Ireno 21
Island in the Sky 45
It Had to Be You 81
It Happened in Paris 123

Jackson, Andrew 67
Jagger, Dean 59, 60
James, Sydney **142**, 143
Jamestown 15
Jannings, Emil 58
The Jazz Singer 21
Jefferson, Thomas 67
Jesse, F. Tennyson 35
Jesse James 46–8
Joan of Lorraine 115
"Joe Palmer's Beard" 131
John Winton 121
Johnson, Richard 147
"Join the Navy and *see* the World" 18
Jones, Jack 146
Jory, Victor 135
"The Judge" 133
Juke Box Rhythm 146

Kane, Joseph 128
Kansas Raiders 123
The Kate Smith Hour 132
Kay, Graham 87
Keaton, Buster 112, 156
Keel, Howard 156
Kempson, Rachel 155
Kennedy, Arthur 145
Kerr, Donnie **56**

KFMB-TV 126
The Kick-Off 17
Killer McCoy 110–1
King, Henry 43
King of Hearts 130, 145
King of the Khyber Rifles 76
Kiss Me Deadly 62
Kiss of Death **107**, 107–9
Kiss of the Vampire 155
Kitty Foyle 113
Klaick, Edgar 7
Kneale, Nigel 139, 141, 142
Knight, Esmond 121
Knox, Mickey 110
Kolker, Henry 48
Kraft Theater 134–5
Kruger, Otto 104
Kwouk, Burt 155

Ladd, Alan 77, 78, 97, **98**, 99
Ladies in Love 38
The Lady Eve 55
Lafayette Flying Corps 7–8
Lahr, Bert 2, 26, 27, 68
Lake, Veronica 63, 77, 78
Lamb's Theater Club 161
Lamour, Dorothy 62, 78, 82, **114**, 115
Lancaster, Burt 112
Lane, Marjorie 44, 90–6, **92**
Lanfield, Sidney 106
Lang, Fritz 1, 2, 82, 83–4
Lang, Walter 114
Langelaan, George 154
Lasky, Jesse 160
The Last Remake of Beau Geste 50
"The Laughter of Giants" 135
Laughton, Charles 80
Launders, Perc **107**
Laurel & Hardy 48, 50
"Lazarus Walks" 131
Leaves in the Wind 163
Lee, Anna 82, **83**
Lee, Christopher 157
Leigh, Vivien 104, 132
Leinster Films 121
Leisen, Mitchell 33
Lemmon, Jack 146
Leslie, Desmond 121
Leslie, Joan 129
Let the Eagle Scream 72–3
"A Letter from His Commanding Officer" 132
Levin, Meyer 62
Levitt, Saul 150
Lewis, Jerry 2, **151**, 151–2
Lewis, Joseph H. 137, 138
Leyendecker, Joseph C. 13–16, 17
Life 87
Life Begins at 8:40 26–7
The Life of Barney Barnato 63

The Life of Floyd Gibbons 62
Lincoln, Abraham 145
"Little Joe, the Wrangler" 54
Little Theater Project 115
Lockhart, Gene **127**, 128
Lollobrigida, Gina 147
London, Jack 37
Longacre Theater 24
Lorre, Peter **39**, 39–40
The Loud Red Patrick 145
Love Me or Leave Me 21
Lovejoy, Frank 135
Lubin, Arthur 120
Lubitsch, Ernst 57
Lucky Jordan 144
The Lucky Stiff **114**, 114–5
Lugosi, Bela 130, 160–1
Lugosi, Bela G., Jr. 161–2
Lugosi, Lillian Arch 130, 160–2
Lupino, Ida 104
Lyles, A.C. 150, 156
Lynn, Diana 102
Lynn, Rita 122

Macken, Walter 135
MacLane, Barton 41
MacMurray, Fred 5, 33, 78
Madness of the Heart 104
The Magic Garden of Stanley Sweetheart 157
Magnani, Anna 121
The Magnificent Heel 122
Maibaum, Richard 63
The Maltese Falcon 78, 157
The Man in the Bowler Hat 115
A Man of Quality 17
Mansfield, Jayne 156
March, Fredric 15, 88
Marshall, Brenda 68
Marshall, George 54, 60, 81
Martin, Mary 64–5
Martingnoni, Phyllis **14**
Marx, Sam 105
Marx Brothers 112
Mary Burns, Fugitive 30–1
Massey, Ilona 69
Massey, Raymond 145
Massimo, Livio 148
Masterson, Whit 144
Mature, Victor 107, 108
Mayer, Louis B. 91, 105
The Mayor of Forty-Fifth Street 72
McCrea, Joel 1, **29**, 48, 57, 71, 99
McDonald, Maria 123
McIntire, Bob 28
McKinley, William A. 40–41
McLaglen, Victor 40, 43, 76
McNally, Stephen 86, 112
McNear, Howard **151**
McQueen, Steve 147
McVey, Patrick 135

Meitner, Dr. Lisa 105
Merinow, Victor 148
Merman, Ethel 21, 32
Merrick, Leonard 17
Metro Goldwyn Mayer 70, 82, 91, 105, 111
Meyer, Emile 157
Mickey 115
Midnight 121
Midnight Taxi 40, 45
The Milky Way 25, 26
Milland, Ray 1, 50, 62, 106
Miller, Joan 134
Miller, Joaquin 88
Milne, A.A. 115
The Minister and the Safecracker 104
The Miracle of Morgan Creek 59
Missile to the Moon 148
Mission: Impossible 157
Mr. Ed 120
"Mr. Liberty Bell" 133
Mr. Smith Goes to Washington 46
Mitchell, Thomas 24, 51
A Modern Cinderella 21
Modern Screen 31
Mohr, Gerald 109
Monsieur Beaucaire 16
Montez, Maria 66
Montgomery, Robert 18
Moore, Charles K. 12
Moore, Constance **63**
Moorehead, Agnes 105, 145
Morgan, Ralph 38
Morosco Theater 23
Morris, Wayne 62
Morros, Boris 71
Moscow Strikes Back 84
Mother's Boy 21
Mount Vernon Democrat (Indiana) 89
Mowbray, Alan 38
Murphy, Audie 123, 124
Murray, Elizabeth 3
My Darling Clementine 108
My Little Chickadee 62

Naish, J. Carrol 48, 128–9
The Name's the Same 135
NBC 132, 152
Neagle, Anna 84
Never So Few 147
New Amsterdam Theater 19
New Colony Productions 121
New York Athletic Club 22
New York Daily Mirror 22
New York Evening Graphic 22
New York Film Critics Circle 76
New York Times 156
Night in Paradise 120
The Night of January 16th 62
Night of the Demon 101
The Night Watch 106

Nightmare **79**, 79–80, 133
The Nitwits 146
No Foolin' 19
No Questions Asked 25
No Time for Sergeants 150
Nob Hill 88
Nolan, Lloyd 99, 124, 161
Nothman, Gastao Raul "Bobby" 27
Nothman, Susan Belinda 27
The Nutty Professor 152

Oboler, Arch 132
O'Brien, Edmund 112, 144–5
O'Brien, Pat 66
O'Connell, Hugh 26, 28
Odets, Clifford 130
"Odyssey to Freedom"' 131
Oettinger, Malcolm 51, 90
O'Flynn, Damian **127**
"Ole Buttermilk Sky" 101
Olivier, Laurence 104, 132
On Dangerous Ground 62
"On the Banks of the Wabash, Far Away" 41
"Once Upon a Time" 81
O'Neill, Eugene 16, 81
Operation Daybreak 82
Original Dixieland Jazz Band 65
Orwell, George 120
Otis, Johnny 146
Our Common Heritage 88
Our Friend Curley 80
Our Hearts Were Growing Up 102
Our Hearts Were Young and Gay 102
Out of the Past 118
Overman, Lynn **47**

Paige, Mabel 133
Paramount on Parade 65
Paramount Pictures 78, 82, 99
Pathe 4
Perfumed Lady 26
Pergola, James 15
Perkins, Anthony 135
Perry Mason 135
Peter Flies High 22
Peterborough Dramatic Festival 24
The Petrified Forest 146
Petticoat Lane 104
Pevney, Joseph 122
Pfeiffer, Julie 104
Phantom of the Opera 120
"The Pharmacist's Mate" 132
Philip, Prince 141
The Pigeon That Took Rome 152
Pilgrim Pictures 15–16
"The Pink Cloud" 131
Pit Stop **158**, 158–9
"The Policy of Joe Aladdin" 135
Potter, H.C. 71
Powell, Dick 112

Powell, Eleanor 90, 91
Power, Tyrone, Jr. 42, 47, 48, 59
Power, Tyrone, Sr. 16
Power and the Glory 55
Power House 62
Powers, Mala 157
Preston, Robert 48, 49, 62
Price, Vincent 59, 112
Pride of the Yankees 132
Prince Valiant 59
Princess Charming 22
Production Code Administration (PCA) 30, 40
Pulitzer Prize Play 132

Qualen, John 86, 88
Quantrill, Colonel 123–4, 129
"Quartet Erotica" 26
Quatermass II 141–44
The Quatermass Xperiment 139–41
Queen Bee 20
Queen of Outer Space 146
Quinn, Antony *47*

Raft, George 77, 88, 156, 157–8
Rainbow 19
Rainer, Luise 116
Raines, Ella 1, 118–9, *120*, *125*, 126, 128
Rand, Ayn 62
Raskin, David 137
Rathbone, Basil 52
Rawhide 135
Red Arrow (32nd Infantry Division) 7–8
Red Harvest 78
Redgrave, Michael 70
Reed, Philip 103
Reform School Girl 146
The Remarkable Andrew 2, 67–9, *68*
Renoir, Jean 121
Republic Pictures 127–9
Return of the Fly 154
Reuben, Reuben 145
Revere, Paul 15
Revier, Harry 8
Reynolds, Quentin 62
Rhodes, Cecil 63
Rice, Craig 115
Richards, Ann 85–88
Rickard, Tex 81
Ride the Man Down 128–9
Rimsky-Korsakov, Nicolai 102–3
Ringside 18, 25
The Rivalry 145, 150
The River 121
Roadhouse Nights 78
Roberts, Curtis 147
Robinson, Edward G. 28, *29*, 30
Robison, Carson 131
Robson, Flora 85
Rogell, Albert S. 110

Rogers, Roy 161
"Rogue River Valley" 101
Rogue's Gallery 157
Rogue's Regiment 112
Roland, Gilbert 40
Romance, Vivian 123
Romance of the Air 8
Rooney, Mickey 111–2, 156
Roosevelt, Eleanor 85, 105
Roosevelt, Franklin D. 85, 105
Roosevelt, Theodore 40–1
Rosalie 19
"Row, Row, Row the Boat" 38
Runyon, Damon 66
Russell, Gail 102
Russell, Jane 121, 141
Russell, John 125, 127
Russell, Rosalind 24

Sahara 80
St. Clair, Malcolm 41
St. John's Military Academy, Wisconsin 9
Saints and Sinners 136
San Demetrio, London 76
San Francisco 42
Sanders, George 45
Saturday Evening Post 13, 88
Schaeffer, George J. 99
Schertzinger, Victor 64, 65
Schmidt, Captain 6
School for Wives 16
Scott, Randolph 60, 61
Scott, Zachary 130
Screenland 52, 74, 90
Scruffy 99
Seek! Strike! Destroy! 76
Seiter, William 41
Seventh Heaven 45
Shakedown 122–3
Shane 157
Sharp, Don 155
Sharpshooters 44
Shearer, Lloyd 121
Sheboygan News 9
Shefter, Bert 154
Shields, Arthur 80
Sidney, Sylvia 30–1, 135
"Silver Saddle" 101
Sinatra, Frank 147
Sinatra, Nancy 122
Sing & Whistle 24
Skelton, Red 2, 111
Skinner, Cornelia Otis 102
Slaughter Trail 126–7
Small, Edward 65, 98
Smilin' Through 20
Smith, C. Aubrey, Sir 84–5
Smith, Don 10
Smith, George *107*
Smith, John 15

Smith, Roger 157
Sobol, Louis 18, 62
Society Girl 23
"Sometimes I'm Happy" 18
Somyo, Tom 121
"Song of India" 104
Song of Scheherazade 2, 102–4, **103**
South of Tahiti 65–6
A Southern Yankee 111
Special Operations Executive (SOE) 27
Stack, James L., Jr. 96
Stack, Robert 96
Stagecoach 46, 51
Stalingrad 84
Stallings, Laurence 17, 19
Stand by for Action 10, 80
Stanwyck, Barbara 40–1, 48, 71–2
Star Stage 135
Stars in My Crown 100
State Fair 86
Stevens, Katherine 71
Stevens, Marla 122
Stewart, George R. 81
Stewart, James 25, 53, 54
Stone, Andrew 104
Storm 81
Stossel, Ludwig 105
Strike It Rich 42
Strike Me Pink 32–3
Striving for Fortune 18
Stuart, Gloria *37*, 38
Studebaker Theater, Chicago 22
Sturges, John 147
Sturges, Preston 2, 23, 55–7, 76, 156
Sullivan, Barry 81
Sullivan, Ed 22
Sullivan, John L. 88
Sullivan's Travels 55
Suspense 131
Sword in the Desert 106

Talent 24
Tamiroff, Akim 56, **58**, 59, 135
"Tangerine" 65
Tantamount 13
Tap Roots 124
Tarantino, Quentin 159
Tarkington, Booth 16
Tate, Reginald 139
Taylor, Robert 40–1, 64, 80, 90
Teagarden, Jack 65
Tearle, Godfrey 105
Tennyson, Alfred. Lord 35
Tension 121
Thanksgiving—November 1941 132
These Are Your Brothers 132
Thieves' Highway 62
Thirteen Hours by Air 33
The 39 Steps 80
Thirty Seconds Over Tokyo 86

36 Hours to Kill **37**, 37–8
This Gun for Hire 144
This Is My Affair 40–1, 72
Thomas, Mary 56
Three and One 24
3:10 to Yuma 146
Three Sheets to the Wind 76, 132
The Three Stooges 145
Three-Cornered Moon 24
Thunder Rock 70
Tierney, Lawrence 122, 123
Time 67
The Times (London) 38, 80, 141
Tobias, Milton 95
Totter, Audrey 121–2, **129**
Tourneur, Jacques 100
Tower of London 52
Tracy, Spencer 23, 57, 81, 86, 87, 105
Transatlantic Rhythm 27
A Tree Grows in Brooklyn 111
The Treniers 146
Trevor, Claire 33–4, 45, 52, 66, 73, **114**, 115, 128
The Trial of Madeleine Smith 104
The Trouble with Women 1, 51, **106**, 107
Truman, Harry S. 85, 105, 124, **125**, 126
Truman, Mrs. 124, 126
Trumbo 67
Trumbo, Dalton 67
Tryon, Glen 53
Tucker, Forrest 1, 125, 127, 128
Tufts, Sonny 88
"Turnabout" 132
Tuttle, Frank 144
Twentieth Century Fox 23, 33, 37
Twerp, Joe 43
Twin Beds 66
Two Years Before the Mast 97–9, **98**

Union Pacific 46, **47**, 48, 71
United Artists 79, 98
U.S. War Department 105
Universal Studios 79, 99, 124
USAAF 63
Up Pops the Devil 21–22, 25

Valentino, Rudolf 16
Valera, Nina 129
Variety 20, 25, 26, 105
Varlamov, Leonid 84
Vass Family 131
Venice Film Festival 41, 84
Vernon, Anne 122
Vernon, Wally 44
Vidor, King 2, 86, 87
The Virginian 99
Voigt, Edward (Congressman) 9
Vox Pop 132
Voyage to the Bottom of the Sea 157

Wachter, Milford 86
Waco 156
Wade, Alan 7
Wagon Master 60
Wagon Train 135
Wake Island 2, 74–6, *75*, 84, 99, 131, 163
Wales, Ethel 32
Walker, Helen 117, 118
Walsh, George 17
Walsh, Raoul 17
"Walter, Walter, Lead Me to the Altar" 44
War Boom 78
War Town 78
Ward, Edith Eddy 122
Warde, Harlan *63*
Warhol, Andy 157
Warner, H.B. 66
Warner Brothers 21
Washington, George 67, 121
Washington Correspondent 79
The Way of All Flesh 57
Wayne, John 52, 76, 132
Wead, Frank 105
"Weather Ahead" 132
Webb, Richard 65
Weisse, Lester C. 5
Wellman, William A. 49–52, 72, 156, 163
Wellman, William, Jr. 146
Wells, Jacqueline 52
We're Going to Be Rich 43–4
West, Mae 62
West Point 9
Westinghouse Playhouse 135
Wexley, John 84
What Price Glory? 16–17, 25, 115
"What's a Kiss Among Friends?" 18
When the Daltons Rode 60–1
A Whiff of Heliotrope 69
White, Herb 161
White Fang 37

Widmark, Richard 107, 108
Wild Harvest 99
Wild Sable Island 121
Wilde, Cornel 81, 137
Wilkinson, June 148
"Willie and the Hand Jive" 146
Wilson, Claude 94
Wings for Democracy 71
The Winner 158
The Winning Oar 17
Winninger, Charles *53*, 54
Winters, Shelley 136
Wirtz, Henry 150
Wizard of Oz 27, 46
Wolfe, Ian 80
Wolheim, Louis 16
Woman They Almost Lynched 129, *129*
Women's Marines Auxiliary 89
Wong, Anna Mae 118
Wood, Helen 36
Wood, Natalie 144
Wood, Sam 113
Woods, Donald 45
Woolrich, Cornell 131
Wordsworth, Richard *140*, 141
Wordsworth, William 141
Wouk, Herman 132
Wren, P.C. 49
Wright, Teresa 1, *106*

Years Ago 161–2
Youmans, Vincent 18
Young, Gig 126
Young, Loretta 38

Zanuck, Darryl F. 33, 34, 43
Ziegfeld, Flo 23
Ziegfeld's Follies of 1931 22–23
Ziegfeld's Follies of 1925 19
Zimbalist, Sam 86